D1260044

The Proper Care & Feeding of Husbands & Marriage

Dr. Laura Schlessinger

ALSO BY DR. LAURA SCHLESSINGER

Ten Stupid Things Women Do to Mess Up Their Lives
How Could You Do That?!:
The Abdication of Character, Courage, and Conscience
Ten Stupid Things Men Do to Mess Up Their Lives
The Ten Commandments:
The Significance of God's Laws in Everyday Life
Stupid Things Parents Do to Mess Up Their Kids
Ten Stupid Things Couples Do to Mess Up Their Relationships

CHILDREN'S TITLES

Why Do You Love Me?
But I Waaannt It!
Growing Up Is Hard
Where's God?

The Proper Care and Feeding of Husbands

Dr. Laura C. Schlessinger

HarperCollins books may be purchased for educational, business, or sales promotional use. For information, please write: Special Markets Department, HarperCollins Publishers, 10 East 53rd Street, New York, NY 10022.

The Proper Care and Feeding of Husbands and *The Proper Care and Feeding of Marriage* were originally published in 2004 and 2007 respectively, by HarperCollins Publishers Inc.

Library of Congress Cataloging-in-Publication Data is available.

ISBN: 978-0-06-191171-2

09 10 11 12 13 /RRD 10 9 8 7 6 5 4 3 2 1

For family and friends who have stood by me—
in humble gratitude.

ACKNOWLEDGMENTS

Without the sensitive, honest, open, generous, and profound contributions of my audience—this book wouldn't have been possible. Thank you all for helping me help others.

Contents

AUTHOR'S NOTE

While the ideas, suggestions, and techniques offered in this book are going to improve your relationship with your husband (or yours with your wife if you get her to read this book), and your attitude about yourself, your marriage, and your life, it is important to qualify this enthusiastically optimistic perspective with a serious concern. As I wrote in my first book, *Ten Stupid Things Women Do to Mess Up Their Lives,* and reiterated in a later book, *Ten Stupid Things Couples Do to Mess Up Their Relationships,* the 3 A's: Addictions, Abuse, and Affairs, are behaviors, in my opinion, that break the covenant and justify the self-preserving decision to end the relationship. Where the behavior of one or both of the spouses is blatantly destructive, dangerous, or evil, this book does not apply.

The Proper Care and Feeding of Husbands has salvaged and revitalized innumerable strained, stagnant, boring, disappointing, annoying, frustrating, and even seemingly dead marriages, as the real-life examples happily demonstrate. I have had women calling almost daily, bitterly criticizing their men, reporting of months of seemingly useless marital therapy (aka "gripe hours"), and at their wits' end about what to do with their marriages. After I ask (well, really nag) them to try just *one* of the hints found in this book, such as finding one or two things to compliment their husbands about (no matter how small) each day for five days, they call me back amazed at the positive results in their feelings about their men, their husbands' demeanor, and the atmosphere in the home. They see progress! They feel powerful! They are happier! Their marriages are experienced as more of a blessing.

My deepest hope is that this book will bring that blessing to your home.

P.S. Reading this book may be of benefit to your health! According to biologists at the University of Pennsylvania, ". . . male perspiration had a surprisingly beneficial effect on women's moods. It helps reduce stress, induces relaxation, and even affects the menstrual cycle." (The *Orange County Register,* March 15, 2003.)

—Dr. Laura C. Schlessinger, 2003

INTRODUCTION

"As a man, I can tell you our needs are simple. We want to be fed, we want our kids mothered, and we want lovin'."

VINCE

"Men are only interested in two things: If I'm not horny, make me a sandwich."

JOHN

"I am a thirty-seven-year-old man who has seen quite a bit in life, and I can offer this to your search for how to treat a man. We are men, not dumb-dumbs, psychics, or one bit unromantic. We need only clear communication, appreciation, honest love, and respect. This will be repaid by laying the moon and stars at your feet for your pleasure. There is no need to 'work' a man to get what you want. We live to take care of a wife, family, and home. Just remember that we are men, and know that our needs are simple but not to be *ignored. A good man is hard to find, not to keep."*

DAN

"A good man is hard to find, not to keep." That sentence should really make you stop and think. As a radio talk-show host/psychotherapist, I've got to tell you how remarkably true and sad it is that so many women struggle to hold on to some jerk, keep giving an abusive or philandering man yet another chance, have unprotected sex with some guy while barely knowing his last name, agree to shack up and risk making babies with some opportunist or loser, all in a pathetic version of a pursuit for love, *but* will resent the hell out of treating a decent, hardworking, caring husband with the thoughtfulness, attention, respect, and affection he needs to be content. It boggles my mind.

What further puts me in boggle overdrive is how seemingly oblivious and insensitive many women are to how destructive they are being to their men and consequently to their marriages. Women will call me asking me if it's alright to go off on extended vacations "without *him*" when they want some freedom or R&R, or if it's okay to cut him off from sex because they're annoyed about something or just too tired from their busy day, or if they really have to make him a dinner when he gets home from work because it's just too tedious to plan meals, or if it's okay to keep stuff from him (like family or financial issues) because his input is unnecessary, or if they're really obligated to spend time with his family (in-laws or stepkids), or if they really have to show interest in his hobbies when they're bored silly by them, or—well, you get the idea.

Let me relate the specific call that prompted me to write this book. Annette is thirty-five, her husband is thirty-nine, and they have a one-year-old son. She is a stay-at-home mom who just doesn't enjoy cooking and doesn't feel it's useful to spend a lot of time doing it. She called wondering if that was detrimental or not to her child. Right away I was alerted to her lack of concern about the needs or desires of her husband—you know, the guy who slays dragons for her and their child every day. In order to really get a feel for this caller, you'll have to imagine the completely hostile and disdainful manner in which she spoke.

DR. LAURA: What do you do for food?

ANNETTE: We eat peanut-butter-and-jelly sandwiches.

DR. LAURA: That's not healthy three times a day.

ANNETTE: No, he's [the child] not eating it three times a day.

DR. LAURA: What do you eat for dinner?

ANNETTE: Well, he's still breast-feeding at one year old.

DR. LAURA: What do the adults in your house eat for dinner?

ANNETTE: My husband might eat beef enchiladas from the freezer, and I might eat cereal or cottage cheese. My husband doesn't much like what I cook.

DR. LAURA: That's not really a balanced, healthy diet. Are you intentionally making awful things that he won't eat or is he some kind of ogre?

ANNETTE: (Sarcastically) No, I'm just not a good cook. [What you can't read is her disdainful, hostile tone.]

DR. LAURA: Okay, Annette, being a better cook is easy to come by. All you do is take a class or get a book of recipes. I wonder if you're intentionally undermining his enjoyment of a home-cooked meal so that you simply don't have to do it. Let me tell you what is detrimental to your child. Dinnertime turns out to be one of the most important functions of a family in terms of a child bonding with parents, their ability to communicate and feel close to their parents—all of which supports their self-esteem. The dinner table is a most important aspect of that bonding. That is the routine time when the family sits down, says their prayers, and spends that pleasant time enjoying their meal together and talking. So, if that means you have to do what you don't like, so be it. Or did you plan to teach your son that when he doesn't enjoy something, he doesn't have to do it at all, or he doesn't have to do it right? In which case you are going to have a child growing up to be a monster.

There are a lot of things we all don't enjoy doing, but they are part of the rigor of life and they are a part of our obligations in our various roles. To be people of integrity, we have to follow through whether or not we enjoy something. So, if you are at home, I think it is important for you to make the effort to prepare pleasant dinners because I think that's part of the joy and comfort for your family. Put in the effort. If your husband can eat frozen, prepackaged Mexican food, with all those spices, it means he has a pretty open-minded stomach—so you must be going far out of your way to mess with him. I don't understand that hostility, especially from a woman who has a one-year-old child. The ability for you to maintain a safe and nurturing home for that child largely depends on the quality and existence of your marriage. I'd expect you to make more of an effort.

Most of the women who complain that they are not getting what they want from their husbands should stop and look at how disrespectful and disdainful they are of them. They should also look at what they put their time and energy into at the expense of him and their marriage. It would be a stunner for them to realize that they try harder to impress strangers than they try to impress the person who is supposed to be the most important to them. As one listener, Gary, says:

"A husband is like a horse. At the end of the day he is usually rode hard and put away sweaty. Like in the movies, if his

master drives and beats him, he'll go just so far before bucking and rebelling.

If you love him, if you coax him, he'll drive himself till his heart explodes before he will let down his master. He'll give himself to death for the one he loves.

Which way should women handle a man?"

I have never gotten a complaint from a male listener in twenty-five years on the radio over my assertion that men are very simple creatures. They agree. I have explained time and again on my radio program that men are borne of women and spend the rest of their lives yearning for a woman's acceptance and approval. Unless you've got a man with a frank mental or personality disorder (the exception, not the rule), men admittedly are putty in the hands of a woman they love. Give him direct communication, respect, appreciation, food, and good lovin', and he'll do just about anything you wish—foolish or not.

With one particular caller, Sandy, I pushed this agenda through to a successful conclusion—but not without a lot of sweat on my part and resistance on Sandy's part.

SANDY: My husband and I have a horrible relationship.

DR. LAURA: And why is that, I wonder.

SANDY: He says I'm too headstrong . . . but I think we are both too headstrong for each other.

DR. LAURA: He says you are too headstrong. And what does that mean?

SANDY: He always tells me I like to take over situations—that I like to control situations and that I go around him when we should discuss these things together. I just go ahead and do it myself.

DR. LAURA: So, why do you do that?

SANDY: I don't know.

DR. LAURA: It is destroying your marriage. Why would you continue to do that?

SANDY: But it is stupid things like going to the store and buying something. Why should I consult him in things like that?

DR. LAURA: Well, it doesn't hurt to have a chat or invite him to come along.

SANDY: I just don't see it.

DR. LAURA: Do we have kids in the middle of this?

SANDY: Yeah, we have three kids.

DR. LAURA: That is why we have to make changes—so that the three kids have a peaceful home. And you can make the changes.

SANDY: We worked on it.

DR. LAURA: No. *We* didn't work on it. *You* didn't change.

SANDY: It is just hard.

DR. LAURA: So what, it's hard. This is about the lives of your three children. Don't tell me something is difficult to do when your three kids are depending on it. That should be incredible motivation for you to behave better in your marriage—to treat your husband better in your marriage.

SANDY: Right.

To help her make some changes, I asked her to make a short list, right then and there while we were on air, of three reasonable things her husband wished she would do differently. She fought this tooth and nail. First, she supposedly didn't know what he'd want, then she complained about him, then she got sarcastic about his needs, then she exaggerated what she'd have to do. Whew! It was tough to get through the resistance to admit that any of his desires or requests were reasonable, much less show any willingness to give him something he wanted.

I explained to her that personal change was difficult, bitching about somebody else was easy. I persisted with my question, offering her the opportunity to make things better for herself and her children. Finally, she relented—well, sort of—you can still read the "edginess."

DR. LAURA: What are three reasonable things you know would please him if you changed?

SANDY: If I took his opinion on things. If I listen to what he says and do it.

DR. LAURA: Okay. That seems fair for a marriage. What else?

SANDY: He would like to see me accept him for the way he is without asking for any more.

DR. LAURA: Generally, I think that means he wants to feel appreciated for what he is and does.

SANDY: Right.

DR. LAURA: And, when you are constantly trying to change him or demand more or different, he reads that as though you don't approve and appreciate what he is offering and who he is. Remember, this *is* the man *you* picked. Okay? So he needs more appreciation. And, what is number three?

SANDY: To just let things slide off my back sometimes. He always says I am too perfect.

DR. LAURA: Okay. Be easier going.

SANDY: Right.

DR. LAURA: Here's your assignment. Do this for a few days and call me back. Number one is *ask him for his opinion about something.* Number two is *show him some appreciation.* Number three is *if it really isn't important, let it pass because nobody likes to be jumped on all the time.* Read them back to me please.

SANDY: Ask him his opinion. Show him appreciation. If it isn't real important, let it pass.

She did call back in a few days and was rather surprised that with seemingly small efforts she had helped to improve her husband's mood and behavior and lighten up the atmosphere in the home, all leading to her own peace of mind.

But that is what I keep telling women. Men are simple straight lines. Generally, unlike women, men do not have mercurial moods (like PMS) or hypersensitivity to interpersonal slights (when was the last time you heard a man complain about his *father*-in-law?). Men usually mean exactly what they say and don't speak in the more indirect style more typical of women. Also, men will typically suffer in silence long, long before they will complain or screech out in pain (isolation and alcohol abuse is where it shows), while women are more likely to use whining and complaining as a form of communication and even entertainment with their girlfriends.

Men are simple. They know it. Women have to learn it if they expect to be truly happy with their man.

Kathryn, another of my listeners, confirms this:

> *"Men really are not as complicated as we think they should be. Men love to hear that their woman is happy and that they are the source of this happiness. Men deserve the same respect you would show a visitor in your home—even more. Men love to be complimented. They also like to be admired. I always thank my husband for working so hard for us, and I encourage the kids to do so, too. Men are grumpy when they are tired and/or hungry. Anything they say while they are in either one of these states is not to be taken seriously. Men don't like it when women talk about them behind their backs. Men are not your 'daddies,' they are your contemporaries and get stressed and scared about things just like you do. And if you were a real friend, you would help ease their burdens, not add to them. Men have dreams, too, and it doesn't matter if it's logical or not, don't walk all over them.*

This doesn't mean that we don't have problems—everyone does—but it's a lot easier to work them out with a man who knows you love and respect him."

I have been sadly amazed by the lack of understanding and appreciation so many women demonstrate for those basic facts. A recent caller to my radio program took the cake with her call. She is married for the second time and they both have children from prior marriages. She is working full-time and is involved in all sorts of activities. She called to complain about her "demanding" husband. It seems he was unhappy in his new marriage because his wife, my caller, was not spending time with him in or out of bed. She described an unbelievably hectic daily schedule, remarking that she just had too much on her plate to have time or energy or impulse to be intimate at all, much less physically intimate, with her new husband.

I immediately suggested that she take a cosmic spoon and dump stuff off her plate to make room for her new marriage, for her husband, for their relationship. She immediately came back with, "But shouldn't he just be understanding?" I almost flipped! He should be understanding about being ignored, about being at the bottom of her priority list? I responded, "Why should he agree to be a boarder in his own home, with no effort at all from you for a personal relationship? Why should he be sanguine about that? Why should he be sympathetic to your choice to exclude him from your life?"

Her answer, so telling, was, "Ohhh. I didn't see it that way at all."

I reiterated that she had to dump much of what was she was *voluntarily* allowing to hog up her plate and make room for him, or he was going to dump her off *his* plate, and that I wouldn't blame him much at all.

These calls are *not* aberrant. They reflect truly typical attitudes of a preponderance of women in today's America. Since

Gloria Steinem wrote that "women need men like fish need bicycles," more than a generation of women have foolishly bought that destructive nonsense and have denigrated men, marriage, familial obligation, and motherhood—all to their own detriment. Normal, healthy women yearn to be in love, married, and raising children with the man of their dreams. However, when their own mothers, much less society, tell them that they don't need men to be happy, or to raise children, and that their own children don't even need a mother raising them (day care will do), it's caused many women to lose the incentive and the ability to treat their personal lives with the love, dedication, sacrifice, compassion, and loyalty that will ultimately bring them happiness and a sense of purpose.

Sonya, a listener, echoes biblical scriptures with her note:

> *"And at the end of the day . . . roll over in bed, close your eyes, give him a big hug, and remember that without him, you are only a sorry excuse for a person, but as half of the team, you are invincible."*

In Genesis God said, "It is not good that man be alone; I will make him a helper corresponding to him. . . . Therefore a man shall leave his father and his mother and cling to his wife and they shall become one flesh."

Contrary to what a good forty years of feminist propaganda has claimed, it is not oppression, subjugation, or abdication of any feminine quality-of-life potential to marry a man, be proud of your bonding, rejoice in your gifts and sacrifices for your marriage and family, and derive pleasure and sustenance from your role as a wife and mother.

Your attitude makes all the difference in the quality of your life. And your understanding of men and what they dearly need will make all the difference in the quality of your marriage.

Kathy wrote:

"I told my husband about the book you are working on and asked him what he thought men want. He said, 'That's simple. Lots of sex and no nagging. What's so hard about that?' "

It's not quite that simple, but Kathy's husband's tongue-in-cheek answer speaks to the truth that women have all the power in the world to determine the behavior of their men. This power is released when women practice the *Proper Care and Feeding of Husbands.*

The Proper Care
and Feeding of Husbands

Chapter 1

THE *IM*PROPER CARE AND FEEDING OF HUSBANDS

"I laughed when I heard the title of your new book. I thought, 'It won't happen. What woman would buy it? Who cares about us men?' There are a few things that men want so bad they would do anything for it. I think a good number of men want respect more than love. They like to feel they have some power. I nearly cry when you tell a woman caller to respect her husband. There is so much selfishness in the world—in marriages. Prosperity has allowed women to be so independent, and thus so selfish. I always feel as though I come last—my feelings come last, my needs come last."

EDGAR

There isn't a day that goes by when I don't ask at least one woman caller on my radio program if she expects to stay married considering her hostile, dismissive, or undermining attitude and actions toward her husband. What is amazing is how surprised they all seem to imagine that their husbands might have a limit to how much they'll take before they tune out or turn away. What is even more amazing is that this *in*sensitivity to their husbands' needs and feelings goes hand in hand with a *hyper*sensitivity about any action or reaction from the men—reactions that are usually more than reasonable.

Here's just one example of such a caller from my radio program the day before I began writing this chapter. This "Christian" woman has been married one year to a "Jewish" man, and they have a four-month-old son. Before they married she promised to raise their children Jewish, even though, obviously, neither one was truly invested in and committed to their religion (because, if they were, they would have married someone with whom they could share their faith). Now that it is Christmastime, she put up a tree and is already revving up for Easter egg hunts. "I don't want my children to miss out on all the wonderful holiday experiences I had as a child," she says to me by way of rationalizing her broken promise.

What was her question for me even after I reminded her of her promise and vows? Of course it was, "How can I get him to stop walking around angry and pouting?" That she betrayed her vow was easily dismissed, I think, by the double standard most women have about what they do and what their men do. If women change their minds, men must take it. When men change their minds, they're brutes.

One male listener wrote to me of his frustration with this double standard. He lamented that women need to understand how frustrating it is dealing with a double standard that only takes into account the woman's immediate needs or desires. It was his perception that everything the woman feels or needs is legitimate and very important, while anything related to the man is unimportant and selfish.

I think, as generalizations go, he has a good point. Try visiting various female-oriented Internet chat rooms, and you'll find cheering sections rallying behind women who trash their men, determined to leave them for trivial reasons ("He's not talkative enough," "I just don't feel complete," "I'm bored," or "He doesn't want me talking to my mother every day").

And while we're talking about double standards, let's not forget what happens in the bedroom. Women expect their men to "understand" when they're not interested in sex, but when the men don't or can't perform—watch out!

What causes this double-standard mentality? In one big, hyphenated word: self-centeredness. And what is the source of this self-centeredness? I believe it's a result of the women's movement, with its condemnation of just about everything male as evil, stupid, and oppressive, and the denigration of female and male roles in families, as well as the loss of family functioning as a result of divorce, day care, dual careers, and the glorification of shacking up and unwed motherhood by choice. These are the core destructive influences that result in women not appreciating that they are perfected, as are men, when they are bonded in wedlock and have obligations to family.

The result is women get married thinking largely about what their marriage and their man can do for them, and not what they can do for their men. And when there is so little emphasis on the giving, the nitpicking and pettiness chews up and spits out what could have been a good marriage.

Cindy's e-mail addresses the issue of "giving" and "doing":

> *"I have been married for ten years and I had a huge problem with* Caring and Feeding *my husband. I did not know the time my mother put into caring and feeding my dad until I was having difficulty in my marriage. It was then she helped me understand a wife's role. My generation (I'm in my 30s) was raised in a very 'me' culture: If we're not happy, then no one will be. Luckily, my mom and dad taught me that in order to be happy and fulfilled, you must help, love, and care . . . for others! Even with a great home life as a child, I didn't know that was so true in a marriage. I just thought you either have a great marriage or you don't—that somehow marriage existed outside your efforts.*

That was just one of my misassumptions. Another was that he should be as knowledgeable about things as my dad, with whom I constantly compared him. I constantly nagged instead of encouraged. Then my dad gave me advice on how the male ego worked. I followed his direction, being encouraging and essentially being his cheerleader. Things changed dramatically.

My mother's advice, after my many mess-ups, was to love him. Now, that sounds pretty basic, but I now truly understand what the word 'love' means. It's a profoundly tender, passionate affection for someone; an affectionate concern for their well-being. God's greatest gift, after life itself, is love. God created him for you. Love your husband with all your heart and treat him like the gift from God that he is."

The notion of love as a gift, as a verb, as an attitude, as a commitment, is a revelation to some. Unfortunately, love is usually looked at as a feeling that comes over you and makes you happy; and of course, *if* you're happy, *then* you behave nicely. Somehow, the notion is out there that you're entitled to behave badly if you don't feel that lovin' feeling. More than that, if you don't feel that lovin' feeling, you're entitled to get it somehow, somewhere, with someone else who's available. This sense of entitlement comes from a culture that has elevated feelings over obligation, responsibility, and commitment.

"I have a right to be happy, don't I?" is not an infrequent comment from callers frustrated that their marriages haven't put them in a perpetual Valium-drip state. And this focus on happiness helps them to rationalize their virtual abandonment of marriage and family, and their replacing it with hobbies, drugs and alcohol, work, affairs, whining in therapy or with friends or family, or hostility directed at those who love them.

This is not a minor issue. When marriages are distressed, the children are hurt and limited in their ability and hope to achieve happiness. This is the point I bring to the attention of many women callers who, with unrealistic demands and outrageously negative behaviors, determine that the solution to the problems in their home is divorce. There are two issues that I force them to look at. The first is that children of divorce will suffer both in the present and in the future. The second is that they are wrong if they think a new pair of pants will change their lives—because the same skirt will be in the room!

I challenge them to do what they complain their spouses won't or can't do: change! I explain that men are indeed simple creatures, and if you change certain aspects of your interaction, like magic you will see changes in them, too. I remind them that their current feelings do not need to change before they can change their behavior. I ask them to behave "as if" things were lovely in their relationship: a call of affection during the day, a kiss at the door, a nice outfit when at home, a request for his opinion about something to do with the family, a comment of appreciation for something well done, a hug, a good meal, a back rub, some alone time after work before dealing with plumbing or financial problems, and a cuddle at bedtime . . . which might get even more interesting.

Invariably, the women protest. Why should they have to be nice when things aren't exactly the way they want them? Clifford, a listener, e-mailed about this attitude:

> *"What ever happened to sweetness? If you act like a Bi★ch, you will be treated like a Bi★ch. I asked my wife once if she wanted something, as she was being unusually nice. She angrily said to me 'I would never be nice to anyone to get them to do something for me. That is sucking up!'*
>
> *So, what is the alternative? Treat them like Sh★t? A man takes care of his woman and a woman should take care of her man! What a concept!"*

What surprised me when I went to my Web site (www.drlaura.com), where I'd asked listeners to send me contributions for this book, was the avalanche of expressed pain from husbands—not so much anger, but pain. It may be a surprise for many women to imagine that their husbands are in pain because of their behavior toward them. In all fairness, men do tend to be more stoic than women; they try to be strong and carry on no matter what. I do not fault that at all. That is a description of masculinity, one that has been under attack from a feminized culture that denies the importance of such inner strength and fortitude. Without those and other masculine characteristics, much of Western civilization would not have evolved. Think about the self-control and self-denial necessary in exploration or combat or survival under ferocious conditions. I do believe that it's to the betterment of men and society that women temper and civilize these masculine characteristics; however, to deny the reality and value of masculine traits altogether is cruel toward boys and men, not to mention foolish, as it undermines the home and country.

That men do not emote pain, hurt, and despair like women do seems to mean to some women that men are not feeling anything. The truth is men suck it up and just try to get along in life in general and with us in particular. Women should not measure or interpret a man's heart, soul, intent, or feelings based upon their own reactions. Women cry and talk; men don't ruminate on feelings, they try to do something about the situation. I guess that makes men lousy "girlfriends," but very helpful "partners" if women would respect their uniqueness.

Ray, a listener, signed himself "Frustrated and depressed husband":

"I hear many of the calls from women who sound so much like my wife. Their disdain for their obligations to their husbands is far too familiar. It is agonizing to listen and to know that I live with the indifference of a woman just like those callers.

I can't describe the frustration, depression, and finally, the utter despair that is the result of twenty-four years of neglect. I can't do justice to the efforts that I have made to salvage a relationship that should be the cornerstone of our family, but is instead a millstone around my neck. I can't explain to you the progression from loving and nurturing husband, through concerned and understanding spouse, to frustrated and repressed male, and angry, depressed curmudgeon, all the way to desperate wretch.

Just know that you must write this book. If you can save just one family, you must write this book."

Ray was not alone in his lamentation. Too many men are living in this pain, having given up any hope of happiness after making every attempt to give their wives what they say they want so that they will treat their husbands nice.

What do women want?

Jill, a listener, sent me this Internet "joke" about "The Perfect Husband":

"A new Perfect Husband Shopping Center opened where a woman could go to choose from among many men to find the perfect husband. It was laid out on five floors, with the men increasing in positive attributes as you ascended the floors. The only rule was that once you open the door to any floor, you must choose a man from that floor, and if you go up a floor, you can't go back down except to leave the store. So, a couple of girlfriends go to the store to find a man to marry.

The first-floor sign reads: 'These men have high-paying jobs and love kids.' The women read the sign and say, 'Well, that's wonderful . . . but,' and wonder what's on the next floor.

The second-floor sign reads: 'These men have high-paying jobs, love kids, and are extremely good looking.' 'Hmmm,' say the girls. 'Wonder what's further up?'

The third-floor sign reads: 'These men have high-paying

jobs, love kids, are extremely good looking, and will help with the housework.' 'Wow!' say the women. 'Very tempting . . . but there's more further up!'

The fourth-floor sign reads: 'These men have high-paying jobs, love kids, are extremely good looking, will help with the housework, and are great in bed.' 'Oh, mercy me. But just think! What must be awaiting us further up?!' say the women.

So, up to the fifth floor they go.

The fifth-floor sign reads: 'This floor is just to prove that women are impossible to please.'"

Oops.

Here's an example of "I love you . . . now change into my perfect husband":

DR. LAURA: Nikki, welcome to the program.

NIKKI: I would like to know when it is appropriate for me to butt into my fiancé's life and when it isn't.

DR. LAURA: Why is it you think you have to butt into his life in many different arenas? You don't like him as he is?

NIKKI: I love him as a person, but there are certain things, like manners, he wasn't brought up with. His parents were hippies and let him do whatever he wanted. When I met him and we were walking across the street and I had high heels on and it was in the middle of winter, he didn't try to help me across the street.

DR. LAURA: In the dead of winter why were you walking around in high heels in the first place if you couldn't walk normally in them?

NIKKI: We were out to a fancy dinner.

DR. LAURA: People can wear sensible shoes no matter where they go. Okay, so you wore silly shoes and he didn't throw you over his shoulder.

NIKKI: What about such things as manners? When he

comes over to my parents' house and he puts his face about an inch from the food and says, 'Wow, this smells really great!'?

DR. LAURA: I think that is very complimentary.

NIKKI: Even if his face was right above the food?

DR. LAURA: Well, how else would he smell it?

NIKKI: I don't know. . . . Okay.

DR. LAURA: Nikki, if you are ashamed of him, get rid of him. If you are ashamed of him, leave him alone.

NIKKI: I'm not ashamed of him. Nobody is perfect. I am totally in love with him. What about him working out and eating better?

DR. LAURA: Nikki, get a different man. Stop beating this one to death. I am really sad that you pick a guy, say you are totally in love with him, but keep pointing out how he is totally unsatisfactory to you. That is insulting. That is not love. If you want an exercise maniac who reads Ms. Manners, get one of those. It is offensive and demoralizing to men when we women types grab on to them and then want to remold them in our image of the perfect man or perfect husband.

NIKKI: That is true.

DR. LAURA: It doesn't make them feel better about themselves.

NIKKI: Yeah, he does feel horrible about himself when I do that.

DR. LAURA: How cruel are you being? How nuts is he to keep taking it?

NIKKI: True. He doesn't have much self-esteem, so he just kind of takes it.

DR. LAURA: There must be a reason you want this kind of situation with a man. I don't know, maybe it gives you a sense of superiority.

NIKKI: I'm sure that's part of the problem.

Ouch. That problem is a frequent one, especially with women overmarinated in the most negative beliefs of the women's movement—that is, that society and men will oppress; they are the enemy; do not submit; terminate or dominate. And men are easily dominated with negativity from their woman. As I pointed out earlier, since men are simple creatures who come from a woman, are nurtured and brought up by a woman, and yearn for the continued love, admiration, and approval from a woman, it makes them vulnerable to their woman's moods, desires, tantrums, criticisms, disappointments, dissatisfactions, angers, and rejections.

Women need to better appreciate the magnitude of their power and influence over men, and not misuse or abuse it. Ladies, it won't make you happier.

One of the most typical ways that a wife misuses power over her husband is by her angry disappointment. Michelle, a listener, expressed this so well:

"My husband and I have been married for ten years. When we first married I started to watch soap operas. I expected my husband to treat me like the lovers of the soap opera stars were treated—without the cheating, of course. I blamed my husband for my unhappiness. If I was unhappy, I expected him to drop everything to make me happy. If he took me to dinner, I would feel neglected because he did not buy me flowers. My friends would readily agree with me that I was neglected and should not have to pick up his dirty socks off the floor. I was miserable and so was he.

I went to a religious women's retreat where we were required to go to a marriage class. God showed me how selfish I was. I learned that my happiness was dependent upon me and not my husband. I learned that my friends should not be a sounding board for my frustrations with my marriage. They always encouraged me to be against my husband.

I have found that most of my griefs are selfish and unwarranted. The ones that are not selfish I tell my husband about lovingly, and I don't nag. I am patient and he does fix it."

I agree that many women get tripped up when they try to measure their husbands' love by what the media or their friends tell them it should look like instead of by the husbands' own unique actions. One listener wrote that she had gotten all revved up for something incredible to happen for her on Valentine's Day. After hearing romantic, over-the-top stories from her friends about what their husbands had done, she expected her husband to sum up his feelings for her in similar grand fashion on this one day. And for five consecutive Valentine's Days, she was ferociously let down and disappointed. Not surprisingly, it showed in her behavior toward him in the subsequent weeks—without him knowing why.

Finally she expressed her annoyance. He devastated her by saying, "I show you I love you three hundred and sixty-five days a year, but if this one day isn't perfect, then none of that counts?" She felt like a complete jerk because she knew he was right. She remembered all the times he'd surprised her with flowers "just because," or took her on a surprise overnight trip, or spontaneously grabbed her in the kitchen and told her all the reasons he loved her.

She realized her husband loved her genuinely and that trying to force him to express it in a way that was more synthetic, while simultaneously discounting all he had done to show his love, was selfish and cruel. She wrote:

"I think if women would stop and pay attention, they would see that their husbands may not have stopped courting them but are actually doing it in a different way. It could be by getting up first when the baby cries, or doing the dishes so she can rest, or making a special dinner. Without acknowledging the more

subtle ways our husbands show us they love us, we rob ourselves and them of that connection. When their efforts are ignored long enough, isn't it inevitable that they'll eventually stop?"

I remember one fax to my radio program from a woman whose husband had died. She commented that she saw a lot of her friends complaining and whining about stupid stuff in their marriages. She reflected on how these women didn't realize how lucky they were to have those little problems in their lives and that they should be happy to have someone to care for and worry over. In short, they lacked gratitude for what they had.

Kaye, a listener, sent me this e-mail to express her awakening to the notion of gratitude:

> *"I must say that an important turning point for me came when I was listening to you on the radio, Dr. Laura. You were listening to some woman grouse about picky little things, and you asked her, 'Does your husband provide well for your family? Are your kids all healthy? Do you get to stay at home with them?' And so forth. She answered yes to all those questions. Then you said, 'So stop whining! You have forgotten to be grateful.'*
>
> *It was as though God took me by the shoulders and said, 'Hello! This is you, idiot!' Right at that moment, in the car, I began to thank God for my husband and for every excellent quality he has. Since then, I have made a conscious effort to do the following things:*
>
> - *Thank God daily for such a terrific guy, mentioning specific qualities for which I'm grateful.*
> - *Look for daily ways to be a blessing to my husband (trying to understand what pleases him, anticipating his needs, etc.).*

- *Chart my menstrual cycle and remind myself on the PMS days that what I'm feeling isn't true and to keep my mouth shut and let it pass.*
- *Avoid books, magazines, and TV shows that describe what marriage, family, and husbands ought to be like, and make a conscious effort to be grateful for things as they are instead of trying to change the people around me.*
- *Take responsibility for my own emotional well-being: Stay rested, don't overcommit and then complain, stay in touch with friends with a positive influence.*
- *Stay focused on making a home for my family and remember that this is my highest calling and responsibility, and that it has eternal value. The more I do this, the happier and more content I am.*"

It is exciting to receive such letters, showing how a change in attitude, and a commitment to quality actions, can bring such deep, profound joy.

I spend hours of my radio program trying to help folks get past the frighteningly pervasive diabolical message that married women at home with the children somehow aren't total women, maximizing their potential, and that men are idiotic, self-centered sex fiends, incapable of contributing anything of value to women or children.

Chapter 2

THE WHITE RABBIT SYNDROME

"And at the end of each day . . . relax. Let it all go; tomorrow will be there whether you worry or not—so let it go. Kiss each other, even if the kids can see. They need it, too."

SUZANNE

"I'm late, I'm late, for a very important date. No time . . ." was the retort of the White Rabbit when Alice was trying to ask him for help in Lewis Carroll's *Alice in Wonderland*. Sadly, this is the same retort many wives give their husbands, who are eager to make an intimate connection. Astonishing.

One of my listeners, Marie, wrote a letter to me detailing her slip down that rabbit hole:

> *"The best pointer I could give to wives about the care and feeding of a husband is to always make time for him. I know wives and moms get so, so, so, so busy. I do not know how I kept up with the soccer games, baseball practices, Scouts, and piano lessons—not to mention dinner, laundry, and an occasional trip to the grocery store or vet. I don't know how I did it."*

She then told the story of one particular day, a day like all other days in that it was filled with errands and activities. But this day was different. This day was her husband's birthday. And she had completely forgotten. No cake. No gift. No card. No acknowledgment at all. She only realized that it was his birthday when his mother stopped over, as she did every year on her son's birthday, to drop off this year's plaid shirt, and innocently asked if she was too late for the cake.

Even her children were mad at her. What did her husband do? *He* comforted *her* when she started crying in embarrassment and frustration!

> *"This is a man who works seven A.M. to seven P.M. five days a week and seven A.M. to twelve P.M. on Saturday so that I can be home with the kids. He certainly deserved better."*

That night, her mother-in-law, who rarely "got involved," told her that she had better take care of the person she had decided to spend the rest of her life with, or when the children were grown up and out of the house, she would be alone.

> *"Of course, she was right. I got so wrapped up in the daily stuff to do that I was not taking care of the great guy who was taking care of me. I started making a point of putting him higher on my list of priorities, and suddenly I was feeling like a wife again and not a frazzled mom.*
>
> *I started the very next day with a little love letter in his lunch box. I got a phone call in the middle of the day when he read it. We started exchanging smiles over the dinner table while the kids went on about their day, and it was so nice to get to know this really great guy I had picked.*
>
> *All marriages have ups and downs, but if you stay focused on why you got married in the first place, you can't lose."*

If the only conclusion drawn from this episode is that the wife now has more to take care of or fret about, larger points have been missed. For example, the outcome for Marie was more pleasure and more peace. Having that loving, attentive, playful connection with her husband *reduced* stress by adding a dimension of shared joy. This is a point too many women miss when they complain about being drained by their husbands' needs, or when they resent their husbands' needs, or when they perceive themselves as being victimized by their lives.

Which brings me to my next point, which is that lives are constructed of choices. Unless lightning has struck your house (obviously out of your control), your life is constructed out of the building blocks of your choices, good ones as well as bad. The bad choices (self-centered, shortsighted, immature, or just plain stupid) can have unpleasant consequences to marriages.

There are only so many hours in a day and only so many things any of us can do and still do well. Prioritizing is a must. Without it—that is, without formally or informally listing in order of importance what is necessary and what is negotiable—the important things tend to slip down on the list. Prioritizing is a moment-to-moment necessity, not just an issue of long-term planning.

Luke, a listener, wrote to me of a call he heard on my program that changed his immediate behavior. The caller had asked what she could do about her husband, who felt that he wasn't the number one priority in her life. I quickly told her that she needed to make him the number one priority or, in essence, her marital vows were hollow. Of course, she resisted, complaining about already having too many demands on her and this just made her life tougher. I commented on how self-centered a perspective that was and challenged her to imagine being on the receiving end of her behavior.

After hearing this, Luke wrote:

> *"I was thinking about how crazy it is to marry and then not enjoy it with your spouse. My wife and I have been married for just under a year, and I really enjoy marriage.*
>
> *Then I began to reflect on what my weekend held, and you guessed it: I was about to neglect our 'Friday Date Night' in the name of studying for my college finals and my lesson preparation for my high-school teaching job. Well, my wife was still at work when I got home, so I got out the books and tried to get as much done as possible. When she walked in the door, I hugged her and told her to get ready because we were going out on the town that night."*

Luke admitted that he had been letting her slip on his priority list—and that it hadn't even taken a year for him to become a meathead. He had justified this priority shuffling with the thought that he would put his wife at number one when he had more time. He ended his letter by thanking me for the lesson learned that no one is immune to occasional shortsightedness and faulty logic.

It is important to look again at what that logic was: that he would put her at #1 when he had more time. What does that mean? That means that she was never to be #1 unless there was nothing else on the list. When was that going to happen?

Julie, a listener, related the truth about what "doing for" a husband actually does for the wife:

> *"Even if I am having a long day, too, I can pick up deli sandwiches, a container of soup, and some parsley. Planning my evening surprise for my husband, strangely, takes away my stresses at work as well, because I am thinking about someone else.*
>
> *At home, I cut the sandwiches into triangles, stick fancy toothpicks through them, pour soup into bowls and add some garnish, set the table, and then greet him at the door with a big kiss and hug.*

How much time did this take? Five extra minutes. How much did we both receive? I had the opportunity to say in a small way, 'We are a team and I support you,' and he felt good that I had taken the extra time to make a simple thing beautiful just for him."

How beautiful is that? She didn't even have to wait to get goodies of gratitude back from him in order to feel good; she felt good simply from the giving. That put feeling good in her control. Get it?

Unfortunately, too many women fail to see their marriages as a source of satisfaction and accomplishment in the way they've been led to believe their careers will be. One caller, Suzanne, forty-three years old and married for more than twenty years, actually demonstrated hostility toward her husband's desire to spend time with her.

SUZANNE: Hi, Dr. Laura. I am a real estate agent, which is an all-or-none profession. I have been in it for about five years. I have just started to build up my career, and this past weekend, my husband gave me the ultimatum of either quitting my job or he wants a divorce.

DR. LAURA: Why?

SUZANNE: (laughing) Because he feels neglected on weekends and evenings.

DR. LAURA: What if he was neglecting you on nights and weekends? Wouldn't you be in some women's group bitching about it? Every time I see a movie with a group of women, they're complaining bitterly about how their men are all focused on their work or something else and aren't paying attention to them. So when we do it to them, it is called . . . what?

SUZANNE: Well, I feel like I earned where I am right now.

DR. LAURA: He feels like he earned the respect of a married person.

SUZANNE: I followed him overseas for five years.

DR. LAURA: This is an ugly payback for something you probably agreed to do. I can't imagine being married to someone I wouldn't see on the evenings or weekends. Suzanne, you are probably going to be divorced. The message you are giving him is that being a real-estate agent means more to you than being married to him. He has warned you. I think you are a foolish woman. With the expertise, knowledge, and talent you have, there are challenging things you could do during the week, and keep evenings and weekends for family time. If family means nothing to you, you will lose it. Your man, in my opinion, is not making any unreasonable demands. And after all these years, and all your nonsense, he still loves you and wants to be your man. At your age of forty-three, see how many other guys are going to say that to you, sweetheart.

I can't understand why a wife would see her husband wanting to spend time with her as a bad thing. They have been married twenty-something years and he still wants to be with her? That's a huge compliment!

This is not about controlling her. This is about wanting to have a life with her. How sad that she might not see that in time.

This mentality is the ugly part of the feminist movement, which supports personal success, acquisition, accomplishment, power, and the feminist political agenda over love, marriage, and family. When Karen Hughes, a counselor to President Bush, decided to resign to move back to Texas and spend more time with her family, many feminist spokes-types accused her of selling out women. Hmmm . . . what ever happened to "choice"?

Ms. Hughes and millions of other women have made the choice to give up their all-consuming careers. Why? Largely because the feminist battle cry of "having it all" resulted in lots of stress over a myriad of competing demands for time, guilt for the virtual neglect of children, and longing for more home-and-hearth time. In fact, there is even a new syndrome ascribed to working mothers called "Hurried Woman Syndrome," a term coined by some in the medical community who listened to women's complaints about their busy lifestyles.

This syndrome has been defined by the symptoms of weight gain, low sex drive, moodiness, and fatigue—all due to the stress caused by trying to do too much, not being able to keep up with it, not feeling very accomplished at any of it, resenting anyone who has any expectations (like husband and children), and ending up feeling hostile and depressed.

Cheryl, a listener, sent me a news release about this and added her own thoughts:

> *"In this world of 'do-it-all moms,' the ones who have babies, jobs, and every activity imaginable for their children, it is not surprising that the medical community has a newly diagnosed 'disease' for women. How does the medical community plan on 'curing' this new disease? Just a little something to think about."*

So much of the mail I receive from young women tells me a terrible story about how they feel compelled to look at life in only one way, and that way leads them to minimize the value of family and marriage to their souls and psyches at the same time they maximize their drive for financial conquest, thanks to the messages of society, the choices of their friends, and even the pressures of their own families. They tell me how they are made to feel foolish, weak, and stupid for wanting to raise their own children (instead of using nannies and day care), or for working only part-time outside of the home, if at all (instead of having equal fiscal strength to their husbands)—even for yearning for marriage at all (instead of shacking up or having babies on their own).

These women tell me how their own mothers or mothers-in-law deride them for being "lazy" for being stay-at-home moms rather than having careers, and how their own girlfriends demean them for wanting to marry and take care of their man, and they talk of the loneliness they feel in their neighborhoods because so few of their compatriots share their family-directed values.

And so the women who choose to focus their lives on family are marginalized, while the women who choose to "have it all" end up with Hurried Woman Syndrome. Generally, the HWS women do not treat their children or husbands well at all. Why? Because when you're tired and stressed out by the requirements of a job you must fulfill (or risk being fired), you tend to make everyone else pay the price (even strangers in traffic) because you have nothing else to give.

I remember just such a woman from my private-practice days. She was married, with one young adolescent boy. She came to her counseling session in her lovely business suit and polished pumps, and with a well-worn attaché case. She paced angrily, furious that her husband had the temerity to ask for some time alone to talk with her when she came through the door after work.

"Doesn't he have any respect?" she fumed. "Doesn't he understand I'm tired from a tough day and I just don't need any more demands on me?"

I looked at her quietly for a moment, then barely whispered, "Yes to number one, no to number two." She stared at me for the longest time, then started up again with her complaints about his insensitivity and selfishness.

Again, I looked at her quietly for a moment, then barely whispered, "*His* insensitivity and selfishness?"

She sat down and started to cry.

Many married women with children are wearing themselves down to the point that ill health and ill temper are the result. The problem is not with the demands of their husbands and children; the problem is with their notion of a full life. "Having it all" begins to approximate a "jack of all trades and a master of none." It is also a self-perpetuating trap. If the work is demanding and draining, and your time is limited and your temper isn't, guilt usually drives one toward more activity for children to "make up" for the neglect and mistreatment. That translates into frenetic schedules of extracurricular activities, which end up overextending and stressing the children as well as the parents. Fast-food dinners on the fly start substituting for healthy, nutritious, joyous, intimate family dinners, resulting in isolation as family members all do "their own thing."

And since the husband is an adult, he's just left to his own devices or attacked as a nuisance for his reasonable expectations for a love life and home life.

I get too many calls from women complaining that their husbands' unreasonable, selfish, insensitive, and annoying demands on a "tired woman" amount to mental abuse! Oh, please!

Tina, forty-six, called with her husband, Jerry, fifty-six. Jerry began the discussion by outlining their debate about the number of times marital intimacy should occur in a marriage:

JERRY: I am saying that for a good, healthy relationship, there is nothing wrong with us making love at least three times a week. She thinks once or twice every two or three weeks is a healthy relationship. I said we should call Dr. Laura because she knows what is healthy and what isn't.

DR. LAURA: Thanks for the endorsement. Tina, you heard what Jerry said. Is that a reasonable rendition of the issue?

TINA: Yes, yes, that is pretty close.

DR. LAURA: Did you ever like to have sex more than you do now?

TINA: Well, it isn't that I don't like it. When Jerry and I were first married, it was a lot.

DR. LAURA: So, what, has it gotten boring?

TINA: Maybe a little boring. But, more important, I am tired a lot.

DR. LAURA: Tina, that is not a fair excuse. It is your *obligation* to keep yourself healthy and fit so that you can be involved with your husband. You can't do the "I am tired" bit every day and have your husband just accept that this important, intimate part of his life is simply going to be controlled by your whim. It is your obligation not to be tired all the time. So take a nap, eat more protein, take your vitamins. What kind of thing is that to pull on him? What if he said, "I'm too tired and I'm not going to work anymore"? You have obligations to each other, and one of them is not to be constantly tired. That is not an acceptable excuse. Now, if the lovemaking has gotten dull, what have you done to spice it up?

TINA: (somewhat disdainfully) What have *I* done?

DR. LAURA: Yes, Tina, what have you done to spice it up?

TINA: Why do I have to do anything?

DR. LAURA: (shocked) Because you are one of the two people having sex.

TINA: Well, sometimes I do the candles, but my complaint is that especially during the week, we both have pretty high-pressured jobs.

DR. LAURA: Tina, your husband isn't complaining that his high-pressured job is leading him to neglect or reject you. Any woman who allows all her other choices of how she is spending her time to interfere with the love and intimacy with her husband is behaving like a fool. Your schedule is too intense for you and you should change it. Your commitments outside your marriage are too much for you. This is making you somewhat hostile and negative to the intimacy that is a great joy and a blessing in a relationship. Also, men need to feel the approval, acceptance, and attachment from their women that comes from sexual intimacy.

TINA: Okay.

DR. LAURA: So that *is* your obligation. It is not to spend yourself all at work.

TINA: (laughing) Yeah, I gave at the office. . . .

DR. LAURA: (laughing) You married him because you loved him and you wanted to make him happy.

TINA: Yes.

DR. LAURA: And I haven't heard too many women express being made unhappy by great orgasms with their husbands. Orgasms will put a smile on your face . . . and release a lot of tension.

There it is. If you decide that the most important thing about your life is your worker-ant role, you'll likely feel drained a lot of the time and resent the obligations you have to your husband and children—obligations that, ironically, will save you from that feeling of being drained in the first place. You are not loved, adored, and intimately needed at work. Check out all the competitive backbiting, layoffs, and computerization and mechanization substitutions for human beings going on in the workplace. Meanwhile, you are a goddess to your children and a queen to your husband. Let's see. Aside from the paycheck issue, which one is more nourishing and rewarding?

Now let me make something completely clear. I am not suggesting married women should not work. I am not suggesting that there is no valid form of personal expression of creativity and special gifts outside the home. Obviously, I have a radio and writing career. I just took up sailing. I love taking on challenges and doing service. But from day one, I have always made it clear to everyone, especially my husband and child, that if anything got in the way of family, it would get tempered or excised. It's one thing to have a tiring, stressful day—or even week. It's another thing to allow outside activities, no matter how seemingly important, to routinely get in the way of obligations to the roles created by holy vows, moral obligations, and love.

Caroline, a listener, learned this lesson and won the spiritual lottery:

> *"One day, after having a rough day at work, coming home to cook, clean, bathe kids, tend to my husband's needs, I told my husband I was too stressed out and he told me to quit my job. And he was serious. He didn't like to see me so stressed out trying to find someone to watch the kids, or just not having enough time to do the endless tasks a wife/mother needs to do.*
>
> *When I made the decision to quit my job, it was not only for the sake of my children, but also to support my husband, who works very hard. I now cook almost every meal during the week as opposed to putting something in the microwave or going to a fast-food joint. I used to ask my husband, 'How did I used to do it? Working full time, going to kids' sporting events, church events, personal life, etcetera,' and he replied, 'You didn't.'"*

The usual way the liberally biased media handles the issue of overextended women is to further condemn men for not picking up the slack at home—for letting their wives take on most of the burden of cleaning, cooking, and raising the children. First of all, it just isn't true—men do and always have helped out. Yes, I know the very phrase "helped out" makes a lot of feminists furious, but that's because they don't see men and women as having different temperaments, needs, attitudes, physiology, or psychology; they see a unisex world. And yet that world exists only in their naive imaginations. In the real world of humans, women have a unique urge toward bonding and nesting and nurturing. Men have a unique urge toward protecting, providing, and conquering. That doesn't mean men can't nurture children or that women can't climb mountains, but it does mean that beneath individual variations in constitution and temperament, women and men are different. Compatibility and harmony are best served when that difference is respected and, yes, even enjoyed, instead of denied or degraded.

Many talented, exceptional women have found that when their feet are firmly planted on family, their creativity has a comfortable place from which to soar. The day before I wrote this page, I received a novel and a letter from a newly published mystery author, Kathleen Antrim. Here is part of the letter she included with her novel, *Capital Offense:*

> *"I feel I have just graduated from the Dr. Laura School of Life. My husband and I decided that when we had children, I would stay at home with them. So when we had our first child, I quit my career in sales and marketing. I'm a staunch believer that you can put your children and family first and still follow your personal dreams! I'm living proof."*

Now, a word of caution. A wife's feet can be *too* firmly entrenched in only *one* part of family. Lynda, a listener, admits to this problem:

> *"The most important thing I have learned about the care and feeding of husbands, after three failures, is that God knew what He was talking about when He said 'forsaking all others' in Genesis. We women forget that, especially when the children come along. I was oblivious to the need to do this when I was married to the father of my children for seventeen years. We seldom went anywhere 'alone' together, and I totally ignored his needs. I always felt my children and their needs came first. I could never put him first."*

Literally hundreds of men have written to me about their pain with being marginalized after the children were born. Once their wives became mothers, they had no time to be wives. The men would even compliment their wives on being great mothers, but expressed considerable pain over not being shown love, affection, or sexual interest. The typical reply from a wife challenged with this was "I only have time to take care of one person, and our child is that person. I'm just too tired for you."

This puts fathers in the ugly and uncomfortable position of feeling competitive with and resentful of their children, whom they love so much. They miss the affection, companionship, and lovemaking they used to share with their wives. They feel put aside and shut out and unimportant.

And then, of course, once this pattern is established, the wives call me complaining that their husbands aren't givin' and doin' what they want them to. No kidding.

Here's a call from one of those women, Lynn.

LYNN: I have a twenty-two-month-old daughter and I am her mother one hundred and ten percent. On Mother's Day, my husband didn't do anything for me—no card, nothing. So I'm still feeling pretty resentful.

DR. LAURA: What's he mad at?

LYNN: I don't know.

DR. LAURA: What would be your guess?

LYNN: Well, I asked him last night, and maybe he feels that he doesn't get enough attention, or that my focus is more on my daughter, but . . .

DR. LAURA: In other words, he's neglected by you, so he's not motivated to please you. Ma'am, it's a very simple matter. Some women tend to get very self-centered when they have babies. They begin to think that their babies are the center of the universe, and their husbands are just supposed to hang out like Uranus and keep revolving around you whether or not they're getting anything back. Doesn't work that way. People start getting rejected, they start feeling alienated. With men, that makes them unmotivated to be romantic back on your schedule.

LYNN: Well, it's hard to snuggle up to a man, though, who hasn't given you a Valentine's Day acknowledgment.

DR. LAURA: That is the consequence of ignoring your man.

LYNN: Okay.

DR. LAURA: Instead of getting on your high horse about not getting a crummy present, take this as a sign that you'd better start treating him like your man if you want him to treat you like his woman. Just because you gave birth doesn't entitle you to ignore your man. And you probably don't pay him ten percent of the attention you paid to him when you were dating.

LYNN: Probably not. So I have to be the one to break the cycle? Is that what you are saying?

DR. LAURA: You're the only one with the power to break the cycle.

She then worried aloud that if she broke the cycle by returning to being loving and attentive, he might not change his behavior toward her, and that would hurt her feelings. The truth is, men forgive just about anything when we women treat them well. They definitely do not hold on to grudges with the tenacity that most women do. Remember, men are simple creatures and very dependent upon their wives for acceptance, approval, and affection. When those 3 A's are restored, all is well in their world.

Connie, another listener, wrote to me, explaining that the "I'm too busy with the kids to love my man" excuse never entered her lexicon. She said that she had gotten the advice to always make her husband know he was the most important person in her life from a male friend who had divorced his "perfect wife" after twenty-five years of marriage. She related that he complained, "When I got home from work, they were all too busy to notice. . . ."

Ken, a listener, pointed out that many wives have a blind spot; that is, "once they become mothers, they fall into a rut and become their husband's second mother." This "second mother" mentality entails "looking like" and "sounding like" a mother on a tear! Ken went on:

> *"They run around in 'mother attire' all the time rather than what they used to when they were out fishing for 'father,' and this continual visual turns most men off or pushes them elsewhere. . . . Not only do many wives look like mother most of the time, they move about the home constantly in mother mode: barking out orders, directing traffic, and beating the family drum. While this is all well and good, they forget to slip into wife mode, woman mode, lover mode, companion mode during private moments with their husbands."*

Women have long complained that their men bring their work home both in their briefcases and in their heads. Likewise, then, a woman should also be alert not to always be obsessed with domestic and mundane issues when she reconnects with "her man" at the end of their mutually challenging and tiring day.

I often hear angry neofeminists whine that it is oppressive that society (read: men) expects women to flit around with the perfect body: no fat, no wrinkles, and no gray hair. Frankly, there are some superficial men for whom that is true, but the vast majority of men feel that attitude, demeanor, and behavior take a front seat to perfect skin. When a wife *behaves* sexily, handles herself *alluringly,* and by the way she *looks* at her husband, *touches* him, and *talks* to him conveys her interest, love, respect, and attraction, frankly, he'll go anywhere and do anything and slay all dragons for his family. On the other hand, if she's too busy whipping him into shape so that her world is ordered, and she forgets to be his companion, his lover, his woman, then he'll forget Valentine's Day, anniversaries, and birthdays. Not hard to understand, is it?

Evan, a listener, confirms this reality:

> *"[My wife] feels that if she doesn't remind me again and again, something won't get done. But the fact is, it makes me feel like her child and that Mommy needs to check up on me. It's degrading. I want to be admired. I want to be acknowledged for being the breadwinner and making sure that we are all well taken care of. My greatest pleasure is when I feel like her hero. Like her* 'man.' *Not her boy."*

As one caller once quipped on my radio program, "My mother always said, 'You had a husband before you had children—don't forget it!' "

It cannot be emphasized enough that sometimes the wife's field of interest becomes so overwhelmingly filled with obligations to her family that she loses sight of her husband's needs and her obligation to him. If there is one basic assumption I believe that most married women make, it is that their husbands are to serve them, and that any demands husbands make are insensitive and selfish. When I tell women callers that they are *obligated* to their husbands for such-and-such, I generally get two reactions: The first is surprise, the second is anger over perceived oppression.

Think about it for even one minute: How many women's mags talk about women's obligations to their men and children? Not many. The typical article is about deserving freedom: Day care vs. child rearing, sex out of wedlock vs. marriage, affairs vs. fidelity, and solo parenting vs. two-parent homes are offered as entitlements for women.

These days, so many young women are products of divorces or never created homes, were neglected by career mothers, were indoctrinated by the anti-family feminists throughout their schooling, and are surrounded by a culture that glorifies selfish gratification over sacrifice, it's no wonder so many of them are "surprised" to not only hear of their obligations to husbands and children, but are also amazed at the gratification derived from doing so. It is for them that this book becomes so necessary.

Many women allow themselves to take on the shackles of obligations to all sorts of family members and friends without at all expressing feelings of being oppressed or angry. Many wives allow destructive friends and relatives to visit or move into their homes against the wishes of their husbands, because these wives have decided this good deed must be done, and then—big surprise—they have no time for their husbands.

One caller, Karen, took this to the nth degree. She's been married six years and has an almost two-year-old son. Soon after she got pregnant, her mother was diagnosed with cancer and moved in with them. When the child was born, the mother's health really started declining and Karen considered herself responsible for taking care of both her mother and her child. She figured, I guess, that her husband could just fend for himself.

Then, one day, she caught him looking at some Internet porn and decided it was time to dump him. She took her son and her mother and moved in with her older sisters so they all could take care of Mom. After her mother died, Karen continued living with her sisters. Two years passed, at which point her husband expressed remorse and regret for having looked at some porn and wanted to get his family back together. Karen expressed her love for him, and while she believes that it is in the best interest of the child to have Dad in the home, the problem is, her husband's job as a vice-principal is in California, but she's back East with her sisters and wants to stay there.

DR. LAURA: But here's the constant, constant problem with you, Karen: It's all about you—your baby, your mother, where you want to be, how you feel. It doesn't seem to ever be about the fact that you're somebody's wife.

KAREN: Right.

DR. LAURA: I'm surprised you're agreeing. However, that is not the attitude of a married woman. It is getting so typical of women to assume that once they get married, they can be all self-consumed and he's just supposed to stand there and take it. Why is that?

KAREN: I don't know.

DR. LAURA: You need to move to where your husband is; he's supporting the family. Isn't that obvious to you? I guess not.

KAREN: Well, he says he is willing to come here and find a job.

DR. LAURA: He has a job. I can't believe you would demand that he give up security for the insecurity of trying to find a job. It's about time you actually left your family. When you got married, you supposedly formed a new one. You had unmarried, unencumbered older sisters around, medical support, hospice help, but you took this all on yourself and abandoned your husband.

What if it had been the other way around? What if all he paid attention to was the child, his mother, and his family, and where he wanted to be living and how he felt and how exhausted he was and how frustrated he was . . . and he completely ignored you? You would be feeling like there was no point for you; that you had no place in his life.

KAREN: Right. That's how he feels.

DR. LAURA: Where did you get this mind-set that made this okay?

KAREN: I don't know.

Actually, she did know—but somehow didn't realize it until I probed. It turns out that there are no men in her family at all—no father, no husbands for the older sisters, no men involved with the family the whole time she was growing up. Her mother and sisters were all divorced. Since men were never an issue, her husband wasn't an issue . . . until now.

DR. LAURA: Well, you know what? I'll bet they're all miserable and have serious emotional problems.

KAREN: Yes, that's right.

DR. LAURA: Do you want to be one of them? Or do you want to be a happily married woman with a child flourishing in the middle of that?

KAREN: Yes, I certainly want to be a happily married woman.

DR. LAURA: Then go be with your husband and make him feel important. Call him up today. Tell him you

> love him and need him and that your child needs him. Tell him you're coming.

Karen went on to explain that her main problem was that she felt so obligated to her family, she didn't know how to get out of it. I reminded her that when one is married, the spouse and children go to the top of the obligation list. I also told her I thought her family was "sick" because not one of them could maintain a functional relationship with a man and they were perfectly content to undermine hers.

At that point, her eyes were opened.

The truth is, there are only so many hours in a day and only so much we can put our energies into. We have to make choices. And if you don't pick you husband as #1, that favor will, sadly, be returned.

Chapter 3

"YOU'RE A NAG!"

"Honey, it is part of your job as my wife to remind me of any duties I am not fulfilling, just as it is my job as a husband to remind you of your duties. You know I try my best, but if I don't know what I'm not doing, how can I do it, much less do it right? There is a difference between complaining and informing, between criticizing and reminding."

BILL

"So my suggestion for your book on the care and feeding of husbands? The number one *thing I want from my woman is to stop complaining. It's easy to moan about how hard your life it. When I do catch my wife in a 'willing mood,' I first have to endure twenty minutes of her complaining about this, that, and the other thing before I get to touch her. I figure if I help around the house to take some of the burden off of her, I would win her affection. Wrong. It is never enough and I am always wrong. A little kindness would go a long way toward making the marriage better."*

BRUCE

Bruce is right on. The universal complaint of men who e-mailed my Web site with their opinions about "The Proper Care and Feeding of Husbands" was that their wives criticize, complain, nag, rarely compliment or express appreciation, are difficult to satisfy, and basically are not as nice to them as they'd be to a stranger ringing their doorbell at three A.M.! These are not men who hate their wives or who were divorced; on the contrary, they are guys who love their wives and are trying to do whatever they can to please them. However, they are miserable and lonely.

Ken, another listener, is a thirty-eight-year-old husband of nine years with two children under the age of three. He wrote to express his opinion about a wife's nagging, explaining that it's not that a wife can never have a negative opinion or a problem with her husband, but that she should state the problem or concern without "bitching, fussing, arguing, guilt-tripping, or whining." Ken believes that a wife should say what is on her mind, discuss the possibility of a solution, and then move on.

I agree. The fact is that men don't like when women just "bitch about stuff," Ken said. In fact, they hate it. If a man can't find peace in his own home, where he should be able to feel relaxed, accepted, loved, and content, he begins to not only hate coming home, but he begins to hate his life. That sad reality is often the precipitator of stupid behaviors like drinking or taking drugs, Internet shenanigans, and inappropriate flirting or worse.

And it's not just issues of domestic disappointment that women nag or complain about; women can also be quite negative, hostile, and demeaning about simple "guy stuff." John and Maria wrote to me about their observations of couples stuck in just that hole. They described wives making fun of guys when they start discussing military issues, sports, or stocks. They wrote, "This same group of females would be livid if the guys made fun of their needlepoint, cooking, spa activities, or shopping tendencies." How true.

John and Maria also wrote about the wives they knew who have joined various all-female clubs and activity groups, who expect their husbands to be home to take care of the kids (which the husbands are glad to do) when they pursue these activities, but go crazy when their husbands want to do all-guy things without them, like fishing or playing poker or even going alone into the garage to hammer and saw stuff. Somehow the husband is seen as neglectful, insensitive, and selfish while the wife was just doing what she was entitled to do because she does so much for the family and needs some time to herself. Talk about insensitive and selfish!

Beyond the issue of complaining about "male stuff" is complaining about his romantic history. These are the calls that really test my patience. Just the other day on my radio program, a wife called to find out if she should confront her husband about a Christmas card he had received from an ex-girlfriend. It seems that this ex (one from a *long* time ago) sent an annual Christmas card, complete with pictures of her happy family and one of those "update letters." My caller was complaining about the personal stuff she shared and how it was so inappropriate.

DR. LAURA: What in the letter was provocatively, seductively inappropriate? And remember, you get one chance to prove your point, so give me the most egregious example, okay?

CALLER: She wrote about surviving breast cancer.

DR. LAURA: You are threatened and angry about a happily married woman who contacts your husband only once a year and only with a Christmas card and who has had breast cancer? Yikes, woman, do you often complain to him about such petty issues that are completely out of his control?

Believe it or not, she was stubborn about how inappropriate she thought this was and how she was going to confront him about it. I frankly felt very bad for her poor husband, who probably won't have a very Merry Christmas.

All of this nagging, nitpicking, and criticizing that men routinely get from their wives (be honest, girls, this is what we do) does not do much for their egos, which in turn results in them trying harder—for a while—and then giving up . . . and then we have more to complain about. Talk about a vicious cycle!

Jim, a listener, described himself as having a master of science degree and working at a college where he teaches a computer course to undergraduates, assists in teaching computer courses to graduate students, helps fellow faculty members with their computer problems, maintains a small research-and-teaching computer lab, operates equipment (dump trucks, tractors, chainsaws, etc.), and advises a student club.

> *"I have always had superlative evaluations on my performance. AT HOME I CAN'T DO ANYTHING RIGHT! I sometimes spend several minutes in thought on a task at hand, trying to decide exactly what to do. After weighing the pros and cons, I make a decision and act. Almost invariably I get, 'What did you do that for? Now I can't . . . ,' or I hear, 'Who put the ??? here?' or sometimes I get a straight-out 'That's stupid.'*
>
> *Many times my wife weighs in on a narrowly defeated second or third option while trashing whatever I had selected. Explanations are not wanted, and if I point out that I have just been called stupid, an argument is more likely than an apology.*
>
> *It is something that wears you down like erosion."*

He means it. And Cathy's husband also meant it—just before he left her. Cathy, another listener, wrote to me of marrying when she was, according to her, "twenty-five and very immature." She admitted being caught up in herself, her home, and her children. Her husband would walk through the door after a hard day of work and all she would do was complain about the kids and the house. She would nag and complain about *her* life, which was, in reality, very privileged. Her husband never got a hug from her. She never sat down and really asked him how his job was or how his day went or if he was happy.

> *"I tossed aside his feelings and I, in the end, lost my husband to another woman and my children lost their father. God, if only I had been as nurturing to him as I was to my children. I am now in my late forties and I could kick myself for my selfishness and stupidity. Boy, have I ever learned from my mistake."*

Cathy remarried and treats her current husband quite differently. She always asks him how his day went, has him describe to her the details of what he's doing, and looks as interested as she can even when she doesn't follow or understand what he's talking about. She wakes up with him and brings him coffee before work and a glass of wine when he gets home—and no jumping on him with house or personal problems the minute he walks through the door. Such simple gestures. Such a difference in her home.

I'm convinced that too many wives don't know what to do or how to communicate if they're not complaining, nagging, or criticizing. Many times on my radio program I have suggested to women that they approach this problem as they would a new puppy. I tell them that instead of constantly screaming "NO!" to every little annoyance, transgression, or difference of perspective, opinion, or style, they should compliment the heck out of the things they like and want. Betcha that way you'll get more of it!

Clarence, a listener, wrote that his wife is very much like

the little girl with the curl right in the middle of her forehead: When she is good, she is very, very good, but when she is bad, she is horrid . . . and abusive.

In order to raise five kids in the country (where his wife wishes to live), he commutes and works a total of thirteen hours a day. Although he's exhausted when he comes home, he always tries to find something that needs doing and would make his wife's life easier . . . and perhaps make her the good girl. He often washes the dishes, and when the drainer becomes full, he dries them.

> *"I would appreciate even a quiet 'Thank you,' but I get, instead, a 'YOU KNOW YOU SPREAD GERMS WHEN YOU DRY DISHES WITH THE DISH TOWEL!' So next time I stop when the drainer is full and work on something else. Response? 'WHY CAN'T YOU DO ALL THE DISHES?' So next time I carefully stack dishes three feet high. Response? 'YOU KNOW THAT I GREASED THE BREAD PAN AND I WAS PLANNING ON USING IT AGAIN, AND NOW THANKS TO YOU CAUSING ME MORE WORK, I HAVE TO GREASE IT ALL OVER AGAIN!'*
>
> *So the next time when I can no longer stack any higher, I wait a couple of hours for the dishes to air-dry and put the first batch away. Response? 'ONE OF THE SPOONS WAS STILL DAMP WHEN YOU PUT IT IN THE DRAWER!' So next time I leave the dishes and spend two hours cleaning the living room. Response? 'WHY DON'T YOU EVER DO ANYTHING AROUND THE HOUSE? CAN'T YOU SEE THE DISHES NEED TO BE DONE?'*
>
> *So next time I stand in front of the kitchen sink with tears running down my face, wanting to help out with something that will be noticed but petrified that I will discover one more way to*

do the dishes wrong. Response? 'I WANT A DIVORCE. I HAVE TO DO EVERYTHING MYSELF ANYWAY!' I would be much happier with a quiet 'Thank you.'"

When discussing this issue of nagging with my husband, who suggested that I had the necessary expertise to write this chapter (was that a hint?), he said that he just figured that nagging was part of the female XX chromosomal information—that it was simply built into the DNA. But even if that were true, would it let us off the hook? Can we say we wives are entitled to nag because it's our genetic destiny?

I think not.

But I believe it is more typically female and that women almost believe it is their birthright and that men would be lost without it.

I think not.

Rachel, a listener, wrote that she also thought nagging was an inherent right of wifehood. Although she and her husband had been married for only about a year, they were arguing every day! She wanted the two of them to go into marriage counseling to help him discover what he was doing wrong. She felt that all her needs were important. For example, she would nag him about how to soak dishes, or get angry at him for forgetting something he'd said in passing three months earlier.

"I had to exercise my right to complain or he wouldn't know when he would be doing things that bothered me. And he, being my husband, was not supposed to get mad—just take it like a man."

More like a doormat, she really means. Obviously, this caused problems in their relationship. She finally admitted that she was to blame, and that meant that she had the answer to the problem: She simply buttoned her lip. A miracle occurred. They argued less. Their marriage got better. She told him she was sorry for causing him so much grief.

She concluded her letter with, "Which brings me to the point: Complaining is not a virtue. Complaining does not lead to anything good."

No, but appreciation does lead to something good. Examine these two scenarios and then tell yourself which you think will get the desired results:

The garbage needs to be taken out.

Scenario 1: Yell at him every five minutes to remind him that the garbage has to be taken out. Then berate him for not having done it yet in spite of your reminders and in spite of whatever else he might be doing. Then start escalating things by bringing up everything else he's done to annoy you in the past decade. Then, once he's finally taken the garbage out, tell him, "It's about time!" Then storm off to your room, pout, and turn your back to him in bed.

Scenario 2: Let him know you've wrapped up the trash and that it's sitting by the back door, and ask him if, when he has time, he would please dump it in the trash bin. Don't bring it up again (why bother, because the trashman isn't coming till morning, anyway?). Catch him just as he's coming back from tossing the bag in the can. Give him a big kiss and tell him that it was a big help because it's hard for you to hold the can lid up with one arm and pitch a very heavy bag with the other hand.

Which approach do you think will ensure that the trash is out of your kitchen every night like clockwork?

Jo, the listener who suggested Scenario 2, wrote:

> *"Men are doers; simple, straight-line types. The reason they have a tendency to rescue damsels in distress is because of their need to be admired for their chivalry."*

Men love to hear, "My hero!" What makes it so difficult for their wives to give them that accolade? Where does so much false pride, ego, resentment, and stubbornness come from?

Charlie, a farmer, wrote about a conversation his wife told him she'd had with a neighbor of theirs. Evidently, Charlie's wife admitted complaining to this woman that Charlie was not willing to do the chores around the house that she wanted him to do, how and when she wanted them done. The other woman told Charlie's wife that she didn't have the same problem with her husband because she "rewards him" for doing the household chores that she would like him to do.

After his wife finished the story, she said to Charlie, "I hope you don't expect a reward for doing the household chores." Charlie proceeded to get his hat and was starting for the front door when his wife asked where he was going.

He told her he was simply going to see if his wife's friend needed her lawn mowed.

"My wife still doesn't get it. I would be much more willing to do the chores she wants me to do if I got some show of appreciation for doing them."

How shortsighted of Charlie's wife. It does seem that many woman see "schmoozing" their men as an example of their being "controlled." Sarah, a caller, and I tussled over this point.

Sarah and her husband have been married fifteen years. She described marrying him because he was so nice. I immediately came back with the suggestion that she made that choice because it put her in control. Now she sees his being "nice" as "weak," and is frustrated with his lack of helpfulness in disciplining the children.

SARAH: We talked about it and I told him that what I wanted from him is to help me.

DR. LAURA: Except he never does it right, right?

SARAH: It's not that he doesn't do it right. It's that he doesn't do anything at all.

DR. LAURA: Because when he does it you criticize him. Whenever he tries something, in your eyes it is inadequate. So now he just doesn't get involved. This is a vicious cycle. I suggest you both go into counseling. The counselor will remind you to hush up and back off and only suggest something to him. He has to move forward on his own and not complain about not having control when he refuses to take it—albeit under the difficult circumstances of you not being willing to either give up control or share it. If he wants to be held in respect in your eyes and the children's eyes, he is going to have to be more aggressive, which is not naturally his nature. He can't blame this all on you, either! Now, I want you to watch yourself all week and observe yourself criticizing when he does exert control. When you do that, he figures, why bother.

SARAH: Right, that is exactly right.

DR. LAURA: So even if he only does whatever sixty percent of the time or sixty percent of how you'd like it, it's better than zero. You see, Sarah, it seems wonderful to be in control, but eventually you become overwhelmed and need help and want a partner. For example, if Johnny intentionally threw the water into the shrub, go to your husband and say, "Can you please deal with that?" and then walk out of the room. Don't even watch it happen. And then—this is the most important part—say, "Thank you."

SARAH: Okay.

It is very difficult for men when they come home from work only to hear how they're not doing enough around the house. When they help with the dishes and only hear about how they didn't do the laundry, they begin to feel like failures. One listener, Chris, had gone through this for so long that he eventually had an affair with a woman who, obviously, treated him more like a hero. Eventually, filled with remorse and love for his family, he ended the affair and has worked with his wife to repair their marriage. He concluded his letter with these important words of wisdom:

> *"If I had to summarize, I'd say, 'Please, ladies, recognize that we men do love you, and although you may not think we do much around the house, we do the ugly stuff like change the oil and mow the lawn and get up early when it snows to shovel a path to your car and start the car so it will be warm when you get in. We would walk through fire for you to get you a quart of cookie-dough ice cream in the middle of the night, because we love you.'"*

Roy, a listener who describes himself as married but lonely, believes he is trying to be a good husband, but that it's hard to be good when the feedback is mostly related to the times he doesn't meet his wife's expectations. He longs to be her hero, but she evidently prefers to point out that he leaves the lights on, doesn't dust everywhere he should, misses spots when he's washing the dishes, interrupts her when she's talking, chooses to drive the wrong way in the parking lot, drives too slowly . . . and so on.

He gave this advice to women:

> *"If you can't accentuate the positive, at least acknowledge it. The world is full of messages to men that there are standards we don't meet. There is always another man who is more handsome, more virile, or more athletic than we are. None of that matters if the most important person in our life looks up to us, accepts us as we are, and loves us even though we aren't perfect.*

Maybe there is a part of the small boy that never leaves the grown man, I don't know. All I know is that the husband who has a wife who supports him and praises him for the positive things he does is the envy of all the other men who have to live with criticism, sarcasm, and constant reminders of their failures."

Ouch.

All of this criticism of men does not make them feel *more* loving, and it also makes the complaining wife feel less love for her husband. That's true; the very act of criticism destroys warm feelings toward the target of that criticism. But on the other hand, the simple elimination or diminution of criticism adds to loving feelings.

Sara wrote that she never realized that she was nicer to telemarketers than she was to her husband, and that many of her married friends would also treat total strangers nicer than their husbands. She never could see the good in anything her husband did—she could only see the mud that he tracked into the house.

She wrote that she couldn't quite remember why or when she started to change. Maybe it was simply that all the negativity became too unbearable for her. Or maybe it was when she realized that she could not have been too happy when she would leave the house without wearing makeup or dressing nicely, or when she would slob around the house in sweats and tees.

"Over time I have adopted ways to make my husband feel like my champion because he is, and for a long time I would go out of my way to belittle him and his significance *in life. I have yet to find out really why I was that way, but life is wonderful now and my changes have come back to me ten-fold. I love my husband more and more each day."*

I often get calls from women who complain about losing that lovin' feeling. They, of course, imagine it's because something is missing from their guy. Turns out that more often than not, though, they've been stomping on their own loving feelings with their mistreatment of their men. Imagine that.

I am often struck by the pettiness of the complaining, and by the complete inability to see another way of handling a situation. Too often the negative perception that seems to always pop up first ends up dominating all emotion and reason.

Tina called me about her marriage of about one year. This was her second marriage and she and her husband had a newborn baby. Now, I give you that at least for the first year after birth, and especially if the mother is actually raising her own child, emotions can get a bit edgy. But this was ridiculous.

She angrily told me that her husband had lied to her about losing his wedding ring.

TINA: He states that he lost his wedding ring over a month ago. He didn't talk to me about it. He proceeded to go to the jewelry store and purchase another, identical ring. I found out by the jewelry bill coming in the mail. It turns out that he found his ring and now he has two rings and a jewelry bill and has lied to his wife.

DR. LAURA: Lied to his wife about what?

TINA: He never told me that he lost the ring.

DR. LAURA: Why is that a lie?

TINA: Because I feel like he should have talked to me.

DR. LAURA: Wondering why he didn't come to you is not the same as him being a liar. He didn't lie. Noticing how you get, I can understand why he didn't want to say anything to you. You seem pretty volatile. So he went out and replaced it before you would find out and get mad. He didn't want you to be hurt, or worried, or angry. He was trying to solve the problem and keep you happy. So you call a radio program and want to hang him.

TINA: I really feel like he was dishonest. . . .

DR. LAURA: You know, Tina, your *feelings* aren't facts, and your *feelings* ought not be weapons.

TINA: So you think he did the right thing?

DR. LAURA: Yes. It was one of a few "right things." It certainly indicates his wanting to not hurt or upset you. And it also appears to indicate that he didn't think he could talk to you about it without you getting angry.

TINA: (sarcastically) I am sure he will be glad to hear that.

DR. LAURA: You know, Tina, I hope you will start treating him a little better, because you have a newborn and you are already down one marriage. I think you should not have your fangs out so quickly.

TINA: Okay. That's reasonable. I guess they are out quickly because dishonesty is a sore point with me.

DR. LAURA: Well, it wasn't dishonest; it was desperate. You are exaggerating everything now because you have some bad memories. You could destroy today.

TINA: I don't want to do that.

DR. LAURA: Well then, when he comes home, I want you to put your arms around him and say you know you were real off base. Tell him how nice it was of him to try to save the day and replace the ring so you wouldn't be upset. Tell him you just got carried away. Don't mention the past. Say "I'm sorry," and it will all be smoothed over.

TINA: I appreciate that and I will do that. I value your opinion.

Obviously, one reason the fangs may come out quickly is that many women, who have cycled through too many intimate relationships, shack-ups, and marriages, have developed a well of pain and disappointment. They don't want to be hurt . . . again. They become hypersensitive and take quick leaps into misassumptions.

Wives need to love their husbands as though they've never been hurt before. Otherwise, they destroy today.

Unfortunately, it's hard for many women to find support for that healthy point of view from their women friends, relatives, or even "help" groups.

Wendi, a listener, wrote to me that during the fourth year of her tumultuous marriage, her husband suggested that she participate in their church's Wednesday-morning "Moms Group." Once she'd done so, her husband noticed changes in her on Wednesday evenings, but they weren't the good ones they'd both hoped for.

> *"The women's group was not the help I'd been hoping for. Instead of finding practical ways to become a better mother, the group was a gripe session for women to vent about their husbands' idiosyncrasies, bad attitudes, and failures in general and in specific. I was becoming trained to complain and whine about real or imagined behavior and look for sympathy from other women. I discontinued participation. My husband and I sought real counsel from a godly couple, our pastor and his wife of over fifty years. They taught us to respect one another, our family, and our privacy. It was important for both of us to be fed from the same trough so that we could work together."*

Grace, another listener, was bolder in her reaction to the "bitching about husbands" that can go on in groups. In her letter she described being with a group of women from the restaurant at which she worked. It seems things started slowly, with women complaining about how their men didn't wine and dine them since their marriage, but then it snowballed into a ferocious male-bashing session.

Grace herself was having marital troubles and her home life was shaky. After about an hour of everyone airing their grievances, someone noticed that Grace hadn't said anything yet. They offered her the platform, acknowledging that she must have some really great complaints. It may have been at that point that Grace had her "revelation." She proceeded to tell the group what she thought.

> *"Most of their complaints were their own faults. They were shocked. I asked them when was the last time they cooked their husbands a dinner and ate it by candlelight on the porch? When was the last time they gave their husbands a back rub? What I was asking was when was the last time they did something for their husbands. All the women just stood there and looked at me.*
>
> *I believe that the give-and-take in a marriage gets forgotten by women. Somehow we feel that once we are married, our part of 'give' is doing dishes, cooking dinner, and watching the kids. We then expect our husbands to reward us for this with back rubs, flowers, dates—but we don't give these things in return.*
>
> *Do we reward him for going to work, mowing the lawn, fixing the cars? He needs to be rewarded for these things, too. But that's not why you should do these things. They are not reward points. You do this because you love him.*
>
> *If you want to keep a fire in your marriage, you need more than the spark—you need to add fuel. So if a woman starts the spark, the man will follow and add some kindling, then she can add more and soon you will have a happy marriage."*

How did so many women get to this unhappy place of not understanding how truly "simple" men are in their requirements and how much benevolent power their wives have over them? Why did notions like assuaging "male ego" and using "feminine wiles" rocket into disrepute? How is it that so many women are angry with men in general yet expect to have a happy life married to one of them?

There are a number of reasons for this, and I believe they all revolve around the assault upon, and virtual collapse of, the values of religious morality, modesty, fidelity, chastity, respect for life, and a commitment to family and child rearing.

With a religious foundation, both women and men appreciate that they become more complete when bonded to the opposite sex in holy matrimony. Without it, though, women may see marriage as either an option equivalent to the usually temporary arrangement of shacking up, or as the threat of oppression, or as an impediment to the fulfillment of some important material goals.

When modesty, chastity, and fidelity were in vogue, women who valued themselves as more than sexual objects or outlets were respected by society in general and men in particular. Now women have to contend with men taught to expect sexual favors as a part of casual dating. As a result, women ignore their true nature to bond, and find themselves getting more and more hurt and bitter as they search for meaning in a culture telling them meaning has no meaning.

When there was awe and respect for life, an "accidental pregnancy" was met with commitment and responsibility because women expected it and men were accountable. Now men expect an accidental pregnancy to result in an abortion because society has trained them to see this as a temporary inconvenience, or they expect to walk away because they've been told men aren't needed to raise babies.

Commitment to marriage and child rearing was once viewed as the pinnacle of adulthood identity, so that women looked carefully for the "right" man for the job, and parents were consulted for opinions and blessings. Now, with so few sustained marriages and children growing up with complex family trees made up of multiple marriages, divorces, and out-of-wedlock children, fewer women look upon marriage and child rearing as stable or even normal.

The feminist double whammy of the elevation of women without men (and children without fathers) and the dismissal of men as unnecessary or even dangerous has certainly not contributed to the kind of positive disposition that women need in order to function well within a monogamous, heterosexual, committed relationship.

This grandiose self-centeredness about the value of women, paired with a virtual disdain for men, leads women to treat men badly. Too many women look at men with a sense of entitlement versus an opportunity for selflessness. Why? All of those forces taken together have given women a false sense of superiority.

Combine this false sense of superiority with the element of not being properly psychologically fed by their fathers and you have a recipe for tension. Women have a hunger for being protected and cared for—whether they want to admit it or not. This hunger is amplified when there was no father in the home. The man or men who then enter their lives become mixed up in their psychological need to replace Dad. This makes for inappropriate expectations about what a man can and should do, which get in the way of a healthy, two-way relationship. While there is always some wonderful mommying and daddying going on in all marital relationships, the compulsion to always give or receive such is a serious problem, as their partner is either force-fed or starved. That lack of balance destroys relationships and corrodes people's psyches.

Sara wrote about her experience with the attitude of entitlement:

> *"I was under the impression, when I was first married, that a husband was supposed to be controlled and bend to the wife's whim. Everyone said men were stupid and they needed to be*

educated and trained. I was becoming more and more frustrated because my husband wasn't bending. I'd demand he act like a 'man,' but failed to treat him like one. I was so concerned about what I deserved that I almost lost sight of the fact that he deserved something, too. I took advantage of his love for me and misinterpreted it as weakness.

As I matured and grew spiritually and emotionally, I realized that it was my actions that made him react the way he did. I now give my husband the respect that he deserves not only as a husband and a partner, but as a human being. He has in turn become the 'man' I never allowed him to be . . . and is wonderful at it. I know that this is one of the most important life lessons I have learned."

Louise, another listener, e-mailed me concerning her understanding of the dynamics of her original family, which clouded her perception of men and marriage. Her father had been violent and mean-spirited. Her response was to fear and hate him. While she wanted to have a happy, loving, well-adjusted family of her own, she was too mucked up in worrying about being "the victim" that her mother herself portrayed. With therapy, Louise came to realize that her mother was not a victim at all, but someone responsible for her own choices, actions, and behaviors. Her mother was hateful toward men, seeing them as spoiled children who must be managed, and she raised her daughters to see life in that same light. "My father was the perfect match for her," Louise recounted. "He bullied her, but she controlled him by allowing herself to be the martyr—the superior person."

Louise came to realize that for her to have a successful marriage, she had to take responsibility for her choice in a mate, and how she would treat him. When she first married, naturally things were difficult because it was hard to *not* put into practice what she had learned in her original family. But now she says, "I am so grateful for my family, and I am proud that we treat each other with kindness, respect, and patience. In short, we nurture our relationship with each other, not our neuroses."

Many of the wives reading this book may feel stuck in some inexplicably angry place. Perhaps this story, told by Louise's minister, will help:

A grandfather was talking to his grandson. "Grandson," he said, "there are two wolves living in my heart and they are at war with each other. One is vicious and cruel, the other is wise and kind."

"Grandfather," said the alarmed grandson, "which one will win?"

"The one I feed," said the grandfather.

That is precisely why I steer women who are troubled in their marriages away from women's groups, where men-bashing is a cross between entertainment and denial of personal responsibility; I steer these women away from the run-of-the-mill feminist-oriented psychotherapists, for whom a happy relationship with a man is simply not necessary; I steer these women away from griping and gossiping with their girlfriends about their annoyances with their husbands. The reason I do all this serious steering-away is explained in the minister's story: The more you dwell on the negative, the farther away you get from appreciation of the positive, as well as the motivation to contribute in a more healthy way yourself!

One small step toward a wife's taking responsibility is to keep lips buttoned over things that *do not really matter.* I'm fond of repeating a phrase sent to me by a retired Marine master sergeant: "Is this the hill you wish to die on?" Frankly, asking myself that question always makes my priorities instantly fall into place and reduces my tension about whatever it is I was worked up about.

Wives need to remind themselves that when their husbands

do something differently from how they would do it themselves, it does not constitute a breach of sanity or a display of contempt. It is merely a *different* way to do something. Instead of immediately correcting a husband, first see if there is something you could learn (could happen, you know?), then see if the job gets done (that was the goal, wasn't it?), and then offer a compliment (you like those, too, don't you?).

One husband, "L," wrote that wives should not "micromanage."

> *"Trust your husband. Recognize that he has his own ways of doing things. They don't have to be done your way to be adequately done. If the toilet ends up clean, it doesn't matter if he didn't give it your 'special touch.' If he has the kids for the day so you can attend a baby shower, don't leave a huge list of detailed instructions. As long as the two of you share the same rules and values, you should trust him to create his own relationship and 'caring style' with his children without your intervention."*

When women micromanage, their husbands give up trying to please them, and then the wives complain that their men don't do anything for them. Wives need to look to the mirror for the typical source of that problem.

Essentially, micromanaging is about controlling. That issue of control makes men feel that they are ultimately not the men their wives wished they'd married. Bill, a listener, shared the example of his first wife (obviously not his last wife) buying him a pair of jeans. He'd carefully written down the size, brand, and color he wanted. He even told her the store with the best price. She came home with Dockers—khaki, the wrong size, and clearly the wrong type. He thanked her for her efforts, explained the inadvertent error she'd made, and asked her to please exchange them for what he wanted. She agreed, and returned from her next shopping trip with another pair of Dockers, not jeans, in yet a different color.

> *"This time she explained that she did not like the way I looked in jeans, and that what I needed, and all I was going to get, was a pair of Dockers. It turns out what she really wanted was a different guy to fill the Dockers. She spent twenty-five years trying to make me somebody else. Know who your husband is and accept him. He is what he is. She clearly knew what kind of guy I was before we married. She just assumed she could nag, lie, cry, manipulate, and scream at me till I became someone else."*

He did become someone else: her ex-husband.

This nonacceptance of who your man is can get even uglier. What horrifies me time and time again is the evil some wives perpetrate in the name of their "feelings." This is an extension of the entitlement issue. And the two expressed "feelings" that can bring almost any husband to his knees are "hurt" and "uncomfortable." I have had innumerable arguments with wives on my radio programs over their over- and misuse of those feelings, which is often tantamount to cruelty or evil in their attempt to control and dictate.

The more typical scenarios seem to occur in stepfamily situations. I'm amazed at how many women marry men with prior marriages and children and expect all of that to disappear when they come on the scene, as though his earlier life had evaporated into the Twilight Zone.

And the men suffer horribly. Brian was one of those husbands.

BRIAN: I'm presently married for three years and have two children, two and three. I have an ex-wife who lives out of state, with whom I have an eight-year-old son. My ex-wife is now divorced again. I don't get to see my son often because of the distance and other factors.

DR. LAURA: Oh dear, that poor little boy has suffered a lot of loss.

BRIAN: Yes, I'd hoped her marriage would work so he would have a male role model.

DR. LAURA: How can I help you?

BRIAN: My question is: I'm supposed to have him for the whole summer. I've never had him that long before, but now his mom is under stress and is willing to let me have him. But my wife is uncomfortable with that.

DR. LAURA: Well, uncomfortable. . . . So what? Everyone is going to be uncomfortable simply because it's new and different. So? Talk about the issues, find ways to deal with them.

BRIAN: Here's my question for you, Dr. Laura. Would it be inappropriate morally to tell my ex-wife that it's just not possible to have him for the whole summer?

DR. LAURA: You're just not going to have me go there, sir. You made him and virtually abandoned him. He's your son, you need to raise him.

BRIAN: I agree with that completely. But my wife says she does not want to have him there for the whole summer. She said she can't do it.

It was at this point that I was ashamed for my gender. Of course I see the strain in raising two small children under the age of three. What I don't like to hear, but hear too often, is women not wanting their stepchildren around because there will be no children before theirs! How disgusting! Even more disgusting is how resentful wives can get about their husband's time, affection, and financial resources being directed at his own children. There is so little sensitivity to the fact that he already has those bonds and that they matter, and that his responsibility to any children he's had is a moral imperative.

What I told Brian, as I tell the many husbands who call with this type of question, is that he needs to *inform* his wife that the boy is coming for the summer. Period. Any difficulties in scheduling, transportation, and activities can be worked out.

BRIAN: And if she says no?

DR. LAURA: There is no "no." You say, "Honey, you married a man with a child. There is no 'no,' there's only 'how.' "

BRIAN: So—no matter what?

DR. LAURA: You're his dad. Period.

I suggested he also watch out for how many times and in how many ways his wife tries to manipulate him by telling him she's "uncomfortable," as though that were a stop sign. Obligations and responsibilities are usually not discomfort-free zones. That's part of what makes rising to those occasions such an extraordinary measure of character and love.

We all think we'd like to be able to control everything and everyone around us. We imagine we'd be safe and secure—always on familiar turf. Frankly, the texture of life does not come from the familiar (which is comfortable), but from challenging ourselves with the unfamiliar.

Tonya, a listener who termed herself a "control freak," got this lesson and shared it with me:

"I take my husband for granted. I know this, as I have recently become an avid listener of your program and have learned from hearing some callers who sound just like me. I am a control freak and I am always trying to dominate my husband. It mostly has to do with our financial health. Somehow I see that

in trying to control his spending, etc., what I am really doing is punishing him. I also like feeling superior to him in this area—that somehow I am better than him as the queen of the checkbook. Just because I don't think he really needs a sander doesn't mean he shouldn't have it. He probably doesn't really think I need all of those candles and Pampered Chef products either . . . but he must be punished for his past mistakes! I'm going to read your book, and I'm sure it will help me find other ways to show him that he is appreciated. And, as I have heard you say so many times, if he feels loved and appreciated, those feelings will most likely be reciprocated."

You can bet on it.

However, the problem is often getting the wife to see, to acknowledge, to accept, to realize that she is, in fact, controlling. While many women are quick to the draw to aim at some extraneous word or deed of their husband's as evidence of his being controlling, it seems that some are blinded to the reality of their own actions.

Crystal, a caller, was one of those women. She'd read my book *Ten Stupid Things Couples Do to Mess Up Their Relationships* and was focused on the chapter whose title she remembered as "Stupid 'Control.'"

DR. LAURA: Actually, it's "Stupid Power."

CRYSTAL: Stupid power. That is my husband and I know I can't change him. I was wondering what I could do to let him know that this isn't going to work.

DR. LAURA: Give me an example of what he does—some behavior you wish would change.

CRYSTAL: Okay. We had an argument. I apologized—actually, I left him a message at his work. When we got home and we were talking, I asked him how his day was. He said he was really busy. I asked him if he got my message. He said that he had but that he is in a really busy, difficult time at work. I walked away. Then I said that it really hurt my feelings that he didn't even acknowledge my apology.

DR. LAURA: Okay. This was your example of his being controlling? I don't see any controlling except by you. Your husband has to—now listen carefully, Crystal—behave in a certain way or you pull out your big gun. And you know what your big gun is? "You hurt my feelings!" He just told you repeatedly that he had a busy and difficult day. None of that mattered to you at all, did it? What mattered to you was a certain response that you wanted at the time you wanted it. Crystal, my love, in your scenario, you are the controller.

CRYSTAL: Really?

Really.

Now, I don't want to give the impression that all controlling of husbands by their wives is a bad thing. To the contrary. It just depends on what's in your heart, the intent in your mind, and the actions of your arms and lips. Pamela's letter was right on target with this issue. She described a conversation she'd had with her husband some fifteen years into their marriage. He'd been loud and clear about the fact that the main reason his first two marriages had ended was that his ex-wives had tried to control him. Pamela smiled sweetly and informed him that she'd been controlling him for fifteen years. He smiled back and said that he knew that she'd been "playing him," but that he liked the way she did—and why.

"1. He knew I loved him unconditionally: He was diagnosed with congestive heart failure six years ago. 2. I like him: He's my best friend. 3. I respect him. 4. I make sure that his needs are met both physically and emotionally: He's a very passionate

Hispanic guy. 5. I make him smile. In return for these things, he showers me with love, respect, kindness, jewelry, anything I want. Recently, I told him that I wanted to quit my job as an executive to start my own consulting business. He didn't bat an eye—because he knew that it would make me happy."

Controlling and giving are opposites, and giving is a more powerful tool than controlling to get what you want as a wife. Moreover, what a wife gets back from giving is offered with enthusiasm and love, not fear or resentment.

Mary Ann, a listener, acknowledged to herself that she was a controlling, moody, nagging wife. Her husband's response was typical: He pulled away and wasn't very loving. Once the marriage seemed to be falling apart, she went to a (good) therapist who helped her understand that the only thing she was really in control of was herself, and she needed to work on herself first before her relationship was going to work.

"I did exactly that and started treating my husband with respect instead of control. I did the loving things that wives are supposed to do for their husbands—cooked his favorite dinners often for him, rubbed his back, let him do his 'guy' things without me and without my complaining about it, stopped nagging about what he wasn't doing and complimented him when he did do things right.

Believe it or not, he started treating me how I had always wanted to be treated as a wife. My advice is that if you continue to nag, control, and be an unpleasant person to be around, then your husband is not going to want to be around you or treat you how you want to be treated. If you love, respect, and treat him how you would like to be treated, he will begin to return the treatment back to you."

Now, I can just hear some wives annoyed that this book is aimed at them. "After all," I'm sure they're saying, "don't men have any responsibility? Why is it on our backs to change for them? Where is her book on 'The Proper Care and Feeding of Wives?' Hummf!"

No, I probably will not be writing about the care and feeding of wives. Why? Because the truth is that when it comes to home and relationships, women rule. This is a book about how to rule wisely and lovingly. If a woman does not marry a sociopath or narcissist, then she's got her basic "male package." And your basic male is a decent creature with simple desires: to be his wife's hero, to be his wife's dream lover, to be the protector and provider for his family, to be respected, admired, and appreciated. Men live to make their women happy.

The cruelest thing a wife can do to a husband is to never be happy. And don't forget, being happy is more an attitude than a reality. When things are going bad, when there are problems and challenges, disappointments and disasters, it is obvious that happiness is going to be undermined. However, when one looks for that little peek-hole in the sky where the sun *does* shine through, then it *is* a lovely day.

And it becomes a lovely day for everyone you touch. As Christine, another listener, wrote:

> *"I also make the effort to pick up the toys, comb my hair, take off the paint-spit-up-yogurt-stained shirt I'd been wearing since six A.M. A little sweet-smelling body spray, lip gloss, some mouthwash, and I'm ready to welcome him home with a big kiss. Some days it's more of an effort than others, but my husband does not want to go anywhere else but to his loving home each evening."*

Chapter 4

MEN HAVE FEELINGS? REALLY? YOU'RE KIDDING!

"Over time, much if not all attention has been placed on men being sensitive and understanding toward women. This has been a good thing. As a man it has taught me well. I am a much better listener. The drawback is that wives believe they have little responsibility to also consider how their husbands feel. I would like the same thing out of my wife that I have been taught to give to her: equal treatment and acknowledgment of my feelings."

CHRIS

"This I am proud of as a wife: I have never, ever said anything hateful to him—even in the heat of anger. Whatever we might argue about will pass, but hurtful words stay FOREVER!"

KAREN

If Karen were in the majority, there would be no need to write this book. However, my experiences in private practice (as a Marriage and Family Therapist), on air, and with the e-mails, faxes, and letters I've gotten from my listeners draw an alarmingly clear picture of, in my opinion, gender abuse. That abuse consists of an amazingly crass disdain of wives for husbands' feelings. And it causes husbands deep pain.

John, one of my listeners, responded to my on-air request for men's input on the subject of the Proper Care and Feeding of Husbands by pointing out the pain men feel, which can drive them to stupid behaviors, such as having affairs.

> *"My experience tells me that since men seem to be afflicted with prurient thoughts about sex about seven times a day, the right hussy with the right words and the right moment and . . . need I say more? Having known several males who have had affairs, I think several things are important to know.*
>
> *While I have known happy men who have had one-night stands (and all regretted it later), I have never known a happy man who initiated or was involved in an affair. Affairs start and are fueled by something missing in the marriage—and it generally isn't sex! The affairs that I have known about started with a man* alone, *crying on a park bench or into an 'adult beverage.' A man in tears usually isn't alone long."*

John continued by noting that the men he has known over the last two decades who have had affairs had been telegraphing their unhappiness for years before they just gave up. Their complaints fall on deaf ears. Then come the affairs. Then come the wife's tears about how *she's* been wronged and *her* feelings are hurt.

While this scenario is not at the root of all affairs, it is definitely common. Whenever I've talked to a man after he's had an affair and ask him, "Why?" he usually first says, "I don't know," which shifts later into, "It's about how she [the honey] made me *feel* about myself."

The obvious issue here is that, frankly, men are generally not all that forthcoming about their feelings, at least not in the way we wives are. As women, we're used to the tears, the desire to talk endlessly about "what happened," the constant assessment of our emotional status, the way we describe things in terms of how they *make* us feel, and, of course, the way we have hurt feelings as a result of just about anything anybody does.

Nope, men are generally not leading with their feelings. They generally don't walk through the door after work with a burning need to talk about what feelings might have gotten tweaked that day. They'll more likely talk about a challenge they've faced, or will have to face. Because they don't cry all of the time, or have to call their mothers or best friends to go over emotional issues a thousand times like their wives do, wives make the mistake in thinking that they don't have feelings.

Oh, puhlease, don't tell me wives can't notice hurt in their eyes, stress in their stooped posture, pain in their silence, fear in their hyperactivity, anger in their tenseness. Or do wives immediately translate their husbands' pain into annoyance that their men are being selfish or insensitive?

Danette, a listener, communicated just that truth. She related a story about the time she was sitting with her best girlfriend, chatting. It was this dialogue that woke her up to the realization that she had never paid much attention to how she was treating her husband. She had asked her friend a question, and ended the question by remarking that she hoped her friend didn't mind her asking—that she wasn't offending her or hurting her feelings with the question. Her friend said, "Nothing you do will ever offend or bother me. But my husband regularly bothers and offends me." Danette, although realizing her friend was half jesting, realized that she was also half serious.

She then got to thinking about her own husband and how he had a tendency to frequently get on her nerves. She started wondering why that was. Later that week she got into one of her typical arguments with her husband, complete with defensive, nasty jabs. It dawned on her at that point that she probably got on his nerves, too.

> *"Then, like a slap in the face, it hit me: I was taking advantage of him without considering his* feelings. *I always considered my girlfriend's feelings because I didn't want to offend her, or make her mad, or lose her friendship. How stupid is that? I didn't have the same consideration for my own husband! It's like I wasn't caring about what he thought or felt."*

I always admire people who are willing to look in the mirror, hold themselves accountable, have remorse for the things they've done wrong, and have the willingness to repair and not repeat their unpleasant actions. That is exactly what I hope all wives will do after reading this book. And if wives can't easily slip out of their self-centered mode ("It's all about my feelings"), perhaps they can at least try to consider that the perspective presented here could give them more of what they want. The main source of husbands' bad attitudes, negative responses, and disappointing behaviors is their wives' attitude toward them and *their* feelings. Plain and simple.

I've even started warning men who are engaged and calling me about some issue with their fiancées' family or the wedding that how they're being treated now, whether or not their feelings or opinions are being considered, will only get more so when they marry. Generally, they just can't believe it. They think that their fiancées' bad, insensitive, selfish behavior is only due to all the stress involved with making wedding plans, and that when folks throw the rice, it will get all better. No way.

J.A., a forty-year-old unmarried woman, wrote to me about her girlfriends' horrible behaviors with their fiancés while planning the wedding. She describes their insensitivity to the feelings of the men:

"It seems that as soon as the ring (and, of course, size does count in this department) is on their finger, women stop responding to their men in a positive, affectionate, respectful way. During the planning of the wedding, men's opinions are, for the most part, completely disregarded. Then the women begin 'complaining' about their fiancés. The women believe their men are there to satisfy every whim."

A call from Jeff, twenty-seven years old and about to wed in two weeks, provides a perfect example of this problem that many wives-to-be have in not taking into account the feelings of their men. Weddings are not just about the one wearing the lace.

JEFF: Basically, we have a full house. Two people on my side RSVPed late, and as a result, my future mother-in-law would like for us to uninvite them based on the space issue.

DR. LAURA: Is it the space issue or the money issue? You can always stick two more chairs and two more plates at a table.

JEFF: We resolved the money issue.

DR. LAURA: Then tell dear mother-in-law that you're not going to uninvite people important to you.

JEFF: Well, I did that, and now my fiancée is all upset about it because it now has become a control issue as to whether or not I will tell my mom that they can't go.

DR. LAURA: This is a control issue between you and your girlfriend—not you and her mother. Maybe you need to step back and see what you might be getting yourself into. If your girlfriend's mother is this controlling and insensitive, and your girlfriend is defensive on the side of her mother, you, frankly, are screwed. And I wouldn't give five cents for your mind in five years. If your girlfriend is already showing disrespect for your feelings and disrespect for the people who mean something to you, I imagine that after the wedding she is not going to show any more respect for either.

JEFF: I see.

I sure hope he does, because men like Chad probably didn't and are now paying the price.

Chad and Sherrie called my program about their conflict. They've been married for three years, and he adopted her two children, ages ten and nine. The current problem was about Sherrie's constant, lengthy visits to her parents' home.

CHAD: My wife has just returned to Springfield, Missouri, where we live with the girls, after spending five days with her family. She now wants and is planning to go back to Iowa for the state fair. She plans on being gone for ten days and we've been arguing over this a little bit, I guess. I believe that being gone for ten days after being gone for five days is pretty excessive. My first pick would be for her to be here and maybe just take a weekend or a four-day weekend up there versus being up there for ten days.

DR. LAURA: Sherrie, do you want to give me your twenty-two cents?

SHERRIE: Yeah. Well, all my family live up there in Iowa. I am a very family-oriented person. I have been with these people my whole life, and it has been hard for me being away from them and moving to a state where I don't know anybody. So, therefore, I try to go up as much as possible.

At this point in the conversation, I asked Chad to hang up the phone and not listen to the radio so he wouldn't hear what I was going to say to Sherrie. I knew I was going to let her "have it," and thought she'd be more likely to take in what I had to say if she wasn't embarrassed by his hearing it.

DR. LAURA: What is in your mind, woman? You got a guy to marry you and adopt your two kids, and you have the nerve to tell him that your family orientation is directed toward your mommy and daddy? This is very foolish. Your husband is your family. He adopted your kids and made them his family. For you to keep running home to Mama is telling him that he is secondary after all he's done for you. You are out of your mind to hurt him this way.

SHERRIE: So the girls shouldn't ever see their grandparents?

DR. LAURA: You can always let them fly to Grandma's and let them stay for weeks while you stay around home and have intimate time with your husband. Don't be making him feel like he is disposable for weeks on end. I don't think you understand what he's done for you.

SHERRIE: Yeah, I do. I'm very grateful.

DR. LAURA: Well, you're not acting like it.

SHERRIE: So I shouldn't go for ten days?

I couldn't believe that after all I said, she came back to herself.

DR. LAURA: Only if you're planning on being divorced sometime soon. I don't understand you. You are so lucky. How many thirty-something women with two kids can get a decent guy to take care of them? You need to not treat that cavalierly.

She never got to the point of actually acknowledging showing him respect or being sensitive to his feelings. Her husband probably falls into the "Stupid Chivalry" chapter of my book *Ten Stupid Things Men Do to Mess Up Their Lives.* In this chapter I describe how men, needing to feel important and valiant, often get into situations that can best be described as "saving a damsel in distress." They believe that if they save her, then she will fulfill their needs and dreams, but in most cases they just end up with a distressed damsel. In this case, Sherrie's feelings are at the center of her universe, and Chad is in an emotional black hole.

Chad was demonstrating his *feelings* of love and his *feelings* of need and his hurt *feelings* of neglect and abandonment by telling her to stay home—with him. What about that display of *feelings* wasn't clear? Should he have cried, screamed, and banged things? Should he have gotten drunk and smacked her? Would these be feelings she could recognize? Certainly, but then he'd be called a rude, insensitive, boorish, violent brute.

And this is the pickle juice in which many a married man marinates.

Brian, a listener, expressed this very annoyance. He gave these four examples to describe his wife's utter disregard for his feelings and her ability to turn it all around on him:

1. When his wife wants to go do something with her friends, she says he should trust her and allow her that freedom. When he feels that he needs some alone or buddy time, she says that he doesn't love her or want to spend time with her—even when she's invited! It's all about her feelings—not his.
2. When she spends money, it's okay because it's something she "needed," and she should have the freedom to spend money when she wants to buy something. When he wants to spend money, she calls him irresponsible. It's all about her feelings—not his.
3. They see her family about twice a week. When he

wants to see his family, she complains that he's not being sensitive to her feelings about her family. It's all about her feelings—not his.

4. "Basically," he writes, "it's her priorities that matter. She'll have the whole weekend planned, while I'd love to have some downtime together. She'll say that I'm not supporting her." It's all about her feelings—not his.

So let's take this time to get to husbands' feelings. Jim, a listener, writes:

"Despite our rugged outward appearance, most men tend to have delicate psyches. I know four very happily married men. In each case their wives make a point of stroking their egos and making them feel *that they approve of them. Consequently, these men practically worship their wives."*

But how can husbands *feel* respected, appreciated, or loved when they are the constant brunt of their wives' negativity about everything?

Melissa, a listener, wrote to me about an incident that occurred during her first year of marriage. She and her husband were at another couple's house for dinner. The wife started complaining about her husband and Melissa started to do the same thing about her husband. What she didn't realize was that although her husband was in another room, he overheard everything.

That night when they were snuggled up in bed, he called her on it and told her that it had really hurt him to hear her talk like that about him. Chagrined, she apologized profusely and made it a point from that moment on to smother her husband with compliments whenever she was with a group of women who were "bagging" on their husbands.

"As much as men's bellies need to be filled with delicious home-cooked meals," she wrote, "their egos need to be filled with 'yummy food' as well. I have found that if I speak blessings about my husband, then blessings are what I get in return."

I believe that women in general have been taught to disdain the "male ego," ascribing to it a sense of phoniness, immaturity, and weakness. Ladies, what makes the male ego issue any different from our "body ego" issue? Our husbands have to tell us our bodies (thighs, hips, and butts in particular) are perfect and that these pants don't make us look fat because (a) we don't want to hear the truth, (b) we can't handle the truth, and/or (c) if they tell us the truth, then we're hurt, they're mean and insensitive, and the relationship is shot down in mid-flight.

We, as women, want to know that we are lovely and desirable *in general* because of our shapes. They, as men, want to know that they are desirable by *us* because of their prowess in providing for their families, satisfying their women sexually, and having the strength and leadership to confront challenges and protect their families and values. They *need* that and they need that from us.

A wife can tear down a husband's necessary sense of strength and importance more easily with a look or a comment than can torture in a prison camp. Surviving the latter *is* a demonstration of a man's strength. Men don't easily survive the former: Their wives' approval is as important as oxygen; surviving their wives' lack of approval is emasculation.

By her own description, Eva was one of the emasculating wives. She wrote that after she and her husband had kids, their marriage felt more like two people who only happened to take care of the kids together, and less like a husband and wife living life together. She had lots of resentment about how her husband "didn't understand her" and "didn't do things right to help her feel happy and satisfied."

This all changed when she finally recognized that "my husband was a person with goals and desires, frustrations and needs, all his own. While I felt he didn't understand me, I didn't understand him, or see him at all, except for what was wrong."

Far from being oppressed in their marriages, most wives are the oppressors. I can hardly remember more than a handful of times while I was in private practice working with couples in troubled marriages that a wife would respond with openness, compassion, and sensitivity to her husband's display of feelings. The typical response would be shock, anger, reproach, threats, and tears. That's oppression, folks.

Thankfully for her husband, Eve was one of the handful:

> *"One night, after my complaining about something, he opened up and spilled out a lot of things I'd never heard before. For the first time I saw the strain of stress from work, fathering, husbanding, home-owning, etcetera, and how overworked and overtired and overwhelmed he felt. It was a bitter and cynical monologue, and I previously would have been very hurt and angry with him—but for some reason this time I was shocked by the depth of his emotion.*
>
> *I thought not of me and my reaction to his words, but of how his attitude got there in the first place and how helpless and horrible he was feeling. I truly felt empathy and concern for him and his situation."*

In the ensuing days, Eve continued to listen without defensiveness, and made suggestions to her husband in an attempt to be helpful. She prodded him to get back into golf even though she'd virtually ripped that from his life because she'd always felt that (1) if he loved her, he'd want to be with her, (2) he needed to do things around the house and with the kids, and (3) she needed a break. She admitted never even considering that maybe he needed a break, too.

This was the beginning of seeing him in a good light and treating him with much more respect for his feelings.

> *"Now, several years later, we both are much more caring about each other, and willing to see the other's needs and point of view. Funny, as I changed, my husband didn't seem so bad. Did he become more pleasant in response to my more pleasant attitude, or was he really not all that bad to begin with?"*

Both.

It's worth reviewing the issue of a husband's feelings and the male ego to point out how vital a wife is to the well-being of her husband. This list of basic points supporting that concept is culled from enumerable e-mails from husbands:

- A man needs to feel strong and needed as a protector for women—basically, to conquer the beast and rescue the fair maiden.
- What every man wants is for his woman to make him feel that he is strong and the head of the household. I am not talking caveman-style, dragging the woman around by her hair, but just as the leader of the family.
- A man wants respect, kindness, and love from his woman.
- A man wants to be put on a pedestal, not so that he can look down on everyone, but to show him that he is the most important thing to his woman.
- A man needs his woman to show him that she needs his strength to help her through life.
- The man should be the major breadwinner in the family. Every man needs a battle or war to win to prove to

himself that he is strong and capable of conquering any and all dragons that life throws his way. Taking care of his family by working and providing are his battles.

- A man needs enthusiastic approval, appreciation, and respect from his wife for being a competent man, husband, and father.
- A man needs his wife to show some interest in his interests, especially when it's an activity she may not "get" or like. Just being there is important.
- A man needs his wife to greet him after work with love and enthusiasm.
- A man needs his wife to care about the day he's had.
- A man needs to know that his wife is sexually satisfied by him.
- A man needs his wife's encouragement in order to be a man.

Some of the hostile input I initially received from women when setting out to write this book concerned their disgust at the notion of men's "feelings," which were perceived as "neediness." And, of course, if a husband has hurt feelings or is needy, then the spotlight is off the wife and she's then required to care-take. It's a bit disgusting that so many women were so up front about not "feeling" that they want to or should have to do that for their men. Yet their expectations about their husbands' solicitousness were resolute and infinite.

The fact is, men probably are more emotionally needy for feedback from their wives than wives are from their husbands. Women turn to their mothers, their friends, their neighbors, their coworkers, their relatives, their shrinks, their hairdressers, their manicurists, and most media to get validation—earned or not. Because of this willingness to gossip and solicit support from the far corners of their personal universes, women in general rely less on their husbands' approval. Which, of course, explains part of why they don't care enough about their husbands' feelings, or fail to pursue those feelings as an issue.

Men don't gossip; they are more private. By and large, they tend to get a sense of approval from their success at work and from their wives' happiness. That makes us wives more accountable for their well-being than we may like to be. So, talking to a grown man, the father of your children and the major financial supporter of your family, in that "mother tone," as though he were a naughty or irresponsible child, is in direct opposition to his wanting to have a wife and family who are in awe of him for who he is and what he does for them.

As John, a listener, wrote:

> *"Nothing discourages a man more from trying to be a good husband than the feeling that no matter what he does, his wife won't be pleased with him. Sadly, I know many men who feel that way. I am grateful to be with a wife who believes in and appreciates me. The more she tells me how much she loves and respects me, the more I want to do nice things to honor her, and the better I feel about myself. Everybody wins!"*

Lloyd, another listener, contributed this analysis about men and their feelings:

> *"Men, whether husbands or bachelors, do not share their thoughts and feelings as readily as women. We do not see any need to bother others with our feelings. We just deal with them. If something needs to be done, we do it. If something needs to be said, we say it.*
>
> *Many times we just don't want to deal with the consequences of saying what we feel out loud. We don't want to*

explain ourselves. So we just live with our thoughts and adjust. Wives must find ways to encourage their husbands to share feelings by allowing them to do so without consequences. Husbands should be encouraged to share their feelings without being accused of being insensitive and stupid. Let us talk. Be supportive. Permit us to have opinions, feelings, and thoughts that do not agree with yours."

The majority of men who wrote to me and commented on the issue of their expressing feelings made that same point. Ken wrote:

"Frequently, when I get angry over something she has said or done and have the temerity to express my feelings, she just dismisses it as me being overtired, or some other trite toss-off. This is akin to a guy seeing a woman angry and saying, 'Guess it's that time of the month again!' "

Other men wrote that when they'd tried to vent about something, their wives would somehow find a way to make it their fault! That goes for everything from their wanting more sex to saying that the lawn mower was broken.

The stereotype of a woman insensitive to a man's feelings is, unfortunately, well-earned. There isn't a day on my radio program when I don't struggle with some wife or girlfriend over this issue. Here are the synopses of several calls that demonstrate the severe magnitude of this problem for men. I am quoting them, with annotation, in some detail, because they clarify the main problems involved in women treating their men's feelings with disrespect or disregard.

This first call has to do with misplaced loyalties the wife has for her original family. Danielle has been married for ten years and has four children. The central point of tension is that Danielle and her sister have always been "best friends." She describes her husband and sister as both having strong opinions and personalities. Her sister and her sister's daughter (note: no husband there!) come to visit Danielle's mom, who lives nearby, for months on end, and her niece then comes over all the time to play with Danielle's children. Somehow that seems to give her sister permission to pop over whenever she pleases, which is a problem because she doesn't get along well with Danielle's husband.

DR. LAURA: If they are oil and water and they don't get along, you need to minimize the overlap.

DANIELLE: I understand.

DR. LAURA: And, frankly, if there is a choice to be made, it's obviously got to be your husband. He is the father of your four children. You don't want to make him feel secondary to your relationship with your sister. If your sister can't come over and be nice to your husband for the sake of your marriage, then she is not a very good best friend. Maybe you need to sit down with your sister and tell her that when she comes to your house, no arguing—just to be nice because you want family serenity.

DANIELLE: Well, he isn't very nice to her sometimes.

DR. LAURA: I wonder if she didn't just earn that. It is his home and maybe you are not showing enough respect for that. What is the ongoing problem he has with her?

This is when the story got even more interesting. The niece was over almost every day for weeks or months. Danielle and her husband have certain rules about behavior—normal stuff—and it turned out that the sister confronted Danielle's husband because he attempted to (reasonably and responsibly) exert discipline in his home.

DR. LAURA: How outrageous of your sister to make your home a day-care center for her kid and then, instead of showing eternal gratitude, come over and get in your husband's face with complaints! And you don't throw her out?

At this point in the discussion, Danielle started to laugh—somewhat out of nervousness, but mostly, I believe, out of an awareness that she'd been caught doing exactly what she knew was wrong: She was intimidated by her sister, desperate for her friendship, and mindless about the destructive impact of her lack of defense on her and her husband's family.

DANIELLE: I knew you would say that. . . . It isn't funny.

DR. LAURA: No, it isn't. You have a marriage you don't respect. You think it's funny that you cater to your sister over your own husband? How can you expect to stay married with that kind of attitude, or doesn't it matter?

DANIELLE: It does.

DR. LAURA: Then act like it.

This scenario of caring more for the feelings of friends and family than for those of husbands is not an unusual one. Women seem to imagine that their husbands can, will, and ought to take a lot of abuse and keep on ticking!

This next call has to do with many women's hypersensitivity to being "controlled"—even by a husband's feelings. Valerie's call, while not unusual, was a whopper. Instead of choosing a friend or relative over her husband, she'd picked a cat! The issue could have been severe allergies (which is more typical in these cases), but in Valerie's case, the cat was downright hostile toward her husband, hissing and attacking. I was so stunned that I responded with pure sarcasm.

VALERIE: I know it sounds crazy, because who would pick a cat over a husband, but I'm having issues with this where I feel like I don't want to have to get rid of the cat. And I don't know what to do.

DR. LAURA: Well, you've already found the solution—just let your husband feel miserable and feel like he doesn't matter. I think that is the really smart way to go. That is the best way to keep a man really lovingly tied in—sarcasm free of charge.

VALERIE: I know—and I know that is probably how he is feeling, because I just got off the phone with him and he said so.

DR. LAURA: But we wives know that what husbands feel doesn't really matter—it is only what we need, what we want. Listen, I have read all the feminist stuff. Men are just oppressors and he is obviously just trying to control you. He is a real bastard about this. What you have to do to teach him a lesson is buy more cats.

VALERIE: I know. And, you know, that is probably what my friends would say.

DR. LAURA: Men are supposed to just go along with what pleases us no matter what they have to suffer, right? He has no right to have these feelings or make these demands or want to be comfortable or want you to make a choice between him and an animal. Right? He has no right. He is just a male.

VALERIE: No . . . he is more than that.

DR. LAURA: How would he know that from you?

VALERIE: (laughing) I know, and I know that's how he's feeling. And I feel just the way you've described. I'm wondering why he is being such a wimp about a hissing cat. So what? She isn't biting him.

There it was: What was emotionally upsetting to him (a hissing cat and a wife having to debate the cat vs. him) was being trivialized. I asked her how she dared trivialize his feelings and then expected him to give a damn about hers.

I saw two options. Either she was superficial, spoiled, and a complete twit, or there was a more significant issue to exhume. I guessed the latter, and I guessed right.

DR. LAURA: Tell me about the part of you where his being hurt or upset really doesn't matter.

VALERIE: Well, I guess because I don't want to be controlled. Yeah, I guess I don't want to feel like I am being told to do something, so now I have to do it regardless of whether I like it or not.

DR. LAURA: Okay. Do you think your husband should feel controlled when you want something?

VALERIE: No.

DR. LAURA: Oh, Valerie, that is so not true. But the trick you do in your mind is this: You don't call it control when you want something. You call that a reasonable request, which should be granted if he loves you. But when he does the exact same thing, it's control. And you know that is true because you are worried about your girlfriends telling you that you have become an oppressed female. You come from a man-hating environment.

VALERIE: True.

I ended the call by telling her that she needed a healthier set of friends and a healthier mind-set about the give-and-take in a relationship. And she needed to find a good home for the recalcitrant cat.

This next call focuses on the issue of wives wanting to control everybody else to create the perfect picture that makes them feel more comfortable. Gina's husband's parents were divorced when he was two years old. Evidently, her husband and his father had never developed any bond or closeness.

GINA: My question is whether or not it is morally right for me to not include my father-in-law in his grandchildren's lives. My husband is against this and very upset.

DR. LAURA: Why would you undermine your marriage to have this "father-in-law" involved with your kids? Why would it be more important to have this distant stranger involved with your kids than it would be to keep your marriage strong?

Astonishingly, she denied she was aiming her gun in that direction. Our discussion pointed out that she knew she was making her husband annoyed and angry, but didn't give thought to that. "So what, he's angry," is the unbelievable attitude so many women express when they're designing life the way they want it, rather than helping their husbands cope with the truth of the way it is.

GINA: A broken marriage is not what I want.

DR. LAURA: Then you have to stop pushing this issue, no matter your rationale for doing so in the first place.

Here it comes!

GINA: So . . . what is important is how *he* feels toward his father?

Bingo! A breakthrough! Or so I thought . . .

GINA: Should he at some point be man enough—

DR. LAURA: Oh, my gosh. I don't believe this. You don't even think your husband is a man because he has made this choice to disengage from his absent, neglectful sperm donor?

GINA: I guess this is the picture-perfect thing that I want. I just don't like confrontation.

DR. LAURA: Well, if you were woman enough, you would handle it. How does that shoe feel on your foot?

GINA: It feels like an ouch, but I can take it.

The next call involves what I call the "world is only on my shoulders" syndrome. Anna is a stay-at-home mom with four children ranging from fifteen months to eleven years.

ANNA: Lately, I have been feeling angry and resentful at my husband. He is a really great guy. He works a lot of hours and the night shift so I can be at home. I feel that he is just someone else that needs something else from me.

DR. LAURA: Anna, do you remember your wedding day?

ANNA: Yes.

DR. LAURA: Aside from the pretty dress and all the presents, do you remember your vows? What were they?

ANNA: To love and honor.

DR. LAURA: Were those vows amended with caveats that you don't have to love or honor if you're tired or annoyed?

ANNA: No.

DR. LAURA: Do you want to stay married?

ANNA: Yes.

DR. LAURA: Then you have to make your husband feel that he is coming home to a woman who considers his feelings and needs important. He has to come home to a woman who rewards him for all he does for his family.

ANNA: It just seems that we are only polite lately—and with the new baby, it is really hard.

DR. LAURA: Yes, it is . . . no question about that. And it is really hard to work two shifts and come home to a distressed wife and four children desiring his attention and love. It's five for him to deal with, too, you know. And, truth be told, you do need some R&R and reward for your day. I'll tell you how to get that: When he walks through that door, give him hugs and kisses and a chocolate brownie if he has a sweet tooth. Tell him how much you appreciate the fact that he has been out all night busting his butt so that you could stay home with the kids. Watch what this tired man will perk up and do for you. . . . *ANYTHING YOU WANT!* That includes sex, a great relaxer, a foot rub, a bubble bath, playing with the kids—anything. You know I'm right.

ANNA: Yes, thank you.

This next call has to do with disagreements in raising and disciplining children. Chris's husband did not think that their fifteen-year-old daughter should go out to a football game on the evening we spoke, because she goes out a lot. The irony was that Chris had given the daughter permission to go, in contradiction to her husband's decision, even though Chris agreed that the girl was out way too much.

I noted that they were actually not in disagreement. I suggested that perhaps they ought to make these decisions together, in private, before presenting the decision as a team.

CHRIS: I guess that the only problem is that quite often we disagree, and when we do, he says I am not supporting him and he says it is like the kids and I are against him all the time.

DR. LAURA: Perhaps he's actually right! Maybe you are protecting "your little girl" and giving her everything she wants and by doing that you are bypassing your obligation to respect his opinion and decisions.

CHRIS: And that is a bad thing?

DR. LAURA: Yes, because the first and foremost relationship in that house is between you and your husband. And this is what your daughter will remember when she makes decisions in her marriage. If she sees you disdainful of a man, she'll likely do that, too. In addition, being this spoiled, she'll have lots of troubles in life when she doesn't automatically get her own way. The social life of teenagers has to be moderated.

CHRIS: Right. I agree with that.

DR. LAURA: Then if you agree with that, you don't always disagree with him after all. I think you need to be more honest about how you are always the "good guy" with your daughter and perhaps all the other children, too.

CHRIS: Now you're sounding like him.

DR. LAURA: Well, it is true. You are doing that. You are focused on "being liked" by your kids, rather than being a parental partner with your husband in raising those children. Now start working with him. He will be blown away that you actually gave a damn about his opinion.

CHRIS: He will. He will be really blown away!

It is of life-and-death (to the marriage) importance that a wife and mother not make her husband feel as though the children are sufficient for her fulfillment. One caller, with her husband on the line, made that very claim. I couldn't believe she could be so blindly cruel to him and expect him to still be there for her in any size, shape, or form—which, believe it or not, was the reason she called: to complain that he didn't do enough for her! One woman, after hearing this call, wrote to me:

"Initially I was shocked that she would say this in front of him, and let's be honest here—in front of you, too! But as I got

real with myself, I realized that what was so shocking was that I have said things that are just as hurtful to my husband. You really hit home with me when you said that behaving this way is cruel and abusive. I wanted to cry.

You also pointed out to the caller that she need not be concerned with her husband behaving in a more loving, attentive manner toward her. Instead, you said, she should concentrate on providing him the love and affection and position of importance he deserves, and that he (since men are 'not as complex as women') will automatically return it to her.

I was frightened as you talked about men leaving their wives for other women who make them feel good about themselves. As you talked to this woman about how difficult it would be to raise her children without this father who provides for the family and loves them, I realized that I never want to be in that situation.

Thank you, Dr. Laura, for opening my eyes to my own selfishness, self-centeredness, and destructive behavior. On this Valentine's Day, I am committing to doing what is right for my relationship with my husband: to nurture him and our marriage with the same energy I put toward nurturing my daughter."

While it is true that men's feelings are not neon fixtures on their person the way women's are, that doesn't mean they don't have feelings. Women, you don't have to see them to know that they are there. Just think. Think about things from their perspective—as though you were in a mini-camera behind their eyes. Imagine his whole day, his challenges, problems, threats, difficulties, frustrations, fears, and exhaustion. You know he has feelings about all of that.

Think about what confronts him at home. You know he has feelings about all of that. Everyone, anyone does.

It's just a matter of thinking about somebody outside oneself. Wives must accept and allow their husbands to have the same feelings, cares, and concerns that they have. Assume it. Don't badger your husbands for female-like expression of feelings—just assume it, and behave accordingly, with understanding, compassion, and support.

I have told innumerable women this. I have asked them to imagine what any human being would feel at the end of the day or at the end of an ordeal. He doesn't have to lay it all out in order for a wife to be sensitive and caring. Men don't need to air out the bitter details of their day. They simply need loving support and reassurance.

The saddest story I received was from a physician. On one particular day, he had performed a cardiac operation on a child. Later, problems developed and he was committed to a prolonged two-hour intense resuscitation effort . . . that was ultimately unsuccessful. The mother of the child, consumed by grief, physically attacked him and attempted to choke him to death.

> *"This, even to a physician, is a severe loss and emotional stress. Upon my arrival at home, the anger at my missing the scheduled time to get ready to go out that evening was apparent and my explanation that the child had arrested was met with, 'I'm sorry, but can we go now?'*
>
> *The expanded facts were never discussed and my responses to a disaster were never considered. I tried to tell her that things were awful, but her response was, 'Well, we have been waiting, so let's go now and I don't want to hear any excuses.'*
>
> *Needless to say, fewer incidents were shared. My summary statement is: REMEMBER YOUR HUSBAND IS ALSO A HUMAN BEING WITH THE SAME EMOTIONAL NEEDS THAT YOU HAVE. TREAT HIM HUMANELY."*

While this story is dramatic, including as it does the death of a child, no matter what the job, husbands come home with stories and reactions. Does anyone at home care?

In conclusion, Bill, a listener, wrote:

"Being married for the second time, to a woman the opposite of my first wife, I am painfully aware of the significance of the Proper Care and Feeding of Husbands.

I know in my heart that my wife loves me by the way she treats me; by the way she looks at me and looks after me and my children. She listens to me about my work, my problems, my dreams, and gives feedback when I ask. I know in my heart that she cares about all of my being.

I would walk through fire for my wife. I FEEL that she loves me. More than anything, I want to make her happy because of all the love and caring and feeding she gives to me. I give back to her from the bottom of my heart, and it is the best feeling I've ever had in my life.

Your question, Dr. Laura, is what do men want from their wives? For me it is to FEEL in my heart that someone truly cares for me and loves me; that I am immensely important to her. I can only get this through my wife's actions. Words are a whisper, but what she does for me is a thunder."

Enough said.

Chapter 5

"HUH? HONEY, WHAT DID YOU SAY? WHAT DID THAT MEAN?"

"Women are disappointed in the man who doesn't read her thoughts. I think that realizing that a man is just that, a man, is the most impossible thing a woman can do. They are different creatures. They think differently, they feel differently, and they communicate differently . . . and they're NOT WRONG for that. They are beautiful, too, in their own garage-grease, fix-it, thinking way."

MARIE

"I used to intuitively expect my husband to be a woman, and felt constant frustration that he didn't think, feel, need, act, and communicate just like me. It took me a long time, discussions with my father, and some reading before I realized that he was simply going to be different and that I needed to accept and work with these differences."

CATHERINE

Catherine continued with the admonishment that younger women like herself, brainwashed into thinking that the sexes are the same to various degrees ("and other feminist gobbledygook"), had better wise up, wake up, and smell the coffee. She remarked that her life has been much better since she got a grip on what is reasonable to expect from a man.

That's a very important point. The bigger the difference between what one *expects* and what *is,* the greater the disappointment, hurt, and, usually, anger. It is therefore important to have realistic expectations. In the realm of husbands and wives, though, women do tend to have largely unreasonable and unrealistic expectations of their men. This happens when women don't accept or respect the unique masculine qualities and quirks of men.

Daniel, a listener who works for an electronics company, sent me an engineer's view of the difference between men and women. His contribution basically consists of a photograph of a rectangular control panel divided equally between the top and bottom parts. The top part has only one on/off toggle switch. The bottom part has some *forty* switches and dials, and *two* switches for on and off. Someone has labeled the upper part MEN and the lower part WOMEN, as a joke about how complex women are, with all those complicated, fine-tuning necessities, and how simple men are in contrast.

Marital communication would go much better if women would accept without rancor that men simply have different communication styles and imperatives. I realize that this sounds like I'm putting the burden of communication problems on women, but perhaps there are some good reasons to do so. Verbal communication is much more important to women, and essential to their being—and that, it appears, is all in the wiring.

The differences between men and women begin in the womb. At first, all fetuses' brains are virtually the same. At about nine weeks of gestation, though, testosterone surges through the male (XY) fetus, changing the direction of general development toward masculinity.

With respect to communication, the result of those differences are apparent early on in childhood. Studies in child development have documented behavioral differences in children even in the first year. In one study, a barrier was placed between the child and his or her mother. The boys, wanting to get back to Mommy, try to get around or over the barrier, or they try to knock it down. The male response is physical, and it's aimed at solving the problem. The female children, on the other hand, verbalized their distress, and their mommies came and picked them up. The female response is verbal.

As children grow up, parents notice that their daughters are unbelievably verbal and usually prone to high drama. These same parents notice that their sons are "men of few words" but lots of action. Obviously, within the populations of both men and women there is variation; nonetheless, these generalizations exist for a reason: They represent the larger population and reveal some focal points of problems between husbands and wives trying to communicate in a manner that enhances the husband and the wife as well as the marriage.

One of the most typical complaints I hear from wives about their husbands is that the men won't sit and talk about things. I'll ask, "What things?" The response usually is, "Things. Just things. Everything. Anything." I might then ask the wife why it is so important to her that he be able and willing to talk about . . . anything, and she will inevitably say, "Because this is how to be close . . . loving . . . intimate."

Men are more likely to perceive their wives as being close, loving, and intimate when the wives wear something revealing to bed, make them a sandwich with a beer, or suggest that they go play some rounds of golf with their buddies. Women are more likely to perceive their husbands as being close, loving, and intimate when the men do what they've been told or asked to do, give romantic gifts, or listen patiently—and without comment—for the nth time to the same emotional account of some old grievances with a friend, relative, or coworker.

The first thing I usually remind women who call complaining about the communication problems with their husbands is that the callers are probably not even communicating but using their husbands as girlfriends or shrinks; the husbands are supposed to show interest, agree, and remain uncritical and unchallenging. Husbands imagine (so foolishly) that their wives are telling them something they actually need to know because they're supposed to do something about it. Otherwise, the men can't imagine why the "communication" is happening at all. It confuses them, then frustrates them, and their response is then to turn off. That's when they unfairly become labeled insensitive.

Therefore, the major mistake wives make in communicating with their husbands is to imagine that their husbands are supposed to be their best *girl*friends. Most women I remind of this error get hostile, as though I'm taking away some entitlement. I inform them that this is simply an erroneous expectation. When they don't want to accept that, I remind them that their way isn't working—the proof is that there is too much rancor and distance in their marriage—and maybe they ought to try seeing what treating their husbands as *men* will bring that's different from what they're seeing now.

John, a listener, can't seem to understand what women don't seem to understand about men and communication:

> *"I dated a woman for a few months, and whenever we drove anywhere, if there was a lull in the conversation, she would demand, 'What are you thinking?' 'I'm not thinking anything, dear.' That was never good enough, and she would spend the rest of the date sulking and planning her retribution against male domination—or something or other.*
>
> *I told her that men aren't bright enough to drive and think at the same time, and that just added more fuel to the fire.*
>
> *We look at the birds, we look at the trees, we look far*

enough down the road to make sure someone doesn't plow through a red light and kill us all; but driving and plotting and manipulating at the same time takes far more hard drive than we were ever issued.

If a man tells you he isn't thinking anything, he probably isn't.

Can't see how that is so hard to understand."

Women, you'll be off track more often than not if you constantly imagine that your husband's quiet is a sign of trouble. He's probably not withholding something from you (unless you're a volatile pain in the butt when he does confide in you), and he's probably not simmering with some secret anguish (because men generally don't ruminate over feelings of hurt or disappointment) unless you notice him sleeping less and drinking more.

The truth is that wives generally overwhelm their husbands with communication. Much of what motivates that communication might better be dealt with through personal circumspection, triaged for significance, selected for true communication (connecting) value, whittled down to its essence, timed better, and expressed more appropriately.

Marla, a listener, admitted that she tended to tell her husband "everything."

"This often included how I felt about people, situations, weather, etcetera. I held back no emotion. From his perspective this was whining and complaining. I didn't see it that way. From my perspective I was just 'sharing my heart.' However, I started noticing that he seemed to want to talk less and less to me.

Years later he was brave enough to confront me and tell me what I was becoming. It was almost as if I were treating him as my dump. Like it was his job to take all the stuff I wanted off my chest.

> *Things have been so much happier in our home and our marriage since I've started taking my problems to God first and trying to deal with my own emotions before 'dumping' them on him. He's more than willing to hear when I have a problem now . . . because he isn't bombarded with them constantly."*

I'm reminded of the theatrical production *Amadeus.* Mozart has just finished leading the orchestra in concert, playing one of his original pieces for the king. His archrival rushes forward and, in front of the king, proclaims that the work was fine but that there were "too many notes."

In Mozart's case it wasn't true; for many wives it is. Terri, one of my listeners, confirms this observation:

> *"I also believe that we as women talk too much in our conversations with our husbands. We say they never listen to us, but let's face it, we usually put in way too many details to keep them interested!*
>
> *I mean, really, would you want to listen if they were telling you every detailed play that took place in a football game they'd seen? I certainly would be bored silly if my husband did that. He can tell me if his favorite team won and he can even tell me a great play that was in the game, but any more than that, I would for sure start to zone out.*
>
> *If we cut down on the details and ask them more questions about their day (without pressure for answers, though), conversations would become more two-sided and more pleasant."*

This is probably one of the most difficult concepts for wives to accept: that they should cut down on the communication as a way to improve it. Somehow, wives have come to believe that with respect to communication, more is better. Wrong. More appropriately selected and timed is better.

Cooper is one wife, and listener, who gets that point. She's been married four years and is a stay-at-home mom to a three-year-old daughter and one-year-old son. She says that she's learned to give her husband at least a half hour when he comes home from work before she bugs him about anything. During that decompression time, she doesn't ask him to talk about anything, doesn't volunteer anything about her day, and doesn't nag him about what he does with that "downtime."

In other words, she lets him unwind. Without that decompression he would be edgy the rest of the evening and unwilling to communicate. Now he is more chatty during dinner and evening activities. Now she can talk and question him about their respective days.

Cooper admits that it is still a struggle to fight against the urge to unload her whole day on him the second he gets home (as though *he* didn't have a "day," too), but that it is becoming easier and easier to wait a little longer for a welcoming set of ears.

Robert, a listener, has a wife who has also learned to temper her eruption of communication.

> *"When I am done with my personal time and come back upstairs, I am relaxed, and I am open to 'hear' what she is saying, and everyone is happier. She has also come up with a catchphrase. When she prepares to tell me something, she reminds me that she doesn't need anything fixed or solved—and that cues me that I'm just supposed to listen, which is what she really wants."*

Some of this caring behavior toward husbands comes from wisdom and practice; some of it comes from maturity. Natalie, a listener, realized that she had to learn how to take care of her own emotions better. She understood that, as a woman, she is more prone to emotions and emotional changes that her husband can't keep up with. "Sometimes I need to deal with my own feelings and not 'work them out' with him," she said. That's where the maturity comes in—realizing that, as a woman, we have responsibilities to our own well-being, and our husbands' sole purpose in life is not to tend to our mercurial moods. A husband's need not to be drowned in an onslaught of verbiage and emotion must be respected. Natalie continued:

> *"Once I thought through my feelings on my own, I could tell my husband how I felt, but I could be RATIONAL (imagine!) while doing it. I guess I basically started growing up emotionally and have pretty much stopped overreacting to situations, ideas, and apparent predicaments that came up . . . and simply react."*

And what makes wives think that communication has to be all verbal? An embrace, a warm look across a kitchen table, a smile, a kiss—these are all forms of communication, too! They aren't verbal, but they are powerful forms, which, like pictures, can be worth more than a thousand words.

I believe that one of the barriers to many women being comfortable with that fact and with those actions is that, for them, verbal communication is a form of control in what they perceive a relationship to be: a power struggle. And yet if that's true, and it is a power struggle, then husbands are generally easy to overpower! All a wife needs to do is tap into his physicality and she's won! Kelly, one of my listeners, figured this one out—to her pleasure, and to the benefit of her marriage:

> *"I believe that while women's needs are mostly emotional, men's are more physical. I make a point to take twenty minutes out of the day to connect intimately with my husband. Most women, I think, feel that with the demands children put on us twelve hours a day, this time with their husbands can be put on*

the back burner. This is a big mistake. By putting my marriage first, my two boys will ultimately benefit from a strong, happy, healthy foundation.

My husband is constantly telling me how lucky he is that we have regular 'alone time' (which meets part of my emotional needs), whether it leads to sex or we just give each other massages. Sometimes we just cuddle!

I think we are definitely not the norm in marriages today—and that is sad. Come on, women! What is twenty minutes a day? Give up the power struggle . . . you will be amazed at the results! Your emotional needs will be met and you just might get some extra help around the house!"

This issue of "power struggles" is at the core of many marital woes. The typical complaint from men: She nags and is never grateful or satisfied. The typical complaint from women: He's insensitive, doesn't meet my emotional needs, and won't do anything around the house. And it goes around and around and around and around as he becomes more disgruntled and she becomes more frustrated. Both husband and wife are unhappy.

Then they go to a therapist, but sadly, much of the psychotherapeutic profession is populated by folks with an agenda: Traditional values are out, men are the bad guys, and women are oppressed. Their cure is either to feminize the husband or suggest divorce. Ken, a listener, confirmed that position when he wrote:

"It has been my experience through nearly all the avenues we have tried (i.e., self-help books, tapes, private counseling, etc.) that today's society insists that it is COMPLETELY THE MALES' RESPONSIBILITY to learn how to understand and communicate on a level that the female can comprehend and digest. It seems that positive improvements to a relationship can ONLY occur if the husband is willing to alter his very nature, to

tune in to his 'feminine' side, and learn how to think, respond, and 'emotionally perceive' the same way his wife does.

If the male has any desires or perceptions that are different, it's only because of his selfish, obtuse, knuckle-draggin' nature, and it is up to him to cleanse himself of anything that might be termed 'masculine' if there is to be any peace in the house."

When I'm talking to wives on my radio program who feel desperate and depressed about what seems like a terminal situation, I ask them to do the seeming impossible: move forward with a new plan and a new attitude.

It's often hard for women to do that; like elephants, we have long memories . . . for hurt. Now, I do feel that there are some behaviors and actions that may defy forgiveness: cruelty, violence, addictions, and affairs. These problems are generally the exception, though, not the rule. I will ask the wife on the line if she chooses to be divorced. Generally, after considering her dreams, children, finances, and good memories, she'll say no. Then I'll suggest that she make a commitment to be different, in spite of old yucky memories or recent hurts.

After all, men can do some stupid things without even meaning to hurt. Jeff, a listener, revealed that in his letter:

"Women need to realize that we are just going to do stupid stuff. That doesn't make it malicious or a personal attack on them. When we do these stupid things, we don't need retaliation. We are usually embarrassed enough on our own. We need forgiveness.

We men will usually walk away from conflict with our wives without hostile thoughts, but unforgiveness on the woman's part will just hold them captive and build into more resentment. Forgiveness is the key to any successful relationship, in marriage or out, and sometimes you should give it if it is deserved or not."

I don't often use the word *forgiveness* in my radio conversations with callers; instead, I talk about *letting it go* so that one is able to grab on to something else, like hope. I remind women that although moving on doesn't mean that old, ugly memories and feelings won't pop up now and then, in both idle and stressful moments, still, they should not always act on them just because they feel them.

That is often a major revelation for them, to learn that not each and every thought and feeling needs to be revealed or acted upon. In fact, part of the maturity process is learning to choose what to deal with from within oneself, and what to take up with others. The alternative is to do what Gary, a listener, described:

> *"Women don't forgive well. They never forget—and stack disappointments up like cordwood. Women tend to blurt out, at what seems to be 'out of the blue' moments, being upset about what seem to be unrelated issues."*

This apparent lack of forgiveness is a weapon in that power struggle I mentioned earlier. That weapon is brandished for several important reasons:

- With the intent to hurt as payback for real or imagined hurts
- As a tool to demean in order to regain control
- As a means to turn the situation around, making the woman the victim when she is unwilling to take responsibility for what she's done wrong

The irony is that at the same time the woman wants to stay (happily) married, she traps herself into unhappiness by not "letting go" and "moving on."

Probably the first thing women need to forgive their husbands for is . . . for being men. Suzanne, a listener, wrote a long letter about the failure of her first marriage and what she learned that's making her second marriage, at thirty-seven years of age, work. Basically, she acknowledged that marriage is a lot of work and that the first thing she had to do is understand the difference between men and women. She explained that the problem, as she saw it, is that women want strong men who are good providers, but also expect them to be like a girlfriend they can always yak with: "We want them to be 'emotionally available.' In other words, WE WANT TO TURN THEM INTO WOMEN." She related a scene from a television movie she'd recently watched, where the husband, trying to console his wife, said, "I don't know what to do. You're not in any physical pain, which is the only pain a man understands." Suzanne wrote that she and her husband just about fell off the couch, they were laughing so hard.

Cary, another listener and husband, wrote:

> *"What I find interesting is that I am always accused of doing what always comes natural to a man. It would appear that my wife wants me to have the characteristics of a woman without losing my masculinity."*

He went on to describe some of the key points of contention between himself and his wife with respect to this expectation and communication. Frankly, they sound pretty universal:

- "I am told constantly that I do not ever listen. In most every case, I have listened—but I failed to read between the lines. Men are generally more black-and-white creatures. Men hate to try to read into everything. Women generally read into everything."

- "Women take offense at the smallest details and it frustrates them that men don't get hung up on every jot or tittle. They get the impression that we don't care."
- "Women generally like to talk and talk and talk and just vent about a problem. Men naturally and instinctively go into the solution mode and try to solve the problem and be done with it! We instinctively wish to protect our families and make sure their lives are secure. We wish only to help."

If women would simply look at their husbands as having characteristics instinctive to male nature, and not fight against those characteristics, they would find there would be less quarreling and fighting. Cary concluded by suggesting that women tend to fight against the natural characteristics of men more than men fight against those of women. I believe he's right.

The fact is that there will always be a power struggle between men and women in a "unisex"-mentality world. Only when women enjoy those strengths they have that men don't, and enjoy the strengths men have that they as women don't, will they be happier creatures and be able to play better in the sandbox called marriage.

One of the unfortunate sequelae of the feminist movement is a lack of respect for the uniqueness and specialness of femininity and masculinity. Many women are now fighting to regain their respect for their own femininity. That will certainly bode well for their ability to be able to accept and appreciate a man on masculine terms.

Sara May, one of my listeners, began that journey when she participated in a religious "Woman's Weekend." Through that experience she began to understand the basic differences between men and women, and how she was expecting things from her husband that he could not deliver. She also began to recognize that by demanding, criticizing, and being bitter, she was working against her vision of a happy, loving, long-term, growing-old-together relationship.

She decided to give those new concepts a try and reports that she feels very much in love in a deeper way than ever.

> *"I learned that the very thing that attracted me to him, his masculine, laid-back, quiet, kind demeanor, was what I was holding against him, instead of appreciating how those qualities enhanced our family—me being the more high-strung partner. I learned to create a brand-new list of everything about him that I loved and appreciated, conveyed my love and appreciation to him in small everyday acts, and made him feel that he was truly my hero.*
>
> *I felt the best of my femininity again . . . and so did he!*
>
> *I also learned to rely more on my female friends for the emotional connections I so craved and had wrongly expected my husband to provide for me, when it was not in his nature as a man to go to the depths that women are able to go on an emotional level."*

That means that if your husband doesn't *say* all the flowery things you think he should because you've watched too many chick flicks, you should look at what he *does.* When he scrapes the ice off your car windshield, that *is* love-speak. Men are made of action. Action is largely how men communicate.

Marge, a listener, described her husband as not overly affectionate or communicative, yet she's unbelievably satisfied with her marriage and deeply in love with what she feels is an incredibly loving man. How can that be? Simple. She's a smart woman—she understands that men demonstrate their emotions and passions in actions more than pretty phrases.

> *"He may not be able to tell me as often as I would like how head over heels in love with me he is or how incredibly beauti-*

ful I am. But he can call the tire place ahead of time, leave his workplace in the middle of the day, and meet me there with my car to get the new tires put on. I don't ask him to do it this way, he just does it—and he does it for me. I have come to appreciate that he has just shouted, 'I love you, baby!' to me in front of the whole tire place. I feel like a real queen. He has done these things for many years. I just had to open my eyes and appreciate them for what they are."

It is easy to challenge a husband when he says that his way of showing love is by going to work and earning money to provide for his family. Of course, he'd be working and battling traffic and corporate nonsense even if he were single. Yes, he would be doing the same thing, but not with the same commitment, intent, sacrifice, and depth of passion that he has when he's doing it for his woman and his children.

Men not only communicate with action and physicality, that's also how they receive messages of love. When a wife wraps her body around her husband's, in spite of being tired or frazzled from her day, he gets the message loud and clear that he is loved, wanted, appreciated, safe, and accepted. And as Cheryl, a listener, contributed so wisely: "When he feels loved and respected, the rest of his care and feeding is just a piece of cake."

When a wife wishes to communicate something important to her husband, the black-and-white approach is the most effective. That means forget the subtle hints. Mark, a listener, complained that "wives give hints and don't just say what they want. If I want something, I just say it. Wives have to beat around the bush and not just simply say, 'I want this. . . .'"

One listener wrote in that her husband always forgets anniversaries and birthdays. Instead of "getting mad and then getting even," she realized that this is not about his disregard for her—it's about his being a guy who doesn't much pay attention to specific details, but is always there for the bigger picture. She began talking months in advance of their anniversary:

> *"Subtle doesn't work for us. Saying, 'Wow! This will be twenty-five years on June 24. We should take a cruise.' Now, that works. We are going to Alaska!"*

Sadly, too many women get caught up in the absurdly romanticized notion that "if he loved me, he'd just know what I'm thinking, what I'd like, what he should say. . . ." Real life requires much more personal responsibility. One listener wrote in:

> *"For so long I expected my husband to read my mind. I thought, 'I can't believe he is asking me that! Doesn't he know by now what I like?' This would include everything from favorite colors to my favorite place for him to touch me during sex. I thought I could talk to him in some subtle, indirect way, and he would surely catch on. No, no, no. I have learned to say what I want and quit playing games that only leave us both frustrated."*

A husband's inability to read his wife's mind, judge her every mood, and be responsive to her every desire does not mean he doesn't love her or that he's an insensitive boob. It more likely means that he's just a normal guy.

And there are those times when these "just normal guys" want to communicate but don't . . . largely because they're afraid.

Men generally feel in a "damned if they do, damned if they don't" position. That means that if they don't say what's on their minds, they're condemned, and when they do say what's on their minds, they're condemned for "not saying the right thing."

Lloyd, a listener, sent me one hilarious letter about this problem:

"Wives continually remark, 'You never talk to me!' or 'You don't understand.'

But when husbands ask, 'What's wrong, honey?' we get, 'If you don't know, I'm not telling you!'

HUH?!

Women constantly and rightly point out that men aren't as sensitive to feelings as they are, but just as consistently completely ignore that wisdom.

If wives really want their husbands to understand them, they're going to have to acknowledge what they instinctively know and actually tell us what we need to know. Wives need to tell their husbands what they are thinking, feeling, and wondering about in simple, declarative sentences using one- or two-syllable words.

Examples:

Wife: Honey, I got my hair cut and styled today. Do you like it?

(Believe me, we men all know how to answer that one correctly.)

Not: Honey, do you notice anything different?

(Huh? Then she gets mad when we ask where the dog is.)

Or:

Wife: I want to go to the movies tonight.

Not: What do you want to do tonight, sweetie?

(Then stomp off into next week when we say, 'Just stay home and watch TV, honey.')"

Lloyd's bottom line is that he want wives to finally "get it" that men, whether husbands or bachelors, do not share their thoughts and feelings as readily as do women—frankly, they generally don't see any need to bother others with their feelings at all. They just deal with them. If something needs to be done, they do it. If something needs to be said, they say it. They largely just live with their thoughts and adjust.

But one big problem men have with opening up to their wives is that the consequences are often unpleasant, something I saw often in marital counseling sessions when I was in private practice. The wife would badger the poor, hapless fellow into revealing some feeling, then she'd pounce on it with a vengeance, accusing him of being completely wrong (with a feeling?), insensitive, stupid, mean, and so on.

That scene has risen to the level of justifiable stereotype. It got to the point where I would say in interviews that women only care about the feelings of their men when those feelings don't threaten them in any way (as in he "feels" she ignores him and spends all her time with her kids and being on the phone with her mother) or compliment them. Most wives don't really want to have to deal with their husbands' feelings, they just want to know that their husbands have positive feelings about them and that they feel for them, and so forth. Any other feelings of their husbands, which may not be pleasant for the wives to face or may be inconvenient to have to deal with, are generally squashed. Admit it. It's true. Many women are stuck in the "There shalt be no feelings before mine" mode. It's a self-centered position that has to be confronted and struggled with if there is to be any real compassion for the husband.

Glen's complaint was right on target:

"Every authority in interpersonal relations says if you have a problem with your spouse, confront them with it. Talk to them and let them know how you feel. Whenever I try this, my wife responds with a very clear explanation of why I should not feel this way. She will share with me every reason why I am wrong to think the problem has anything to do with her!

After thirty-five years of marriage, she cannot understand why I close myself up in my study and avoid any substantive discussion with her, why I don't share my feelings with her. I am not an idiot. I am a retired educator, with a thirty-year career behind me, who has, over time, been shrunken to a level of insignificance that is crippling.

I have loved my wife, raised three kids to adulthood with her, and have been completely faithful to her. Our lives would be so much better if she could listen and actually hear me rather than contemplate her 'defense' as I speak."

How painfully sad his letter was. All too often men will not speak because their wives will not let them say what they, the wives, don't want to hear. So the husbands are shut out. Then the husbands shut out their own feelings. Then they shut the wives out. I've received hundreds of letters from husbands expressing the same pain Glen did. It is remarkable that most of them still said they loved their wives and families, remained faithful, and didn't leave. Talk about the loyalty of an abused puppy!

And whether the husband is just being "a guy," or has actually backed off from communicating to his difficult wife, there is always the issue of the Patton-technique of getting a man to "open up." Roberto, "a guy" listener, wrote:

"One thing I find very frustrating is when my wife insists on digging out an answer or opinion when I'm not ready to talk—or I haven't figured out how to word the issue/opinion without her personalizing it. I believe that for most men, and I'm certainly in this category, it takes us time to process things verbally. Sometimes we need to start painting a room, play catch, or do something else physical to find the right words to convey, or decide to let it go and not 'die on that hill.' I just wish my wife would let me have time to think nonverbally."

Roberto's letter expresses an important position. I believe most wives simply want to be loving and helpful to their husbands, but when they don't take into account the "male" nature of their husbands, they often end up doing damage out of that good intention. Wives have a habit of questioning their husbands to death about their issues, feelings, etc. Men generally don't want an interrogation—open ears will do.

Since it's not in men's nature to "open up" about feelings, it's counterproductive to bombard them with questions and push, push, push. Let's get back to that "male physicality" point—mostly husbands just want to be heard, hugged, and supported. Which means don't overanalyze, or as Garry, a listener, wrote:

> *"Don't put everything a man says through a fem-filter and then expel what you believe is his real meaning. Men are never taken at their word; it all must be fem-filtered to find the true meaning of what it is that the man has said. Then he is blamed for the hurtful words that he never said in the first place!"*

Women should take whatever a man says at face value. Women tend to overanalyze men when men are just not that complicated. Wives need to give their husbands a break and respect that "guys" just have different ways without judging that difference as inadequate.

Charlie, another listener, points out this problem very clearly:

> *"The lack of respect for differing opinions seems to be a common frustration. What I find is an attitude from some women that if I think differently from them, it's because men are a-holes, or stupid, or just plain wrong. Name calling and insults are very difficult to ignore. I'm weary of sharing my opinions and feelings if I think there might be the slightest chance that they're not mainstream* female *points of view.*
>
> *And the sad thing is, when a man falls for this type of*

manipulation, and attempts to smooth out the rough male edges his wife despises, she's now even less attracted to the wimp she created!"

What follows are the common mistakes wives make in trying to communicate with their husbands. These were all submitted by male listeners:

- "Women are very good at dropping subtle hints when they want something. If I don't figure out what is wanted, then I am insensitive, uncaring, or oblivious. If they could make a simple request, like, 'Would you please do this or that for me?' it would give me a clear idea of what is expected. Also, women who espouse an acute sensitivity to feelings are often only sensitive to their own feelings and needs and not to their husbands'."
- "I don't know how to tell the difference between my wife wanting advice and just venting. For example, she will tell me that she has no time to fix dinner. I offer to take our sixteen-month-old daughter out for a walk. My wife will get upset that I don't understand. If she tells me a problem, I look for a solution. How can I know when I just need to listen . . . without dinner?"
- "I was married thirty-two years and then divorced. A man needs to know what a woman wants and needs before little things build up in reality or in her mind. A man is not a mind reader; don't nag, but you must be blunt sometimes. A wife needs to communicate the serious things in a special way so the husband will pay particular attention and not consider it just an ordinary, run-of-the-mill conversation. Do something different, like hold his hand and say, 'We need to discuss something very important to me.'"

- "A man wakes up in the morning with a clean slate and the thoughts in his head are something like this: 'Hmmm, what should I do today? I could work on my car, or the wife and I could go do something—I wonder what she wants to do? If she's busy, maybe I'll go find [friend's name] and see what he's doing. . . .' There's not a hint of malice there. So then the wife walks in and says something like, 'Well, what are you going to do today, work on the car all day in the shop? Well, fine, I'll just go find something else to do. You know, we never spend any time together anymore . . . blah, blah, blah.' What was the girl really trying to say? Probably, 'I'd like to spend some time together today with you, the man I love. I like to be with you and I miss you.' But what did the man get? 'I have already decided that you are uncaring and I don't have to take this!' What is the man's reaction? 'Heck, babe, I haven't even had my coffee yet. Why are you complaining about something that I haven't even done? I'm made to feel guilty of a crime I didn't commit, and whatever it is you want to do now, I feel manipulated into and will likely resent.' Women: Be direct!"

- "If there is something you wish to talk to us husbands about, begin with the subject. Don't work your way toward it; tell us up front you want to talk about, for example, discipline for the children, spending habits, or something about us you're dissatisfied with. Don't drop hints that are hard to follow or unintelligible. We need to be alerted to whether this is about small talk or something serious. For example: The wrong way is to say, 'How much did it cost you to play golf over the weekend? [Pause] Isn't that a lot for golf? [Pause . . . silence . . . lots of time . . .] Why won't you ever talk about money?' The right way is to say, 'We need to talk about money. I'm worried that we're spending too much.'"

- "Men are not mind readers. Many a time I have been in the situation where I have apparently done something wrong with no clue what it was or when it happened. I just know from the atmosphere in the house that something is not right. The silent treatment is a dead giveaway. When I ask my wife what is wrong, or what I did, the answer is always the same: 'Nothing.' Basically, I told my wife, 'I can't fix a problem if I don't know what it is.' Life is much better now."

It was heartening to read the many letters from wives who had turned the corner with many of the issues that the men brought up. Mary, a listener, had been married to her husband for ten years when (at forty-seven years of age) she started to take a long, hard look at how she treated him. She concluded that it was not his responsibility to read her mind. She used to think that because he was her husband, he should automatically and magically know how and what she felt and what her needs and desires were. She grew ashamed of how she'd let her expectations of him to read her mind allow so much hostility to creep into her mind and out her lips.

"It's amazing how I let myself get irritated if a laundry basket of his clean underwear and socks stayed at the foot of the stairs for days because I expected him to know that I thought he should put them away. Now I just tell him that the laundry in the basket is clean and ask him if he would please take it with him and put it away the next time he goes upstairs. And he does it with no problem!"

I believe that Mary hit upon something very important when she expressed awareness that her husband actually never intended to irritate her, and that a lot of what she was getting angry over was a result of how she interpreted his actions or inactions.

"You are right, Dr. Laura, the care and feeding of husbands is really a simple task. I had to stop complicating it with internal commentary."

Actually believing that a husband has a wife's welfare in mind, actually believing that he doesn't intend to hurt or disappoint, and being able to see the positive amidst the negative are the keys to the good feelings a wife can have about her husband. Kelly, a listener, wrote about her turning point with her husband over these issues. She remembered one argument (though she couldn't remember what it was about!), after which she stormed off to another room, and sat and stewed, thinking that if he loved her, he'd go out and buy her flowers, because he was the one who was wrong. She fumed and pouted every minute he didn't come in with flowers, thereby proving that he really didn't love her! Then she realized that this was getting them nowhere, that she was putting "winning" over her marriage.

She thought about what her husband would like and went out to the store to get him some chocolate milk and flowers. When she got back, they had a wonderful conversation about all the things they valued in each other, and realized how unimportant their disagreement had been.

"As simple as it sounds, treating a husband well hinges on the Golden Rule. Instead of stewing over what you're not getting and turning it into a tug-of-war (you demanding more, him pulling away defensively), try giving him some of what you'd like. Look at life from his perspective. It never hurts to come out and tell him how much you appreciate how hard he works to support the family, instead of just complaining that he's late for dinner again."

It's also important to not keep score with "gotcha" points of compliments. If you picked a good, decent man in the first place, you're going to get a lot of love reflected back to you if you concentrate on the giving rather than nag about receiving. You and your husband will be happier because your marriage will be stronger.

Alexis, a listener, wrote a very telling letter, which sums up this whole topic of communication. She talks about the way to properly care for and feed a husband, while at the same time getting what you want—assuming, of course, that what you want is reasonable. Alexis had an ongoing issue in her home, one that is ongoing in most homes: getting the husband to do something around the house, or to do *more* around the house, whether it be cleaning up or fixing up.

Alexis did what most wives do: argued, got angry, nagged, threatened, condemned, and punished. None of it worked. One day, when she was very fed up, she took a deep breath and asked her husband in a sincere, loving way, "You know, honey, when I ask you to do something around here, am I asking you to do too much? Are you doing as much as you could be doing or should I be doing this?" His response was, "No, I could be doing more." And all Alexis said was, "Okay."

> *"This could have turned into something big, but I just thought that we've argued about it so much and that just wasn't working. We women have to be smart. We need to make our husbands feel loved the way we want to feel loved. My husband's complaint before was that I kept track of everything he did wrong and what he didn't do. Men have feelings, too."*

And so Alexis's husband stopped trying to please her. She quickly changed her own tactics and began approaching him in a positive manner, as in, "That makes me so happy when you remember to take out the trash! Thank you very much!"

Now, it might make a wife wonder why she is thanking him for something he "should do," because, after all, it's his house, too, and women are not slaves . . . and here come all those negative thoughts and feelings to ruin the day. But the fact is, everyone deserves and needs appreciation and approval for what they do—whether it's their duty or not (or why do we give soldiers and other heroes medals?). As Alexis said:

> *"The more I acted positively and made a big deal about what he did do, the more he would do it. People will do more of what you praise them for. When I approach him like that, he's not defensive anymore."*

By the way, her husband always starts his evening prayers now with, "Lord, thank you for my wife."

In conclusion, I give you Ron's list for wives who wish to communicate well and properly care for and feed their husbands and their marriages. He wrote that most women didn't realize how easy it is for them to get what they want from men. Here are the points he made:

- Men are impressed by honesty, not manipulation (nagging, coercing, yelling, crying, or emotional blackmail).
- If a wife's request gets too complicated, we tend to either forget or lose interest. So if wives can make sincere, short requests, we usually love making those requests happen.
- We love being able to expertly solve tough problems for those we love. If you treat us like the expert, we quickly become that, probably due to our need for ego strokes.
- Asking us anything in a loving manner will assure that you will quickly and easily put us into the mode of doing what you'd like. If there's enough real reward (appreciation, affection, approval, admiration), we will

do almost anything for the source of the reward—almost as loyally as dogs.

- When you ask us to do something, be aware that distractions happen: Emergencies threaten and obstacles can become factors. If you remind us, again in that loving way, of your original petition we'll get back on track.

Gary, a listener, summarized all of the above with:

"The Proper Care and Feeding of Husbands? Be somebody he can respect. Then love him like you've never been hurt. And let him return the favor."

That's what needs the most communicating.

Chapter 6

WHAT'S SEX?

"I think women use their bodies as tools for controlling men. Once married, they go on to other tools. It seems to me we have this backwards. Girls ought to be more modest, and wives ought to be less so—around their husbands. Instead, single women show thighs and breasts, and wives dress like Eskimos. I saw a lot more skin in my dating life than I do as a married man—and I was a virgin when I married!"

BOB

"My wonderful wife has put it best: "Sex is to a husband what conversation is to a wife. When a wife deprives her husband of sex for days, even weeks on end, it is tantamount to his refusing to talk to her for days, even weeks." Think of it that way, wives, and realize what a deleterious impact enforced sexual abstinence has on a good man who is determined to remain faithful."

HERB

"We need more sex. Once a day is fine."

STEVE

If I were listing rules for the Proper Care and Feeding of Husbands, Rule One would be to . . . be a "girl." Sounds simple, doesn't it? Obviously, wives are female; women; girls. So what is there to actually "do" in order to be a girl? Lots.

After marriage, and definitely after having children, too many wives contract the "Frump syndrome," the symptoms of which include wearing flannel pajamas and socks, or sweatpants with oversized T-shirts, to bed instead of some girly thing with lace; not shaving legs or grooming nails; not washing, styling, or even combing hair; taking off (instead of freshening up) makeup from the day just before your husband comes home; using the toilet with him in the room; not making an attempt to smell sweet (with a little perfume or body oil); and never putting on sexy outfits . . . in front of your husband.

When women have called in to my radio program to say that they are unhappy in their marriages, but nothing particular is actually wrong, I ask them if they have contracted this ailment. Almost universally, the answer is yes. When I suggest the obvious cure, I am confronted with some angry, annoyed, resentful, defensive women! It's worrisome when women embrace the notion that once they are married, they are entitled to be loved, adored, protected, gifted, romanced, obeyed, and provided for without question, without reciprocation, and definitely without any effort on their part to create the emotional and psychological environment that would more likely get them all those desires.

Sam, a female listener, wrote:

> *"Women expect to be wooed yet be allowed to look haggish and frumpy. It's hard to romance a hag and come off as being sincere. I will admit that I have fallen into the trap of letting myself go, but I have been clawing my way out of that hole. I now put the extra effort into showering and doing my hair and makeup before my darling comes home from work, and well, it has certainly paid off!"*

As if in rebuttal, the wives will give themselves amnesty because, "He . . . (something to criticize him for)." "Well," I'll say, "that may be so. But you're the one calling me, unhappy. And you're the one who can decide to make this situation better." I remind them that "men are simpler," and that they, the wives, really have the power to change what is happening in the relationship because, as I've said earlier, men forgive easier and are more easily corrected in their behaviors with positive feedback than women are.

What attracts men to women is their femininity, and femininity isn't only about appearance, it's also about behaviors. Looking womanly and behaving sweetly and flirtatiously are gifts wives give to their husbands. This gift communicates that the husband is seen as a man, not just a fix-it guy, the breadwinner, or the sperm donor. And if it's romancing a wife is hungering for, presenting oneself as an appealing "woman" will get more romancing than presenting oneself as only a child-care worker, or house cleaner, or the other wage earner.

Kelly, a listener, wrote that she remembered how much effort she put into her femininity when she was dating her now-husband. She would look forward to cooking him romantic meals, and buying sexy outfits to flounce around in. She loved the way he "wanted" her and she loved the feeling of wanting him.

After marriage, there were bills to pay, two careers, a home to keep up, and children to raise. After the second child she gave up her career to take care of the home and children. She would spend the day cleaning, doing laundry, grocery shopping, playing with the kids, and balancing the checkbook. When her husband came home, immediately there were things she wanted him to do . . . now! And, of course, none of those things had anything to do with romance, intimacy, or any other lovish activities.

She discovered that she was becoming more naggy, hostile,

and bitter, with a growing feeling that she was being cheated out of life. When her husband came home, she stopped going to the door with a hug and a kiss, stopped showing affection, stopped having sex, and even stopped the good-night kiss.

Basically, she was blaming her husband for her unhappiness, insisting that it was up to him to go out of his way to please her and pamper her to make up for how difficult her life was. Never mind how difficult his day was—which was only amplified by his wife's angry discontent.

It was only when a female relative came to ask Kelly for advice about marriage that she realized she was not practicing what she was preaching. She acknowledged to herself that she was using her husband as a scapegoat for her own emotional struggles, and was so busy blaming him for what she felt he was not giving her that she wasn't noting what she wasn't giving him.

> *"I am on the road to fixing that. For starters, I began by realizing how lucky I am that I have the ability to stay at home and raise my boys. I wouldn't have that luxury if it weren't for my husband's hard work. I still have that excitement to do things to make him happy because it also makes me happy. I give, he gives. I give more, he gives more. I realized that it isn't all about what I'm not getting, it's about what I'm giving that makes the difference."*

There are two important issues in Kelly's letter: appreciation for what one has and the realization that giving begets getting. And it needs to be emphasized that the most important thing a wife has to give to her husband is herself; therefore that "self" needs to be taken care of and then shared. That a wife cleans the house or drives the kids all over town or argues a big court case is all wonderful, but it's not giving of herself to her husband. While fulfilling the obligations and responsibilities of taking care of the house and family is an essential part of giving in a marriage, other folks could be hired to do it. The real essence of giving is more intimate, sensitive and vulnerable, and up close and personal. Since fidelity is an essential part of trust and commitment, no one can or should be hired to take care of any of the tender, loving, sensual, sexual aspects of marriage!

Romancing a spouse is supposed to be a two-way street, but I'm wracking my brain trying to think of one movie, book, play, or conversation on the radio, when I've heard a man describe his wife as romantic. I can't think of one time. Is it that men don't need romancing? No, don't believe that. Is it that men define romancing differently? Probably. Is it that men don't get much romancing? Definitely.

But let's first go back to the differences in defining romancing in the minds of men when it pertains to their actions or their wives'. When men think of being romantic, they think of what women like: sweet words, flowers, perfume, dinners out, and gifts. When men think of women being romantic toward them, they think less of what she can go out and buy or specifically do; they think more of how she presents herself to him as a woman and how she reinforces his ego by treating him as desirable and competent. It's how she makes him feel like a real man and her hero.

In order for a wife to do that, she's got to tune out of herself and tune in to him. For many wives it means tossing out their bags of petty, bitter feelings, resentments, disappointments, and overreactions to basic annoyances. While that is often a daunting task, the rewards are worth it in the long run.

It might seem that I'm suggesting that men are totally superficial, requiring that their wives look like *Playboy* centerfolds, and while that's a popular stereotype, my research in preparation for this book demonstrates otherwise. It's not "absolute perfection" that men desire from their wives (although a "10" walking by will get any man's attention); it's the effort the wives put in to pleasing their men that seems to make the most impact. That's not a superficial concept. It means that men appreciate that their wives care about their "male nature," which responds dramatically to visual stimulation.

One husband wrote:

> *"Almost every man I've ever spoken to is not infatuated with big breasts (even though women are). They don't find attractive the terribly skinny models featured in women's magazines. They like normal, naturally shaped women, much like Jennifer Lopez or Marilyn Monroe. They like women who are naturally attractive, what many women would consider plain-looking. Men generally don't like a lot of makeup. What many men are concerned about is if their wives let themselves go, gaining huge amounts of weight.*
>
> *Men actually find their wives' bodies attractive, though, even when they carry a little extra weight. Husbands have an intrinsic need to enjoy their wives' bodies 'visually' for their emotional well-being. And both men and women have a responsibility to keep their appearance up, within reason."*

Frankly, men like to look at their wives' bodies naked, watch the simple act of them undressing, see them in something sexy. Men need this visual excitement, and they should get it from their wives, not from adult bookstores or the Internet. The men who wrote to me commenting on this issue surprisingly were in agreement that there was no absolute rating system in their minds about perfect female bodies when it came to their wives. Most of the men were describing their desire for their wives to dress (and undress) and behave somewhat coquettishly. Their sense of well-being was very tied into their wives indulging them with visual input and seductive behavior.

Ralph, a listener, expressed his frustration with his wife's just not caring about this part of his being:

> *"The number one thing my wife doesn't do is take care of herself. After the courting and the 'I do's,' attention turns to other things. On your radio show, when you get a caller who is now less interested in their relationship, you advise them to go back to what attracted their mate in the first place. For guys that is generally to be romantic, bring flowers, take her to an exciting place, etc. For women, it is to fix themselves up, put on something nice, and be sweet.*
>
> *Guys have a natural and deep desire to be with a woman who cares enough about herself to look good for her mate."*

In reading all the letters from men, I was struck by their depth of sensitivity about the issue of women's appearance. It wasn't an impersonal, animal reaction (as it is with women the men don't personally know), it was a deeply personal one. The wife's comfort with and appreciation of her own body and femininity, and her willingness to share that with her husband, actually fed his sense of well-being, his feeling of being loved as a husband and valued as a "man."

Shahina, a listener, wrote about her sad story of divorce after ten years of marriage. Her husband left her, complaining that they had so little time together (because she was over-involved with her "mommy and daddy") and he no longer found her attractive. It seems she had gained a tremendous amount of weight by eating too much and exercising too little. I can bet that the reaction of most women upon reading that is to get their hackles up and proclaim her husband as shallow. Frankly, that hostile reaction itself demonstrates a shallow self-centeredness. The impact on our bodies of natural aging, illness, pregnancies, and so forth is a simple fact of life. The inability to accept these realities betrays immaturity or worse. At the same time, though, the unwillingness to accept responsibility for the upkeep of one's physical or emotional well-being should be met with consternation by a spouse because it is an assault on the marital covenant. And the disregard of the unique feelings and needs of one's spouse is a selfish insult.

Shahina's letter went on to say:

> *"I would try to tell him that I would go on a diet and exercise to lose weight and become more attractive. I thought I would do these things for him so that he would find me attractive. I knew deep down that I did not want to do those things because I wanted him to love me and accept me just the way I was."*

This is not an unusual sentiment for me to hear from women, who express hostility that their husbands would like them to clean up, dress up, and tone up. They act like their husbands are selfish, sex-crazed, superficial, insensitive barbarians, which isn't the case. The "If they loved me, they wouldn't make a fuss about such things" point of view is simply irresponsible and destructive. As I said in my chapter on communication, verbal exchange is but one means of communication. A lot is also said by one spouse to another by the willingness to fulfill each other's needs. Men have the emotional need to see their wives as desiring them, and the way the wives take care of and present themselves expresses that love.

The natural extension of these positive attitudes and behaviors is sexual intimacy. Phil, a listener, introduces us to this issue beautifully:

> *"God made men the way they are; men have hormones and urges. I believe that too many women think that men are oversexed, but in this area men are not self-made. For men, it does not take a super sex partner to keep a man happy. Making love with the wife, even at low frequency, keeps a man healthy and*

> *home. But when sex is withheld, the need for and lack of it becomes a constant state of mind for men. It forces men to turn their thoughts outward.*
>
> *I believe that most men would not settle for a fast-food burger when they have prime rib at home, but when they are hungry, they will find a way to get fed. I believe that most men do not want to leave their wives—they are driven out by a lack of physical love, compassion, and understanding in the area of sexuality."*

Male sexuality is yet another subject that seems to elicit hostility in many women. Much of that hostility is the product of defensiveness resulting from the realization that they, the women, indeed are not putting their husbands' needs anywhere prominent on their to-do lists. Kim, a listener, got that straightened out fast when her husband came to her and asked her if a divorce would make her happy. She was shocked! She could not understand what he meant because she felt extremely happy with her life, her marriage, and her children. She immediately suspected that he had a girlfriend, but that wasn't the case. The truth was, he thought *she* must be getting her sexual satisfaction somewhere else because she rejected him sexually just about all the time.

He went on to tell her that he loved her and wanted her to be truly happy and that he was sorry if he failed in doing this. According to Kim:

> *"The truth was I had an excuse every time he wanted to be intimate. I'd say, 'I'm tired,' or 'The only time you show affection is in the bedroom,' or 'I just don't feel like it.'"*

Her husband then confessed to her that he had looked at pornographic pictures on the Internet. Kim's first reaction was disgust, then deep hurt . . . then humility as he explained to her that as empty and guilty as he felt while doing that, still it was easier than coming to bed only to be rejected again. He told her that she's the only one he wants but she won't let him have her. He said that he was frustrated by the intensity of his desire for her, and wished he could be neutered like a dog to diminish his suffering.

He remarked that being rejected is always bad, but being rejected when one is at his most vulnerable—naked—is devastating. Kim wrote:

> *"I was saddened and humbled by my lack of selflessness. Yes, every day I give to my kids, my home, my friends, and even to myself in many different ways, but I have failed to give in the right ways to the most important person in my life: the person who makes my life complete, happy, and possible—my best friend—my husband.*
>
> *My truth: Before I was married I used sex to get what I wanted. Now I have what I've always wanted (more than I deserve) and see sex as useless. I have taken him for granted and pushed aside his emotional and physiological needs."*

"I've pushed aside his emotional and physiological needs." That is a powerful admission. Since that time, Kim has changed her priorities. She now pays attention to her husband as a man. She writes that he is incredibly good looking, fit, and a great dad. Since she's begun to look at him with a "new eye," she's grown more in feelings of love and begun to see the sexiness that she missed for so long. She reports that the children's bedtime has changed from nine to eight, all electronic devices are turned off, and "the house is rocking!"

Still, it is astonishing the extent to which female society denigrates a man's sex drive, reducing him to merely a rutting animal with no deeper context. After reading all the mail from men about the Proper Care and Feeding of Husbands, though, there's no way to hold that position.

Most men actually pointed out in their letters that their desire for sex wasn't just about a "release" (although that is a great need for both men and women). As Chris, a listener, wrote:

"I don't understand why women don't understand that sex is a man's number one need from his wife. It's not just the act and sensation of pleasure, but it's the acceptance by a woman of her man. There's a communion that happens during intercourse that will bond a man to his woman, and he in turn will then begin to give of himself emotionally to her.

When that need isn't met, the man begins to look at his wife as just a roommate who doesn't pay her share of the rent but continues to harp on him about leaving the toilet seat up."

Ron, another listener, describes himself as a romantic, sensitive, and helpful husband who believes that women need to be more open to discussing sex rather than immediately dismissing all men as just "sex hounds."

"I am tired of women putting all men down for wanting and needing affection. Aren't people in love supposed to want to kiss, hug, and make love? That just makes sense to me."

Ron pointed out that sex and affection are healthy ways for couples to connect and should be given freely and eagerly in a good relationship. He believes that if women thought sex and affection were as important as any other part of a marriage, there would be fewer breakups because there would be more mutual satisfaction and bonding.

Jessica wrote with a critical female perspective on this issue:

"You're willing to scoop poop off of chubby baby thighs, clean vomit out of cars/car seats, wipe colorful snot off of drooling

> *children's noses . . . I think you can be willing to have sex with your husband!"*

A stay-at-home mother, Jessica belongs to a number of groups, and the talk about sex is always anti-male. She wrote that the majority of the women are just tired and see their husbands as selfish for "wanting some." She reminds them that they are communicating negative messages to their husbands when they're willing to get up several times during the night for their child but act like spending a few minutes nurturing their husbands is such an unnecessary chore.

> *"I think that there is a myth out there that* men need to ejaculate. *I asked my husband, 'If I just lay there and let you get your physical needs met, is that satisfactory? Is that what you need?' He was disgusted! He wants to interact with me. He wants me to participate with him. This is not just a matter of a physical outlet for him.*
>
> *I also asked him, 'After we have sex, do you feel physically relieved, or closer to me, or happy about our family, or just totally blank or relaxed/stress free?' His reply was that he feels good about his family and our relationship."*

I wonder how many women have the guts to ask their husbands that question . . . and respect the answer?

In addition to the obvious physical pleasure involved, men desire sex in order to feel emotionally closer to their wives. So perhaps more wives should say, "All my husband wants is to feel close to me," instead of "All my husband wants is sex from me." That would make it much harder to dismiss the husband and his unique male sexuality. Sex is the way men communicate their emotions to and about their wives.

When wives are hostile or rejecting about sexual intimacy and physical affection, men begin to believe that their wives no longer have interest in them in any personal, profound way. How lonely, how neutered will a man feel before disconnecting from his wife altogether? Ron, a listener, says:

"I believe that most wives who feel secure in their marriages believe that because their husband loves them, they no longer need to address the sexual part of the marriage like they did in the beginning. What most men want is a wife who still desires her husband, and the fulfillment of that is the closeness in the sexual experience. From a man's point of view, if this does not happen, his communication, moods, and masculine well-being suffer."

Another listener, Don, wrote that as a man, he seeks out intimacy with his wife as a means of expressing his love, as well as his desire to put aside any small differences that have cropped up. To be turned down is extremely hurtful, and is very harmful to the relationship because as wives remove the opportunity to experience that depth of closeness, both physical and emotional, men find themselves losing all positive and caring feelings toward their wives. Yet wives expect husbands to ignore their own neglected needs and hurt feelings and do for them whatever they want . . . or else.

Mike's letter was one of the most touching I received. He began by saying:

"Dr. Laura, you have been openly supporting husbands. And that is contrary to the popular 'man-bashing' that I usually have to endure. Because of this I will share my thoughts on this topic."

Mike went on to describe himself as forty-four years old, with three children, all adults. He is in his second marriage, with a woman who already had two adult children. He talks about the care and feeding that he needs in order to "feel like a man." Mike sees his role as providing for and protecting his family, and is willing to work as hard as it takes to do both. He says that the appreciation he needs can come from a kiss at the door, or his wife reaching for his hand or drawing him into a hug.

> *"When I feel that my wife feels safe in my arms, then I know that I am doing my job. To be desired is an extension of this closeness."*

Unfortunately, he reports that affection and physical intimacy are gone from the relationship—and he doesn't know why. He reaches out to her, but only coldness and rejection are returned.

> *"When I am feeling the most rejected, I ask myself, 'Why am I here?' and 'Who cares for me?' To me, I am still doing my job of protecting and providing, but I get nothing in return.*
>
> *When months pass without sex or affection, the message that I get is that I am undesirable and have no value. If I were appreciated, I would be 'loved.' Caring and nurturing is what I need to feel healthy and happy."*

I get so many letters like Mike's, and it tears up my heart to read about the depth of hurt men feel from their wives' sexually rejecting them. This isn't physical frustration, it's real emotional hurt.

Interestingly, one male listener wrote that when wives constantly belittle and neglect their husbands' sexuality, the men become emotionally suppressed and then their wives don't get what they need from them. He further indicted that he believes these women are displaying the "moral equivalent of infidelity." This latter statement deserves some attention. When we normally think of infidelity, we think of a spouse having an emotional and/or sexual relationship outside of the marriage, whether with a "real honey" or a "synthetic honey" on the Internet. That is an obvious breach of marital vows as well as a violation of one of the Ten Commandments. However, don't the marital vows include and imply words like *love, honor, protect, care for,* and so forth? So when one breaches those vows by neglect, is that not also a form of infidelity? Perhaps we should start looking at the act of intentionally depriving a spouse of his legitimate needs as infidelity, too, because it stems from being unfaithful to the intent of the vows.

Sex is a serious point of contention for many women. I can remember one female caller in particular who complained that her husband wasn't understanding about how tired, burdened, and overwhelmed she was. He still wanted sex. I asked her what was wrong with that since most people expect monogamy in marriages, not celibacy. That seemed to startle her . . . but only for a moment.

She hit me back with the challenge, "Should I be expected to have sex when I don't want to just because he wants to?" I took a deep breath and answered, "Most of the time, yes." She was horrified and likened my response to a call for some form of slavery. I reminded her that she expected him to go to work and earn money to support the family even on days he didn't feel like it. I added that she expected him to visit her relatives whether he liked them or not, or was even treated very well by them. I threw in that she expected him to submit to her decisions regarding their social calendar in spite of his personal preferences. "It's called," I reminded her, "loving obligation." This time she was quiet a little longer.

I then went on to ask her about the times she "didn't feel like it" but did it anyway:

DR. LAURA: Didn't you get turned on at some point in the lovemaking?

CALLER: (giggling) Yes.

DR. LAURA: Well then, sometimes the pump just needs a little priming. . . . And didn't you feel great about him and life in general after a good orgasm?

CALLER: (giggling again) Yes.

DR. LAURA: Then why the hell would you want to keep that from your own life? Never mind for a moment that you've been suffocating your husband. Think about what you've been missing! Don't cut off your nose to spite any part of your body!

So many women seem to get so compulsive about everything else in their lives besides intimacy with and compassion toward their husbands. Of course, regular sex is not in and of itself the panacea for troubled marriages or troubled spouses. But if women would show more compassion for a man's physical needs, they would find themselves happier and better able to survive and confront all the annoying challenges of life.

When women call complaining that they are turned off to their husbands because the men seem to have a never-ending need for sex and only do affectionate things when they want sex, I remind them of something one of my listeners, Clint, wrote in:

> *"She says that I don't want to cuddle her without having sex, because I get aroused when we touch. I say that if someone is starving and you put a plate of food in front of them, you can't expect them to just nibble on it. Give them a full stomach, then they will snack."*

Based upon that concept, I have told wives that the way to cut down on their husbands' seemingly voracious appetite for sex is to take control by initiating sex play themselves—and at reasonably frequent intervals. When these women call me back, they all report the same results: (1) They're having more fun in their lives, (2) they feel closer to their husbands than ever before, and (3) their husbands don't seem to be nagging about sex at all.

Magic.

Douglas added his opinion:

"If you are not really interested in having sex at a certain time but your husband is, say something to the effect of, 'Come on, big guy. Show me what you got. Let's do it just for you.' Then tell him to skip the foreplay on you and just do his thing. Be extra enthusiastic and active. He will come sooner and think you are terrific. You might even find that you yourself are more interested in having an orgasm that you thought!"

But remember, do it with enthusiasm. As Scott wrote:

"What's worse than rejection is a begrudged spreading of the legs so we can get it over with and go to sleep. How is a man supposed to feel like he is pleasuring his wife with an attitude like that? The most pleasure a man can get from sex is to know he is pleasing his wife."

It ought to seem obvious that when you love someone, you aim to please them and make them feel loved and contribute to their happiness. One listener, Michele, was quite blunt about this by saying that although she might not always be "in the mood," she is always ready when he wants it.

"It may sound stupid, ladies, but I want to make sure he gets what he wants. He's too wonderful and I love him too much to disappoint him. That's how I nurture and respect my husband: communication, understanding, support, great chocolate chip cookies, and GREAT SEX!"

Now, honestly, does Michele sound oppressed and miserable? I'm convinced that most of the oppression women experience is of their own making—through their misguided choices and attitudes.

Lounelle, another listener, concurs with Michele's positive attitude:

> *"I have felt like sex is the last thing on my mind for different reasons, but it never fails that if I give in and enjoy the attention my husband shows me that my attitude changes, and not just for the moment."*

Barbara wrote to me after hearing a particular female caller on my radio program who didn't want to give her husband sex because she said she wasn't getting the little displays of affection from him she needed to make her feel good. Barbara was stunned that she recognized herself in that call! She had begun to resent the sex her husband always seemed to want, and because of her actions, her husband didn't feel very affectionate with her and didn't do those little things she wanted, which only served to increase her resentment . . . and so it went around and around! Barbara described herself as pretty cold and aloof, acting most of the time like sex was a chore and hoping he would just get it over with. But then she changed. . . .

> *"Man, oh man, did the affections get showered all over me. I began realizing how incredible my husband was, and my prayer and devotion life in the morning began to center around being a better wife and then mother. I began to look forward to seducing my husband, and he was so amazed that he felt that he had a new wife! He began again to show me all the affection that I missed from the beginning of our marriage because I once again showed him how much I loved him.*
>
> *Your caller cannot expect her husband to shower her with affection when she is so resentful of the intimate part of their life that means so much to him."*

My on-air conversation with Anna, twenty-five years old, married for five years and with two children, one five and the other nine months, provided me with one of the most startling exchanges concerning marital sex.

After she became a mother, Anna was worn out and didn't much feel like having sex. That is not unusual for new mothers, considering the hormonal changes and the challenges of little sleep and the relentless needs of a new baby. Nonetheless, affection between parents at this time is important on so many levels: Their bond needs to be confirmed, they need each other's support and tenderness to help with the transition from "us" to "family," and they could both benefit from the fun and release that sex offers.

In Anna's case, she rejected her husband so often that she got sick of doing it. Her solution? She told him that she would pay for him to seek out a prostitute. Now, four years later, he told her that while he followed her instructions, he wasn't able to go through with anything once he thought of their daughter. Neat guy.

DR. LAURA: What is your question for me?

ANNA: I just don't know if I should end the relationship.

DR. LAURA: You want to dump a man with whom you have two small children because you refused to have sex with him and told him to have sex with a prostitute? He tries to do what you told him to do, but he didn't really go through with much of it, and he tells you four years later, and you want to dump him? Frankly, of the two of you, he looks better.

ANNA: He should have understood me.

DR. LAURA: Anna, one of the big mistakes women make is to think that because he marries you, he's obligated to stay there, obediently and docilely, no matter how you treat him. Of course being a new mother is difficult. But isn't being a new father difficult in its own

> way? When you tell a man that you disdain him intimately enough that you can't be bothered to hug, kiss, or make love, for any reasons, in an ongoing way, and then tell him to go pay someone else for sex and leave you alone—but you still expect him to come home and love, cherish, support, and understand you—then you've got wires loose.

This call had a positive ending. I reminded her that she hurt him first and that, because he loved her, he was not holding that above her head. She agreed with that. I also reminded her that he wanted to have a long, wonderful life with her and that she needed to return that favor by never throwing this incident in his face again.

ANNA: You're right.

DR. LAURA: So when he comes through the door, I expect some slurpy kisses, a good, hot dinner for him, and, uh, you know, put the kids to bed early.

ANNA: Thank you so much, Dr. Laura.

Women, as Anna expressed, expect their men to be understanding about them not being in the mood for sex. But women need to reciprocate that understanding and not be critical when their husbands desire *them*. Likewise, they need to get it into their heads that their husbands are not just "wantin' some," they are desiring closeness with and acceptance by them!

"Accepting" a husband's sexual/affectionate advance is not the only way a wife can lovingly demonstrate her openness and caring. How 'bout actually being the aggressor! Jeffrey, a listener, wrote for all husbands:

> *"PLEASE be the sexual aggressor almost 50 percent of the time. If you chase him around the house/bedroom/bed enough,*

he will be too tired, and pleased, to even give another woman a passing thought . . . well, a good man won't.

Do you know what it means to a man to hear his woman say aloud the words 'Would you please make love to me?' or 'Would you please———' (you fill in the blank with some sexual invitation). Don't spend a lot of time in front of the mirror wishing you were something you are not. Your husband is likely not a movie star either, and he loves you anyway.

Your 'sexual personality' determines a lot in how your husband sees you. The most beautiful woman in the world who says 'no' all the time to any and all sexual suggestions or overtures becomes ugly in his eyes in a big hurry. A supposedly 'plain'-looking woman who is a more-than-willing love partner with a good imagination in the bedroom, living room, shower, backseat, secluded woods, etc. (you get the idea), becomes one of the most beautiful women in the world.

Please, PLEASE, if we aren't doing something right sexually—PLEASE communicate. Go ahead, whisper naughty and loving things in our ears, we'll take your lead. And say 'I love you.' What? You thought only women love to hear that?"

A lot of women have called my radio program telling of their reluctance to "ask for some" or to "ask for it to be done a bit differently." It's understandable—nobody wants to look foolish or risk rejection. But remember, that's the same emotional issue that your husband has! *He* has to communicate one way or another and risk *your* response.

And don't worry about looking "slutty" to your man. Not one of the hundreds and hundreds of faxes and e-mails from men included the notion that if a man's wife "came on" to him, he'd be dismayed or horrified. The universal response was one of great longing and potential glee.

In addition to all the good that can come from the wife being more available, agreeable, open, experimental, and seductive (i.e., sharing more responsibility for the marital love life), there is also that building up of the male ego, which contributes a lot to a husband's sexual satisfaction. It's that "hero" thing again. As one woman wrote:

"When Viagra hit the market and everyone was talking about it, a friend asked my husband if he was using it. I quickly responded, 'Are you kidding? They come to our house to get his blood to make the stuff!' He beamed with delight and saw that I considered him as he was twenty years ago and began to act the part!"

She ended her letter with something very touching and interesting. She talked about a Bible verse:

" 'Faith comes by hearing. . . . ' If we say hateful things about each other, we begin to believe it and it just keeps escalating until our 'faith' in our marriage is over."

Her husband wakes her up each morning calling her his Proverbs 31 Woman. And every day, she reports, she tries to live up to it. That means she builds him up so he can be on the same kind of pedestal he's put her on. How beautiful a sentiment is that?

Helen, another listener, has two rules when it comes to sex in her marriage. First, she never turns her husband down. She describes him as very passionate and someone who likes to make love several times a week.

"Unless I have just had major surgery, or am very, very angry with him, I don't turn him down. I am past forty and, honestly, I have found my own drive diminishing. Dr. Laura has said on her show that even if you are not in the mood, once you start it, it's fun. She's right! I don't want him hesitant to approach me,

nor do I want him looking elsewhere. He knows his wife, lying right next to him in his bed, is always warm and eager."

Helen's second rule about married sex has to do with "experimentation." Evidently, her husband is quite creative. When he tries something new, she doesn't let her first reaction be one of rage or disgust without considering the possibility of it being something she might like, and maybe giving it a go. She says she draws the line at pain and other people, but believes that the creative side of their lovemaking is part of their exploring possibilities together.

But let's get back to that problem of diminishing desire. It is not an issue of normal aging, and any woman who leaves it at that is fibbing. Ask her about her lustful fantasies about some suave, buffed-up movie star or neighbor. It is true that when life gets routine and mundane, the excitement is often replaced by a kind of sad lethargy. Some of that is good, as it makes life more comfortable. But some of it isn't good, because it makes life predictably boring. That's when you've got to get into gear and do something.

Lisa, a listener, was precisely in that "bored, tired, uninterested" place. When she got into bed at the end of the day, she only wanted sleep, but her husband "bugged" her about sex. Then one rainy afternoon, she called her husband at work and said that it was the perfect day for him to come home early and crawl into bed with her. Even though he couldn't, because he had an important meeting scheduled that he couldn't get out of, later he told her that he couldn't stop thinking about her all day and couldn't wait to get home to her. How many wives hear that after fourteen years of marriage?

It's got to be ego-boosting to have a husband still "want" his wife, to find her desirable even with her varicose veins, stretch marks, and C-section scars. Women often talk about being depressed about their lives, but if they would only jump-start their sexual interaction with their husbands, and be lavished with all that emotional and physical feedback, I think that would beat any Valium cocktail they might consider taking.

Sex, like any other part of the marital relationship, needs respect and nurturing. So no TV in the bedroom—keep it a beautiful sanctuary. The bedroom is the foundation of the marriage and family. Don't underestimate its importance and its power to generate the energy by which every member of the family flourishes.

Chapter 7

A MAN SHOULD BE RESPECTED IN HIS OWN HOME

"My father's advice when I married was, 'You are marrying a man. Always treat him like one and he will always act like one.'"

TAMMY

"It is easy for a woman to love; that is the way that God made her. It is more difficult for her to show respect."

WENDI

"I think men need respect—and the more respect they're shown, the more love they give in return."

JANETTA

The day before I began this chapter, I received a call on my radio program from a husband and wife together. The husband began the conversation by telling me of the latest in a series of typical incidents involving his mother-in-law. Frankly, the wife's behavior and point of view stunned me into silence!

It seems the husband, wife, and several children had gone to

Grandma's house for dinner. Afterward they all left in separate cars to come back to the callers' home. For some reason, the car with Grandma and some of the children stopped in a parking lot of a large department store. The twelve-year-old boy, suffering from a bad cold, needed to clear his throat of some mucus, which he spit out on the parking lot ground. Evidently, Grandma went ballistic, yelling at him that he was "no better than someone from the ghetto."

When everyone arrived at the callers' home, one of the daughters turned to Grandma and told her that it wasn't nice of her to hurt her brother's feelings. The twelve-year-old was crying.

Dad got into gear and started questioning Grandma about her behavior, and she immediately got defensive and hostile, eventually "flipping the bird" at Dad. At this point, according to the father, he told his mother-in-law in no uncertain terms that she was not going to disrespect him in his own home!

I asked the wife if she concurred with her husband's rendition of events. While she agreed that he'd described the events accurately in a general way, it was stunningly clear that her loyalties lay with her mother. For example, she criticized her son for coughing up on the parking lot ground, where "other people have to walk." She also said that her husband had raised his voice excessively. Clearly, she was most motivated to justify her mother's (mis)behaviors.

I was surprised, quite frankly, to hear a mother not jump to the defense of her child; sadly, I am more used to wives not jumping to the defense of their husbands, especially when their "mommies" are involved. When I addressed her condemnation of her son ("He was choking on sputum—a glass of water or a paper towel could have been used to clean up without embarrassing the boy"), her reaction was to discount this suggestion and to reiterate her mother's position that the boy was "bad."

The real stunner was when she turned on her husband. In the most horrible, disdainful, sarcastic manner, she imitated him saying, "A man should not be disrespected in his own home." She particularly emphasized "man" and "own home" with her snotty disregard for him.

I quietly said, "You *don't* think a man should be respected in his own home?" She flippantly came back with, "I think everyone should be respected everywhere." I repeated, "You *don't* think *a man* should be respected in his own home?" She wouldn't answer that.

I tried to reach her, but frighteningly, she clearly saw nothing wrong with her manner or attitude. After the call, I expressed out loud that I felt deeply sorry for this man and his children.

Another female caller the day before did "get it." She and her husband already had a cat, when she decided to get a second one. He strongly protested about getting another animal in the house. She called me to find a way to convince him to agree to what she wanted.

DR. LAURA: What? He doesn't have the right to his position?

CALLER: Yes, of course he does. It's just that I don't see any good reason to not have another cat.

DR. LAURA: A good reason is that he doesn't want to live with multiple animals. Why isn't that a good enough reason?

CALLER: Can't I keep pushing him to specify his reasons? Doesn't he have to justify his position? I just want to know why he feels that way.

DR. LAURA: No, you don't. You are not really interested in *understanding* his position. You just want him to enumerate his arguments so you can shoot them down so that you can have the cat. You don't want to "understand," you ultimately want to "manipulate." In general, men are more easily beaten down by the relentless arguments of their wives than the reverse.

CALLER: Yeah, I guess that's so. But I really want this other cat!

DR. LAURA: Obviously, you want that cat more than you want to show your husband respect and love.

CALLER: No, that's not so.

DR. LAURA: Yes, it is—and you know it. You aren't simply grateful and satisfied with one animal, you want to impose another on him against his will. You are acting like this is your home—not "our" home. You are acting like what *you* want is important, and what he wants is only an impediment to you. You are telling him that his home is not his safe, peaceful haven.

CALLER: Oh, my gosh, I didn't really see that. Yes, I guess that's right—that's how he probably sees it.

DR. LAURA: And what do you think you'll ultimately get in return for that attitude?

CALLER: Got it.

Some of the more cynical types might say that this caller is oppressed by her husband's whim, but those "types" are not going to ever be happily married to someone happily married to them. There is a necessary give-and-take, a benevolent cooperation between spouses that results in each feeling and believing that they deeply matter to the other. That, of course, is more important than simply getting another pet or getting one's own way by overpowering the other.

Whether it's whims or tastes should not be the important issue—being fair and loving is. Think about the typical home; it is largely decorated by the choices and tastes and whims of the woman of the house. Real estate agents have told me that they really need to sell a house to the wife because it is generally her reaction that motivates the man. Husbands defer to their wives because they love them and want to please them, and because (girls, we have to be honest) we make life hell for them when they don't. Since men live for our approval and acceptance, they are too easy to manipulate inappropriately, insensitively, inhumanely, and unlovingly.

One female caller to my radio program provided a great example of such manipulation. It seems that her husband has always hated chicken, even from as far back as when he was just her boyfriend. He probably ate some bad chicken when he was younger, or became ill after a meal and assumed it was the chicken. Just about everybody has had some experience like that, and we just don't want to ever eat that food again! No big deal.

But it was a big deal to my caller. She had been cooking him chicken cutlets and such, and telling him that it was turkey, since he had no problem eating that. She called to ask me if she should tell him the truth.

DR. LAURA: Why would you do that?

CALLER: Because, well, two reasons, actually. I wanted to prove to him that he didn't hate chicken. And it's just too annoying to cook chicken and turkey when I can just cook chicken.

DR. LAURA: You never cook something separate for the children or friends or relatives?

CALLER: Yeah, I do . . . but that's different.

DR. LAURA: How?

CALLER: (avoiding the question) Well, anyway, I want to know if I should tell him that he's been eating chicken, and see, it's fine!

DR. LAURA: No, absolutely not. And I think you should be cooking him turkey—as he asked you and as you said you were. If you want to offer him a bite of your

> chicken to see if he's still sensitive to it, that would show real caring and respect.
>
> If you tell him what you've been doing to him to (a) risk getting him sick and (b) getting him into a "gotcha" moment, he's going to feel betrayed, humiliated, and definitely disrespected.

While the "chicken caper" may seem like a small thing, it isn't. When one adds up all those little moments when a husband is proven wrong or overpowered, we end up with one unhappy man. Then I get the calls about his not coming home on time, not being romantic, not listening, not—well, you get the idea. And, no wonder, because when you put garbage in, you get garbage out.

Steve, a listener, responded to my on-air discussions on how a wife should treat her husband. This is not, he remarked, a subject one hears much about.

> *"In today's world it is assumed that men are pigs and women suffer. With all my efforts (car and lawn maintenance, tending to children, working full time) I am not appreciated. It's never enough. It is common for the woman to expect the man to do uncomfortable things to help the relationship. I do not particularly like buying flowers or presents, shopping, having chitchat, dressing nice . . . but I do it because it is important to my wife.*
>
> *However, for some reason, if there is anything at all I would like, but my wife feels 'uncomfortable,' it is out of the question! She feels that as a woman she should not have to do anything uncomfortable. Double standard!*
>
> *The other double standard is that it is okay for women to criticize, put down, become grouchy, but if I'm feeling similarly, it is called verbal abuse. When I asked why that is so, I am told it's because I'm a man and they abuse, women don't!*
>
> *I've got news for everyone: Men are hurt just as much by*

abuse, or hurtful words, as women. Any form of coercion to get a man to do what you want is not only unproductive, it is damaging. Just because I am married does not make me a slave. Men are human beings."

Steve's final sentiment, about being a "human being" and not a "slave," reflected a common grievance from the men who wrote to me about this subject. Most women think that their husbands should have a sense of humor about how "difficult" women can be, with their hormonal cycles, emotionality, (hyper)sensitivity, changeable minds, and so forth. Well, some men do, some men don't.

The men who do have a sense of humor about the mercurial and mysterious nature of women are husbands who get respect, appreciation, gratitude, and compassion; they get love returned in a way that's meaningful to them.

The men who don't share that sense of humor are the men whose wives feel that doing the laundry, cooking dinner, or taking care of the kids is adequate compensation for their husbands' work. While these things may be appreciated, by and large, they're things she'd be doing even if she were not married. Those are not acts, specifically and personally, directed to "her man." And it is definitely those personal acts that make the difference to a husband who yearns to be treated like "a man," and like "her man."

The destructive anti-male subtext of the modern feminist agenda is to blame for some of this because those folks argue that catering to or deferring to a husband is slave-like submission to the male. In fact, after the Southern Baptist Council published a statement on "submission," the media went crazy, railing against their so-called backward, oppressive notions about women.

The Reverend Shane Cornutt, from Alabama, was one of many in and out of the clergy who wrote me to clarify this issue:

"Over the past couple of weeks I have noticed that some of your lady callers have had questions on a wife's submission to her husband and how it deals with their Christian faith when faced with a moral problem.

Nowhere in the Bible is a woman told to blindly submit to the will of her husband. In fact, the first act of submission is on the husband's *part! The husband is to submit himself to Christ and the will of God. When he does this he is not setting himself up as master, but rather as servant of the Lord. Only then is the wife to submit to the will of her husband—because the will of her husband will be obedience to the Lord. So the wife is not submitting to the husband, but to God.*

As soon as the husband steps outside this and acts contrary to scripture, the woman is under no moral obligation whatsoever *to her husband to transgress the moral law! Women are not, and were never meant to be, set up as servants to men in the kingdom of God.*

A man is supposed to love his wife as Christ loves the church. That means that a husband is required to love, care for, nurture, protect, comfort, and even be willing to die for his wife. That is love."

The reverend ended his letter with an admonition to men, suggesting that if any man is upset because he feels his wife is not in "proper submission" to him, the problem is with the man!

Whether or not a wife is Christian, or religious at all for that matter, the issue of respect is too often confused with a fearful notion of blind submission, and that becomes a stumbling block to the simple act of *giving.*

Rather than see this, though, for many women, it's easier to wallow in that self-pity mode. Lisa, a listener, is a married mother of two children, one six years old and the other nine months. She's new to being a stay-at-home mom and has adjusted her life to include an at-home business. When she and her husband did not have children and both worked full-time, they were more like equal partners in making a mess all week and then feverishly cleaning up on Friday night to afford themselves leisure time over the weekend. Now that she is at home, he leaves the household issues totally to her—and she's angry about it.

> *"I just get so frustrated that I find myself complaining loudly throughout the day as I pick up the mess left the night before. I really resent at times that my role as companion has changed to housekeeper, maid, and nanny. Listening to the Dr. Laura show helps balance my views. I really need the reminders sometimes that Joel, my husband, works very hard to support us at a job that he does not enjoy, and that is physically taxing.*
>
> *I really respect that he rarely if ever takes a sick day. I know he works hard and I think he would love to be able to stay home as I do with our children. I try not to let the negative thinking overwhelm me. I still get mad when I have to pick up glasses from the living room or clothing from the floor, but I married a wonderful man who has never intentionally done anything to make my life more difficult. I don't have it so bad after all.*
>
> *It helps to reflect on reasons I married Joel in the first place. I married a man I truly respect, knowing that he is faithful and loving."*

I get many calls from at-home wives who complain that when their husbands get home, they, the husbands, do not do various household chores. I generally challenge the women in return, asking, "Do you go to his work and make some of his calls, go to some of his meetings, help with filing or other clerical necessities?" Of course, the answer is, "Well, no . . . but." The point is not that the husband should be able to treat his wife like his personal maid, butler, or valet. The point is that in a division-of-labor situation, each has responsibilities, which, all totaled up at the end of the day or week, combine to take care of a family and household.

As one listener, Joanne, pointed out, "The care and feeding of husbands is, bottom line, to walk a mile in their shoes." Joanne's story is quite dramatic and instructive. She and her husband have two children; one has severe learning disabilities and the second has slight mental retardation. Until about five years ago, Joanne was the children's primary caretaker because her husband worked long hours. She felt deep resentment that she was alone at home fighting the battles with and for her children and their disabilities as well as doing all the household chores.

> *"And, of course, I let him know that I resented his long hours, though now looking back, that was a selfish thing to do because he was the major breadwinner. And he also did maintain the outside chores, i.e., lawn care, fixing up the house, painting, etc."*

Five years ago their lives changed dramatically. After a serious injury on the job, Joanne's husband was no longer able to work like he used to. The situation at home has completely reversed, and he now does the bulk of the household chores, including the outside chores he always has, such as lawn care, car care, etc. And according to Joanne:

> *"NOT ONCE does he complain! He makes sure the boys are taken care of. He is even teaching them how to drive. As I look back on how I acted toward my husband's long hours, I feel guilty. After all, he was supporting us so that I COULD stay home and raise OUR two wonderful sons. I realize that now. The boys needed me then and they need their father now. And because of all this wonderful time with Dad, they are turning*

into wonderful, productive young adults. Because of my husband's health problems, our sons do a whole lot around the house to help their dad and me. They have learned a lot of responsibility and see how important it is for a family unit to come together during hard times as well as good times."

The issue of "roles" in a marriage and family is often a sensitive one. Stay-at-home moms as well as hardworking, primary-breadwinner men are not given much respect from our society-at-large. Feminist educators and activists keep trying to squeeze men and women into niches that may simply not be a good match for their innate qualities as individuals as well as their unique masculine and feminine drives.

It is more in the female nature to nest and nurture. It is more in the male nature to conquer and protect. Frankly, the more we ignore the true, inherent masculine and feminine qualities of people, the farther apart we pull them.

Most all of the women who call me who have reversed the traditional societal roles—that is, have a husband at home with the children—are troubled by the fact that they seem to have less regard for their husbands as "men." Likewise, they report a diminished sense of their own femininity, and suffer ferocious guilt over not being their children's primary caretaker. This does not mean that this situation is not workable, but it is a delicate balancing act and it requires husbands and wives to be creative in complementing and augmenting their partner's feminine and masculine needs.

Interestingly, a major study reported in April 2002 at an American Heart Association forum concluded, after following patterns of heart disease and death among nearly four thousand participants for ten years, that men and women who defy traditional societal roles may suffer more health consequences, such as heart disease, than those who adhere to traditional roles. According to an ABC News report:

"The investigators did not find that high amounts of job stress, characterized as having high demands with little autonomy, was associated with an increased risk of heart disease. However, they did find that women who were in positions of high authority with high job demands suffered higher rates of heart disease than other women, although their male counterparts did not. Similarly, men who dubbed themselves primarily as house-husbands—about 10 percent of the participants—had an 82 percent higher ten-year death rate than men who worked outside the home."

The researchers took into account such factors as smoking, age, anxiety, stress, household responsibilities, blood pressure, weight, cholesterol levels, diabetes, and others.

While obviously the differences in individuals would make it wrong to limit or judge personal choices, I believe that ultimately the well-being of both men and women is maximized when acceptance, attention, and nurturance is given to what is innately different and special about men and women.

And, with respect to the Proper Care and Feeding of Husbands, we can take direction from folks like this listener:

"Although at thirty-one I am still unmarried, I've noticed that my father reacts much better to my mother when she needs him and acts like he's an important and integral part of her life."

Curtis, another listener, adds:

"All of us men have been told for years now that a woman 'needs' to be listened to. We're told not to try to solve the problem or to advise her, just listen and be sympathetic to her needs. Most women don't understand why men haven't learned this by now. Here's why! What she doesn't seem to understand is I really do want to be her White Knight. I really do want to come

riding to her rescue. I really do want to sweep her off her feet and carry her away and live happily ever after."

The most poignant part of Curtis's letter followed. He talked about the never-ending job of listening without rescuing that he was supposed to do for his wife in order to be a sensitive husband. However, when she was finishing venting, and felt better having gotten whatever it was off her chest, the problem for her was gone, but the problem for him had just begun.

Because he's supposed to just be a listening board (like a girlfriend or shrink?) and not help solve, repair, or attack her enemies, he is quiet. Why? Because he's failed, in his eyes, to be a man, her man. He's worthless, impotent to help her, to stop her pain.

"I've been relegated to being the warm, soft, cuddly teddy bear on her bed, instead of the white knight in her bed. I don't feel like a man. My self-esteem is in the bottom of the well. I just want to be a man with the woman I love in my arms."

This is an important lesson that not too many women appear to be getting from their own mothers or because of the modeling of their childhood family life. Amber, a listener, wrote that about a year ago (and seven years into her marriage), she and her girlfriend decided to learn how to be better wives to their husbands.

"And to our shame, we really learned a lot. In essence, I've learned what you teach, preach, and nag about: that my mother's four dysfunctional marriages and our culture taught me to disrespect my husband and to take his love for granted. I freely and cruelly criticized him, privately and (shamefully) publicly. I tried to control everything, especially finances, because

I erroneously thought that he couldn't handle things as well as I could. I couldn't bear the thought of anything controlling ME, so I had to be the one in control."

After studying Scripture, reading, and listening to my program, Amber realized how destructive her attitudes toward her husband had been. She asked herself the following very important questions, which every wife should ask herself: If I really believe all the things I say/think/complain about him, why on earth are we married? If I love him so much, why do I act so unloving and disrespectful? What will make him continue to love me if I continue to act this way?

I have been using that latter question lately on my program to get women to pause and think about the destructive nature of their behavior toward their husbands. For example, recently a twenty-something female caller asked me whether it was fair or not to get her husband to shave off his beard. He didn't have one when they were dating, or at any time since they married some three years ago, but had grown one recently. Shamefully, she had already told him that she didn't find him as attractive with the beard.

I responded with sadness in my voice. "Tell me, how much more indignity could a husband experience at the hands of his wife than not being allowed to decide for himself whether or not to have facial hair?"

I further surprised her by calling her comment to him about not finding him as attractive with the beard *abusive.* It is sad how much abuse (criticism, nagging, blaming, yelling) women can heap on men without seeing it as hurtful and abusive, even as they themselves are so hypersensitive about any apparent (even unintended) slight or reaction of their men to them. Double standard, I say.

Wives do tend to be controlling—in ways we perhaps don't even recognize as such. Just before I went to bed last night, I turned on the television for a last-minute news update, and in going past channels to my usual news station, I paused at a sitcom. I don't know the characters or the plot, or even the name of the show, but I saw what appeared to be a father talking to his grown son in his son's fiancée's presence. The father said something like, "Son, you are a man and you can make any decision you believe in and feel is right . . . until you're married—then your wife will be making all your decisions for you."

While the laugh track did its thing, I immediately realized that the controlling of men by their wives is so taken for granted that a sitcom could use it as a source of humor with no one imagining it was a true slap against women.

Alexis, one of my listeners, struggled with this concept of controlling and changing a husband into a wife's perfect picture of a mate.

> *"I remember a perfect example of how I set myself up with high expectations. Before we were married, I was going to his house for dinner, and on the way I had this image playing in my mind that I'd get there and he'd come to the door and hug and kiss me and his house would be spotless and he'd have a big bouquet of roses for me and the table was set and the dinner was ready and soft music was playing, etc.*
>
> *I get there, knock three times, and finally just open the door myself. He's lying on the couch watching sports, dishes are in the sink, no food, no flowers, no music, and he says with a smile, 'Hi, babe,' no different than any other time . . . and I was mad at him.*
>
> *I realized I had set him up in my mind to be something I know he isn't. He's casual and unromantic. What you see is what you get. But he's moral, loving, and has a very strong religious faith. He stands up for what's right. He's funny and intelligent and he loves me for who I am, so shouldn't I love him for who he is?"*

When you put it that way, what's a little bit of facial hair?

Instead of appreciating a man for his unique and manly qualities, too many wives constantly complain—to the husbands themselves and to friends, neighbors, family, and sometimes even to the children.

One caller recently asked me if she was wrong to "vent" her annoyance with her husband to her ten-year-old son. She said that her husband told her that she did that to recruit their son to her side in their issues and thereby undermine his bond with his own child. In her own defense, she said that she thought her son had a right to know what was going on—and, she admitted, she wanted his sympathy.

Not only is this disrespecting a husband and father in his own home by trying to make him look bad to his family, it is completely inappropriate and psychologically abusive to burden children with parental issues and force them to give up one parent for the sake of the other.

I suggested, and she was agreeable, that she apologize to her son for triangulating him into their skirmish, and that she apologize to her husband for such dirty tricks.

Another listener wrote in to confess that she used to be hypercritical of her husband. Now she's learned that he may not do things the way she would, but that he gets the job done.

> *"And in the end, it doesn't much matter that they eat PBJ sandwiches for breakfast, lunch, and dinner for a day or that one tooth brushing gets overlooked or whatever little thing that used to set me off!*
>
> *What matters is that our sons have learned that their daddy is an awesome, competent, and loving caretaker. More important, I have learned that I set an example for my sons of how a wife should act. Would I want my sons to marry someone who treats them the way I used to treat my own husband? NO!"*

Showing respect for a husband in his own home not only sends him a message that he's loved and appreciated, it sets the game plan for the next generation's marriages. How much more important could it get?

Becky, another listener, wrote that her mother warned her early on not to come to her with complaints, criticisms, and gripes about her husband.

> *"My mother, I believe, had the best advice; in fact, I follow it to this day as a married woman. The general idea behind her words was simple: If you want me to love and respect the man you date and eventually marry, don't come to me with complaints about all his faults and weaknesses. You may forgive his words and actions easily; I, however, am your mother, and I don't like to see you hurt. It will take more for me to accept his apologies than it will for you."*

Becky admitted that at times this great advice wasn't easy to follow. There were days when she just wanted to vent to someone all of her frustrations on some point. However, when that happened, she would stop and think about what her mother had told her and, as she said, realize that "no emotional outlet is worth damaging my husband's reputation."

In opening this chapter, I quoted one of my listeners, Wendi, who said, "It is easy for a woman to love; that is the way that God made her. It is more difficult for her to show respect." This is a sad but important truth. Wendi's letter continued: "Respect means treating someone in an edifying manner, never denigrating or attacking."

She acknowledges in her letter that when she and her husband married sixteen years ago, they did not know how to communicate with fairness and respect. Although like all newlyweds, they promised to be friends, they fell into that familiar trap of too much "familiarity," treating each other worse than they would treat strangers or acquaintances. They would say they loved each other, but their actions and words would appear to disprove that sentiment.

Finally turning to a more religious, spiritual course, Wendi chose to see her husband as a gift from God, thereby someone deserving of respect.

> *"Even when times were difficult, I tried to look beyond what was happening and see him as God saw him. When I began to show my husband respect, he did not reciprocate—at first. And it was difficult to do what God required when no progress was obvious.*
>
> *But God was working on his heart, healing old hurts and wounds that I had created, allowing him to know that he could trust me to stick to our vows. The change in my husband from that time forward has been dramatic. We are a team. We respect one another. We try to place the other's needs above our own, in full confidence that our own needs will be met by our spouse.*
>
> *Learning to see beyond and reflecting God's love to my husband made all the difference. Making the decision to respect the man God had given me made all the difference."*

What does it actually mean, in concrete terms, to treat one's husband with respect? To start with, a man likes and needs to be treated like he is "the man." That seems to be difficult for a lot of women to do, partly because they have been brought up with notions of "unisexuality," the sadly mistaken and destructive belief that men and women have no differences—and whatever men want or do that women don't appreciate is stupid, wasteful, and self-indulgent. Well, the fact is, men and women *are* different physically, psychologically, motivationally, and temperamentally. Anyone who has had exposure to babies and children can tell you that boys and girls respond differently to the world right from the start. Give both a doll and the girl will cuddle it, while the boy will more likely use it as a projectile or weapon. Give them two dolls and the girl will have the dolls talking to each other, while the boy will have them engage in combat.

On my radio program, I have related an experience that vividly points out the subtleties of masculinity and femininity in parenting. I was at a swimming pool, watching a mom and dad play with their infant child. First, the mother, holding the baby against her chest, cooed to the baby and playfully swooped him up and down. After a while, she passed the baby to Dad, who immediately turned the baby's face outward, and swooshed the baby forward and up into the air. My conclusion? Mom equals protection and nurturance. Dad equals autonomy and adventure. It is that perfect balance that helps produce a functional, secure human being.

When a wife treats her man like he's one of her children, when she puts him down or thwarts his need for autonomy, adventure, risk, competition, challenge, and conquest, she ends up with a sullen, uncooperative, unloving, hostile lump.

Tammy, a listener, learned to follow her father's advice, cited earlier: ("You are marrying a man. Always treat him like one and he will always act like one.")

> *"I have noticed that in every area of our marriage, work, home, family, children, career, David excels when I treat him like a man.*
>
> *I mean by this that I do not demand he do things. I ask. I suggest options for his problems and then let him pick one. I never differ with him in front of the children. I do not deal with his family in an unpleasant situation—I let him deal with his family.*
>
> *I never do anything to embarrass him or make him feel less manly in front of his family, coworkers, children, neighbors, or friends.*

Let me tell you what this gets me. It gets me a man who is so comfortable with his masculinity that he can focus on being tender and loving and giving to me constantly because he is never concerned about protecting his ego or proving he is the 'man of the house.' I do that for him."

I believe most women don't appreciate how much they are responsible for the tone of the home and the entire family. This statement is not about placing fault or blame, it is about acknowledging the incredible power women have in impacting those around them. Both children and husbands are inexorably dependent upon the approval, appreciation, and acceptance of Mom. Without that, they are desolate—and they behave badly.

CJ, another listener, wrote to me that she was about five years and four kids into her marriage when resentment hit. She was tired of her schedule—the cleaning, the kids, the dinner, the shopping, the everything! She even began to lose her sense of being in love with her husband.

And so she decided to develop a sense of humor. She started to cut back on "chores" and focus instead on paying more direct attention to her husband. This is, of course, the complete opposite of what pop psych and women's magazines suggest. These sources generally recommend that when a woman is "fed up" with her life, it's time for spas, solo vacations, more girlfriend time, plastic surgery, affairs, or divorce. This is all in the search for "getting one's own needs met."

But CJ decided to turn that energy into affection and attention toward her husband. How did that get her needs met?

"I started to ignore the house and pay more attention to him. Instead of just telling him I loved him, I told him I adored him. I made those little calls during the day just to remind him. When he came home tired, I started to indulge him, and not resent him. When in mixed company, I always went out of my

way to compliment what he's done for me or the kids. I always brag about what a great dad he is.

I realized that I CHOSE this life, so I made myself appreciate ALL I had, and pretty soon I believed it!

You may call it stroking his ego, but it paid off. The more attention I paid, the more I got. He was not as interested in a perfect house as he was in having an adoring wife. I became her and thus fell back in love with my husband and life.

In return, he showed his love for me. I learned that MY MOOD set the mood for the house."

And since when did sincere stroking of a husband's ego fall into disrepute? Probably when the feminists decided that caring for a man was tantamount to a betrayal of the sisterhood. Too many women lost too many wonderful opportunities to have a happy and fulfilling life by buying into the destructive notion that a woman becomes more if she sees and treats men as less.

On my radio program, I hear from too many women who believe that they are somehow entitled to have all their needs, wants, desires, and whims met by life in general, and by their men in particular, no matter what choices they've made and no matter how poorly they treat their men.

The two major categories for these complaints are domestic and emotional. Kelly, a listener, wrote in to respond to a caller on my program who went on and on about her husband not meeting her "emotional needs." Kelly acknowledged that she, too, had been caught in that trap during most of her thirties, but she now reflects on that time as a waste of a decade because she spent countless hours husband-bashing because he wasn't meeting her emotional needs.

"This is such a pitfall of pop psychology and really has more to do with the baggage that one brings into the marriage than the truth of the matter: Marriage is a lot of hard work. And when

you are raising kids together, with Mom staying at home, it creates an awful burden on the husband to do what he has to do in order to financially support the entire family on one income. I never fully gave my husband credit for, as you say, Dr. Laura, 'slaying the dragon' all those years while I stayed at home—all the while complaining that he wasn't meeting my emotional needs."

Kelly's perspective changed when it was discovered she had a brain tumor. Her so-called "emotionless" husband sat by her bedside in the hospital for nearly three days straight, became both father and mother to their children for her nearly three months of treatment and recovery, and somehow managed to still get himself up and off to work every day to provide for the family. She became a firm believer that God will do what He must in order to get your attention at times—and she learned the lesson.

She developed a new appreciation and love for her husband. She learned to respect his masculine approach to life, family, challenges, and problems.

Men rescue, repair, provide, protect. Men don't sit, stew, and rehash. Men are active and proactive. They do that out of love, duty, responsibility, and character. That needs to be respected and appreciated if a woman is to have a happy life married to a good man. A good man is just that—a man. A good man is not a best girlfriend.

Stephanie, a listener, wrote:

"I am so excited that someone is finally tackling this issue. I did not realize how destructive I was to my marriage until I heard you say a few times that for the spouse who chooses to stay home with the children, it is their responsibility to cook, clean, do laundry, and perform all those mundane tasks that keep a home running so that the other spouse can go out and earn the money that helps this family succeed."

Stephanie had been married for almost two years and had a nine-month-old baby boy—a surprise that took her out of the workplace and into the home. It only took her a few months to become resentful at what she interpreted as her husband's "freedom" compared with her feeling chained down at home. She never spoke about her feelings; instead she took them out on her husband by "not being in the mood for sex."

She, like many women, found it difficult to give up the work world since she had defined herself by the position she held with her company. She missed the daily kudos and the calls she would receive asking for her opinions. She missed the excitement of travel and the constant challenges and new input.

At some point, though, she had an epiphany: "I am fortunate beyond what I deserve." She describes a family that has most breakfasts, lunches, and dinners together, a husband who is the most well-balanced executive she knows.

> *"Nothing is more important than our marriage and our son. I appreciate my husband more than he will ever know. Since I had this epiphany, our marriage has changed. It's romantic, loving, respectful, and intimate.*
>
> *Our greatest hope for our son and future children is to learn what it means to be a family and to make sacrifices for the betterment of others and give of themselves by seeing their family growing stronger every day. My husband and I will be giddy when our son and his future wife provide our grandchildren the same loving and nurturing environment.*
>
> *Maybe family values will become popular again, and this craze of women destroying their families in the quest to have it all will become passé."*

Perhaps the feminist notions about women having power if they do it all has obstructed too many women's ability to realize that in real life we all make choices, and that the true joy and meaning of life is not in how many things we have or do, but in the sacrifice and commitment we make to others within the context of the choices we've made. The Tenth Commandment, about coveting, reminds us that none of us can have everything there is to have nor everything we want. Without enjoying and appreciating our gifts and blessings, we create hell on earth for ourselves and for those who love us.

Jennifer called my show complaining about her emergency-room-physician husband.

JENNIFER: I am my kids' mom. I have a five-year-old and a three-year-old—both boys. My husband voluntarily takes extra hours at work to make up for a pay cut that happened this year. We don't need the extra money. And I need him at home.

DR. LAURA: To do what?

JENNIFER: To be a father.

DR. LAURA: What hours is he working?

JENNIFER: Twelve-hour days, four days a week, and he's sometimes on call.

DR. LAURA: You were aware when you were sold in marriage from some Eastern Bloc country that you were marrying a physician, right? Perhaps you didn't understand the life of a physician's wife—which means assuming much more personal responsibility for home and kids.

JENNIFER: I know he measures everything by his wallet, whether he's successful or not, and he wants to try to retire early. I understand all that. Is it wrong for me to go about what I'd like to do while he's at work—go see my sister and do the things that I want to do? And would it be unsupportive if I'm not home when he gets home?

DR. LAURA: Yeah, that would be unsupportive. Go see

your sister, but get home in time to have a hot dinner there. Because that's your part of taking care of the family—and he's doing his part.

JENNIFER: But we don't need that extra money.

DR. LAURA: Because he's trying to make up for the money he lost when he got a pay cut, somehow he's a greedy, avaricious type?

JENNIFER: I don't think that.

DR. LAURA: That's what I got out of what you said. You have a lot of hostility. You didn't marry a nine-to-five type. You married someone with a profession—a calling. He works in urgent care. That requires a special mentality, dealing with life-and-death crises, allaying people's anxiety, fixing body parts.

You need to be supportive that you have a man who is trying very hard to take care of his family and get them in a position where there is no financial problem. The hours he works sound very much like those of a fireman. You have to do your part—he has his.

You can take the two kids and go to a movie in the middle of the day while he's cleaning up blood and pus. I don't really want to hear your grumbling about the hours he's working because they are not glamorous hours—they're pretty nauseating, considering most of the things he has to do.

You have a tremendous amount of freedom to do whatever you want. When both kids are in school, you can use those hours in constructive ways. I think you ought to be more grateful to him that he's working his buns off to keep all of you really solvent and independent *and* that he's doing something that is just a blessing to the earth: helping all kinds of people who are sick and dying in pain. I think you need to

> show more respect for what he's doing for them and for you and your family.
>
> So go do what you want to do all day, and make sure a hot dinner is there, served with a smile and a hug, when he gets home. Because the more you create an atmosphere that shows you appreciate what he does when he's out there, the more he's going to want to be home.

Finally, one husband sent me a copy of a letter to his wife he'd been up until two o'clock in the morning writing. He considered it a significant coincidence considering the announced subject of this book.

Evidently, he'd been trying to communicate to his wife his feelings and thoughts about the texture and direction of their marriage. Her quickie solution to their problems, it seems, was to suggest a two-week visit to Disneyland. He did not feel that trip would be the miracle to improve the marriage.

This man's letter, I believe, represents a universal truth that has been denied and largely lost by a culture hell-bent on measuring human value through power and money. That truth is that the family needs a woman and a man, a husband and a wife, a father and a mother, much more than it needs the equal power of two career-oriented people.

He writes to his wife:

> *"I'm learning more as the years go by that you are a career-oriented person who doesn't have a clue or understand the essence of what it means to be a wife and mother. Call me traditional if you like, but I firmly believe that mothers need to spend more time at home, perhaps 100 percent of their time at home, to nurture a family and develop a home.*
>
> *Far too often, there are too many things that get overlooked by you as a wife and mother as it pertains to this family. Our kids lack focus, training, and discipline. They have no routine*

and there's no order about anything that they do. Mothers, in my opinion, are nurturers and teachers who ought to spend as much time with their kids to teach them things, skills that they will use to cope with life. To put it bluntly, you haven't been a mother. Our kids have been left too often to cope and figure out things for themselves.

When it comes to being a wife, you put no effort. And I think you don't love me anymore. Making love is not high on your agenda of things to do, and showing any intimate interest in me isn't either.

I'm feeling less and less interested in you and less and less motivated to keep this family together. I'm feeling like you are married to your job and that you are more committed to it than to us as a wife and mother.

I'm not claiming that I'm the perfect husband and father. You and I both work too many hours, but I believe you underestimate the importance of the mother in a family. Mothers and fathers play different roles in a family. I've never discouraged you from pursuing a Ph.D., but I don't think it's high on the list of priorities of what I think is best for us as a family right now.

I want to love you, be with you, and support you, but I must confess that I'm feeling like we are losing each other and our kids. I don't know what the complete answer is, but I believe it has to start with us spending more time at home to grow, develop, and nurture our family and our relationship."

The notion of "fixed roles" is inflammatory and controversial. It shouldn't be so. I've said many times on my program that women have become denigrated by that part of the feminist movement that dismisses marriage, child rearing, and homemaking as insignificant and insulting to women. Promiscuity, shacking up, abortions, illegitimacy, rush-hour traffic, and office politics are a boon to women?

I am a working wife and mother, and I appreciate the

opportunity to use my skills and talents to be creative in something I believe is meaningful. Nonetheless, I consider my first and foremost responsibility to be "my kids' mom." I work my career around my family—and not the other way around. My deepest satisfactions in life come from a tall, skinny but muscular teenage boy saying "I love you" (even in front of his buddies) and a husband of almost two decades who still calls me "beautiful."

As long as women disrespect what they have to offer as wives and mothers, they will continue to disrespect their men who serve as husbands and fathers. No one benefits. No one is happy.

Chapter 8

GUY TIME

"A woman would do well to understand that an honest, faithful husband who goes on a three-week hunting trip is not telling her he doesn't love her. He just wants to kill something. Nothing more complicated than that."

JOSH

Sabino called my program to ask me who was right, him or his wife. The situation causing the problem concerned a weekend trip to Seattle he and his wife had planned as a little get-away time. Then Sabino happened to mention the trip to his buddy, a married neighbor with kids just down the block. His buddy thought this weekend jaunt was a great idea and offered up himself and his family to Sabino as company on the trip. Sabino didn't want to disappoint or hurt his buddy, so he said, "Fine."

Well, it wasn't fine with Sabino's wife, who had been looking forward to quiet, intimate family and personal time.

Sabino wanted my opinion. Was he kidding?

This is not an example of legitimate, healthy, even necessary "guy time." This is an example of insensitive (and stupid) behavior that demonstrates a profound lack of maturity and responsibility within a marriage. When a fellow is more concerned about disappointing his buddy than his woman, he has virtually cut up his "manhood" card and retrieved his adolescent-male card from what should have been his past.

It seemed that Sabino had his definitions backward. He thought being a man meant standing up to his woman and standing with his buddies. But a real man can stand up to his buddies and stand with his woman *and* believe that this highlights and intensifies his masculinity rather than diminishes it—because he is not about image, he is about substance, and that substance consists of respect and commitment.

Now, on the other side, too many women are outright hostile and pouty about a man's need for guy time. I can't tell you how many calls I get from wives who are deeply resentful that their men want to take some time for themselves and maybe spend it with their male friends. Usually what they end up doing is playing some sport (like golf, basketball, or baseball), watching some sport (that generally includes nachos and beer), going on a trip (oftentimes to fish, hunt, or rock-climb), or something as tame as playing poker (more nachos and beer).

Where does that wifely resentment come from? While the arguments given by these wives to explain why they object to their husbands' guy time vary tremendously, the core issue seems to be insecurity. This insecurity could be about a fear that their husbands might not really enjoy their company, or that they don't know how to be alone without feeling bad about themselves, or that they are envious of their husbands' ability to have hobbies and friends, or that they worry that their husbands, while out of their influence and control, might not evaluate their relationship and family situation as desirable. Also, many women have the notion that everything in the marriage and family must have them at the center to be valid and acceptable.

Recently, a woman called about her military husband, who is in a band. She was upset because he'd agreed to a gig on Valentine's Day, without checking with her first, and she called to ask if it was reasonable for her to be upset.

I took her back to the time before her marriage and asked whether her husband had been involved in music then. She reported that he's always been into music, and joined up with his current band while they were engaged.

"Honey," I said, "you've got to learn to accept what kind of animal you brought home. You can't knowingly bring home an elephant and then expect it to curl up in your lap and purr."

This is a big problem for many women. They believe that after marriage, the husband will become completely domesticated and she will be the master; the whip will be *her desires and feelings.* Men do put up with that to a certain point . . . and then they don't.

I suggested to her that she rent a room at the hotel at which her husband's band was playing on Valentine's Day, go to his gig, and then take him upstairs to wine, candles, and a sexy negligee. I reminded her that her main dilemma was the acceptance of her own choices.

One listener wrote in about this very dilemma. However, she finally figured out what kind of animal she had brought home and stopped trying to threaten it into being the kind of animal she thought she wanted. It paid off. She wrote:

> *"Early in our marriage I discovered myself resenting my husband for all the Saturday and Sunday afternoons he spent playing golf. It became a constant source of tension between us until it finally dawned on me that he was not playing any more than he had during the two and a half years we were dating; I simply hadn't noticed it as much before we were living together.*
>
> *I told him that I would stop badgering him because, after*

all, doing what he enjoyed made him a happier person and a more content husband.

He now asks if I mind before he sets up a golf outing, plays less often overall, and pays more attention to me when he's not playing—all because he appreciates the change in my attitude."

This wife was smart. She thought about the two candidates in the election: candidate #1, being angry all the time and ruining her own life as well as her and her husband's life together with her constant resentment, or candidate #2, accepting the kind of animal she brought home and reframing his traits in the positive. She ultimately voted for #2, and it changed everything. Why? Because he no longer saw his wife as somebody chipping away at who he was and what he did. He saw a wife appreciating the man he actually was—and that made him want to be more of that for her.

It's worth repeating that men yearn for, first, their mothers' acceptance, approval, and appreciation, and then their wives', and when they get those three A's, they'll do just about anything to please their wives.

Brian, another listener, wrote about what he saw universally—not just in his own home—as a double standard regarding time spent apart.

"When the issue of friends comes up, it's usually that she's allowed to go out almost at will, with little regard for what I might have planned. But if I were to want to spend some time with friends, it's usually a fight waiting to happen! She says she feels like I should trust her and allow her freedom. However, when the shoe is on the other foot, and I want to spend some time with friends, according to her it's that I don't love her or want to spend time with her. Even if she's invited!

I feel this is a form of manipulation: wanting to have things her way and not wanting to give me the same. Basically, it's she that matters."

And that is the message that too many husbands get. They begin to realize that their feelings, needs, and desires are really not that relevant to their wives, or are perceived only as annoyances and impediments to the wives' more important motivations.

This is not the way to keep a man happy—or to keep a man at all. As one listener, Jim, wrote:

> *"Wives want romance, hugs, kisses, and surprises. They would get more of these things if they hadn't just told hubby he was stupid or that a night out with the guys was tantamount to abandonment . . . or that four hours out of 168 to myself is being overly selfish or self-indulgent."*

When men call my radio program to complain about not getting support from their wives for guy time, they let me know the magnitude of their frustration by listing all the things they do for their wives and families, as a way of defending themselves against charges of being selfish, uninvolved, or negligent. These men are involved in family activities and outings, and work around the house on the weekends and evenings when needed. They cook, do dishes, fix the cars, repair the house, mow the lawn, trim the hedges, go to kids' sporting events and school functions, drive kids to and from their activities and school, stop off at the market on the way home, even "baby-sit" the kids when the wife wants to go off to shop, eat lunch out with her mother or girlfriends, or go to aerobics.

Not only do these men suffer criticisms for the precise way they do or don't do all of the above, they are begrudged the guy time they need in order to blow off steam, work off nervous tension and energy, reconnect with their animal-level masculinity, briefly relieve themselves of the stress of responsibilities, or just have some fun to keep sane and happy.

Many times wives will undermine these efforts by scheduling family visits or doctor appointments, or by complaining about being ill or so exhausted from their week, or so emotionally distraught from some interpersonal problem, that they need their husbands home.

I believe that women basically take men for granted and want to mold them into an image they have in their own minds of what a husband—their husband—should be. This takes me back to the metaphor of the "animal you chose to bring home." Women will often be attracted to the athletic, musical, accomplished, involved, outgoing kind of guy for not necessarily the right reasons. If they are attracted to these active men because they admire those qualities, and expect to support those qualities, that's good. But if they are attracted to these active men because they are like groupies who bask in the men's glow, who think they can acquire a value and identity by association with "greatness," that's bad. The former means that they are a good match. The latter means that they are a match that will light the fuse for a big explosion.

Another listener who married a musician shares this story about her transformation from the "latter" to the "former."

> *"First, my husband and I were married after just four months of serious dating after knowing each other for one year. He was really into playing music, but I didn't figure that it would still take the number one position in his life. I thought that I would. For many years I would be very angry when he would leave for his practices and performances. It took me about seven years to realize that I could not change him and his desire for his music. He told me once that it was his escape.*
>
> *After many angry nights, fights, and threatening to leave, I have accepted the fact that he does need this escape. Now I have learned to use the time that he is gone to have some private time of my own. Now it seems that if his practice is canceled and he is home, I am a little bummed because I don't have that special quiet time of my own.*

We've been married for nine years, and after listening to your show, I have put much of my silly things aside and have realized that my husband is a truly good and loving husband . . . just not in every way that I 'expected' him to be."

Her letter reveals a very important point, which is that many women expect their husbands to always bend to their, the wives', whim and will, but that their lives are like a letter, completely dependent upon someone else's writing. In other words, marriage should not mean that either partner takes complete responsibility for the other's well-being, activities, or state of mind. Marriage does mean we share—but it also means we support the individuality necessary for mental and emotional health, and for the ultimate well-being of the relationship.

Without this healthy balance, a marriage can decay or dissolve. Tansie, a listener, reveals that she learned this the hard way:

"I learned that husbands need to have interests outside of me! *Whenever my now-ex-husband would visit his brothers or sisters or friends without me (which he only did for a few hours once per month or so), I would complain and act like a spoiled brat for days! Why didn't he want to spend every waking moment with me? Obviously, he didn't love me!*

After a very painful divorce and lots of therapy, I have learned that husbands with friends and outside interests are happier. It adds to their happy relationship with you when you gracefully support their relationships with others and not behave like a spoiled brat who wants to control their lives."

Tansie now has a new "sweetheart," who loves to spend a few hours a week with friends and is always very excited to call her afterward to share how much fun he had. Tansie has cultivated hobbies and friends of her own now and is not depending on her man to be her *everything.*

Frankly, in order for either party in a marriage—as well as the children—to stay balanced and centered, a reasonable amount of quiet time, alone time, is necessary. Now, the desire and need for this time may fluctuate depending on what's going on in your life, but in most cases it's a good antidote to stress, and stress is a by-product even of everyday obligations, tasks, and responsibilities. Think of stress as a kind of static electricity on the brain and soul that has to be gotten rid of with either quiet contemplation or a complete change in activity. Don't begrudge yourself or your partner this necessary outlet, without which one's life and one's marriage can become an overfilled pressure cooker.

I believe that it is a responsibility of both spouses to refresh themselves so that they can give their best to their relationship and their family.

Sometimes the issue of schedules can become a good-intentioned bargaining chip! Keith, one of my listeners, writes:

> *"My wife has interests independent from me. In other words, she has friends and work and isn't totally dependent upon me for her happiness. While we are a team and work together on issues and do most things together, we also can enjoy some time on our own.*
>
> *The flip side is that my wife allows me some independence to play golf once in a while, to watch sports, etc.—in other words, lets me have some life on my own. She has let me bargain with her so that I can watch football on Sundays if I do the laundry. Talk about a win-win!*
>
> *I am not advocating total independence for each partner. But I believe one of the major reasons for our success is that in moderation we are able to pursue our own interests, and in comparison with other wives that I have observed, mine doesn't need*

> *me to provide for her entertainment twenty-four hours a day. Having other interests makes both of us more interesting to each other."*

It didn't escape me that Keith used the words "allows" and "lets me" when referring to his own opportunities for downtime or guy time. I don't believe these references necessarily suggest that he is hen-pecked, I think they point out a universal truth that I have mentioned numerous times in this book: that men are raised by women as children and are embraced by women as adults and look to women for those three A's. This gives women tremendous power over men, power that ought not be abused or overused; it is just too easy for a grown man to turn into a rebellious child.

Women generally have tremendous opportunity to "hang with their own kind." Wives should not begrudge their men the necessity to do the same. Men need some space away from femininity and domesticity in order to reassert an important yet societally denigrated reality: Basic, fundamental, animal masculinity needs to be respected. When men get their time away, they come back to us better men.

Allison, a listener, has come to peace with this reality:

> *"My husband and I have what we consider to be a very happy marriage. Besides not trying to change each other, I have no problem letting him have his 'guy time' with his buddies. Mostly they get together in our garage (pool table, fridge) for cards on Saturday nights—but not every week. They usually don't start until after our kids are in bed, so there is no extra burden on me.*
>
> *He works hard all week and I believe he deserves some time just to be a guy and do guy things. I usually use that time to enjoy having control of the TV remote, work on the computer, or do something just for me.*

He also gives me my time—it's not one-way.

Most of his friends' wives don't feel the same as I do, and they see the get-togethers as a bone of contention.

I think having that time makes him a more relaxed husband."

Allison is a smart woman and a smart wife.

Now you know how to be a smart—and happier—wife, too.

The Proper Care *and* Feeding *of* Marriage

Also by Dr. Laura Schlessinger

Ten Stupid Things Women Do to Mess Up Their Lives

How Could You Do That?!: The Abdication of Character, Courage, and Conscience

Ten Stupid Things Men Do to Mess Up Their Lives

The Ten Commandments: The Significance of God's Laws in Everyday Life

Stupid Things Parents Do to Mess Up Their Kids

Ten Stupid Things Couples Do to Mess Up Their Relationships

The Proper Care and Feeding of Husbands

Woman Power

Bad Childhood—Good Life

Children's Titles

Why Do You Love Me?

But I Waaannt It!

Growing Up Is Hard

Where's God?

The Proper Care *and* Feeding *of* Marriage

Dr. Laura Schlessinger

HarperCollins*Publishers*

To all who yearn to love and be loved

Contents

Preface

Is there really ever such a thing as a *perfect* marriage? The answer to that question is, "YES." I know you're stunned. Stay with me here: "perfect" doesn't mean that everything goes right, or your way for that matter, or that you're feeling romantically perky all the time. There are just too many unpredictable events, challenges, and tragedies in life for any of us to feel content and satisfied for any prolonged period of time. Yet even in the midst of misery, you can still feel and believe that your marriage is perfect *if* you have the right attitude; and I don't mean that you think *positively*—I do mean that you think *outwardly*. When you do so, married life becomes perfect no matter what difficulties you're going through.

I took a call from Michelle, a seventeen-year-old high school student, which will clarify:

Michelle: Hi, Dr. Laura! It's a pleasure to speak with you. My question is this: this Saturday is my boyfriend's and my senior prom. As it turns out, we have a conflict because it is also his championship lacrosse game at the same time as the dance. He has told me that I could decide which one we should do.

DrL: Really? So what's your decision?

Michelle: Well, personally, I want to go to the prom because it's our senior prom and it's our last dance together, it's meaningful, you know? But it's also his major opportunity because scouts will be at this game for college recruitment. So for him the best choice would be for the game but I want to go to prom . . . selfishly.

DrL: Do you love him?

Michelle: Of course. Yes.

DrL: Do you imagine you're going to marry him? I'm asking you that because I just want to know the depth of your compassion and caring for him.

Michelle: I can see it. I can definitely see it working, but I'm only seventeen. . . . Yes, I care for him a lot.

DrL: Well then, I guess he's going to his lacrosse tournament.

Michelle (sounding deflated)***:*** Okay.

DrL: Because that's what we do when we're in love—we give them gifts . . . that doesn't mean you go to the store and buy something. It means you give up something that's very important to you to give them something that's very important to them. O. Henry wrote a short story called "The Gift of the Magi." There was a young couple, very poor, married, and very much in love with each other. Christmas is coming and there is no money to buy gifts for one another. Her prized possession was her long, lovely hair which she had grown since childhood. His prized possession was his solid gold pocket watch—an heirloom, passed down from generation to generation.

Come Christmas morning, she hands her beloved a package. It is a solid gold chain for his pocket watch. He hands his beloved a package. It is a bejeweled comb to hold her beautiful hair in a bun on top of her head. They both cried with joy even though he no longer had the pocket watch, as he had sold it to buy her the jeweled comb, and she no longer had long hair, as she had sold it to buy him the gold chain.

Neither could use the gift the other had given them from a store—but look at the gift each truly got from the other.

Michelle: WOW!

DrL: So when you love somebody you give them what they really need—and your boyfriend needs you to be supportive of the fact that this game is important to his college career—for scholarships. If you do get married, you'll be dancing together for the rest of your lives.

Michelle: That's true. Well, I guess he'll be playing this game and I'll be sitting on the sidelines cheering.

DrL: Good for you! That's the kind of woman a man should marry.

Michelle: Thank you so much, Dr. Laura

Oh, wait a minute, friends! The story does not end there. A few days later I received this e-mail from Michelle:

"A few days ago I called in with a dilemma I had with the prom because my boyfriend's championship lacrosse game

(with college scouts) was the same night. You told me the story of the 'Gift of the Magi,' and that if you really loved someone you would be willing to give up whatever was most important to you—which for me was the prom. I took your advice and called up my boyfriend telling him that we would be going to his lacrosse game instead of senior prom. He explained to me that he knew I would decide to go to his game, so he went ahead and bought our prom tickets so we would go to prom.

"So, basically, I was willing to give up senior prom for him, and he was willing to give up what was most important to him, his championship game—proving the story of 'The Gift of the Magi.'

"But hold on! The story gets better! Yesterday we found out that because of some unknown factor, his championship game was changed from 7 o'clock to 3 o'clock in the afternoon. Is this a God thing? I think so! Now we not only get to go to prom and his lacrosse game, but we have the knowledge that we are both willing to sacrifice what is most important to us because our love is stronger.

"I know that I am only 17, but I think I found a keeper!! Thank you so much for your wonderful advice to let my MAN know how important he is to me. This experience not only made me grow as a person, but is strengthening our relationship as well."

Now, dear friends, even some seventeen-year-olds can understand the beauty and meaning of having somebody care enough about you to put themselves aside for you—that beats every prom and game imaginable. And when you are living this scenario, no matter what grunge is going on in your life, your marriage is PERFECT!

The Proper Care *and* Feeding *of* Marriage

Introduction

This is not your typical marriage manual—not by a long shot. I'm not going to present the usual psychobabble nonsense that has been dominating the marital therapy field since the sixties which condemns masculinity and disdains femininity, considering both some kind of disorder while striving for the destructive lie of unisexuality. This sort of thinking takes the obvious concept of *equality* in the eyes of the law and the Lord, and morphs it into a false concept of *sameness*. In addition to being utterly ridiculous, believing in "sameness" generates a sense of lack of respect for and a denial of your need for the qualities of the other gender. A respect and admiration for the qualities of the opposite gender will feed you in ways you've ignored or never imagined.

Sometimes this book will seem like a smack in the face, other times it will feel like a big hug. But it will always be about the truth: men and women are as different as bananas and peaches. Sure as fruits they have commonality, but differences in texture, consistency, flavor, color, response to heat and cold, and nutritional content dictate a uniqueness that is to be appreciated, not criticized or dismissed in some bizarre notion that it hurts the banana if the peach is pink. I believe that the single most horrible problem for marriages today is the lack of understanding, not only of what is needed by a man in a woman but also what is needed by a woman in a man. The very acceptance of the polarity of masculine and feminine is what makes a tight, loving, long-lasting bond—not the more mundane issues like equal effort in housekeeping.

I remember growing up with the jokes about the "war between the sexes." That war was simply that men wanted sex without marriage and women wouldn't give sex without marriage. Men were clear on the kind of girl they would bring home to mother, and have as mother of their children. That was just a friendly skirmish compared to what the war is today where the feminist demands by women have made, in my opinion, men *and* women have less respect and regard for women, femininity, motherhood, men, masculinity (am I the only one sickened by metro-sexuality?), fatherhood, family commitments, and marriage.

Today's brave new world is frightening. It is a world where abortion is easily available, the creation and wanton destruction of human life reduced to whim. It is a world where instead of marriage, we have shacking up—where two become . . . two. Instead of marital procreation and meaningful intimacy, we have "hooking up," where sex is for recreation; instead of mothers raising their children we have institutionalized day care; and instead of intact families we have women who are unwed mothers by choice or irresponsibility, intentionally denying a father's love and guidance to children, and way too casual multiple divorces and remarriages, with minor children cruising between homes and parental affairs—with no actual homes of their own. Issues of love, commitment, security, self-respect, values, vows, obligations, and responsibilities have become ethereal vapors rather than the promises of a good life.

As a consequence of all these social experiments, and the normalizing of amorality, men no longer visualize "motherhood." Whom do they look to? The nanny? The day care employee? When they think about apple pie, they wonder, "Which grocery?" Men see women as sex objects when women act like unpaid whores and wage earners who will keep working till they drop and buy that BMW. They have become shell-shocked from the anti-male hostility that women have demonstrated since the 1960s. Now it is difficult to find a male who values virginity, purity, and innocence when females dress like babes and perform oral sex and intercourse without even having to be fed dinner; who puts any rational stock in protecting and providing when women have said they can do and be it all without a man? Men now figure they can benefit with less pressure of responsibility and use women to insure the acquisition of more goodies. Who cares about vows—after all, why buy the cow when the milk is free? Who sees any point in sacrificing for what they see are emasculating ball-busters. They think, "Open your own door, get this seat first if you can, get a job so I can relax, you said you're equal so you pay for dinner, you said you could have/do it all . . . so do it!"

Chivalry is largely dead, and feminism is the murderer. It soured both males and females on the joy, awe, wonder, excitement, thrill, satisfaction from, and mystery of femininity and masculinity. The war between the sexes is today an all-out war. Spouses more likely suffer from behavior that resembles sibling rivalry where there is competition for resources and power versus "giving," and "sleeping with the enemy" where men are the "evil empire" and women are self-centered, complaining, and demanding bi★★hes rather than two folks who thank God every day for the blessing of their marital partner and the opportunity to live for something other and outside of themselves.

You may be wondering which came first, the chicken—feminism—or the egg—male selfishness and immaturity. I believe the answer is feminism. From the first day that *The Feminine Mystique* hit the bookstands, feminism did not focus on equal pay for equal work, but on how marriage, husbands, men in general, and children in specific were the enemies and the oppressors of true womanhood. All, and I mean all, women's studies programs in high schools and universities brainwashed women into believing that they diminished themselves with motherhood unless they were just a receptacle for birth and didn't actually raise their own children, and marriage, which was twisted into an acceptance of patriarchal control and domination.

Societal pressures have determined to destroy the truth: a real man needs a real woman to be complete *and* a real woman needs a real man to be complete; which is why you don't get too far into Genesis without a demonstration of the polarity of Adam and Eve and that they are part of each other (i.e., the "rib").

Happily, and hopefully, I have many listeners who are aware of the beauty and wonder of the masculine/feminine polarity and interconnectedness and interdependence that brings the best out of both. Dick, a listener, wrote:

> *"Your regular commentary of the differences between men and women is refreshing in a social atmosphere where dogma insists that there MUST NOT be any difference. A wise man (or perhaps woman, I really don't know) once said that if you want to insult a woman, call her a whore. If you want to insult a man, call him a liar.*
>
> *"Perhaps there would then be some truth to the assumption that a wife who loves her husband is faithful because she loves him, and a husband who loves his wife is faithful because he has promised her that he will be."*

I believe that one of the most egregious problems standing in the way of folks having good marriages today is an almost total lack of understanding, appreciation, and respect for what is feminine and what is masculine—and therefore what it means to be the counterpoint to the other. This is the reason I will spend time reintroducing you to what masculinity and femininity are and how each can bring the best out of the other as well as bring joy and pride in being a man or a woman. Without this understanding, marriage becomes one of two competitive, neutered drones trying to make sense out of the incomprehensible, stumbling in the dark, confused, trying to get love to little avail and ending up with the worst kind of loneliness and bitterness.

The second major issue standing in the way of a satisfying, happy marriage is the level of selfishness that has become acceptable in our society. Debbie, a listener, wrote:

> *"I believe that one of the basic mistakes that men and women make in marriage is a lack of commitment and sacrifice. Nowadays it seems like people are much more committed to their careers, their interests, etc. I think that people see their marriages and children as dispensable and other selfish pursuits as necessary. We live in very selfish times. The true needs of spouses and children are neglected for the wants of one or both spouses. Marriage and children are a huge sacrifice and commitment. The last few generations have not been taught these basic moral principles. Our society has come to believe that momentary pleasure without obligation is the most important of life's pursuits."*

The feeling of love, which I haven't mentioned yet, is a little understood, yet highly valued *emotion*. It is normal for people to enjoy that *feeling* of love. Unfortunately, like chemical addictions, it can become an end in itself, as the self becomes the center of the universe—like an infant's perception of the world. "Early love is when you love the way another person makes you feel. Mature love is when you love the person as he or she is. . . . It is the difference between passionate and compassionate love." (*Time* magazine 2/15/93, "What is Love")

An anonymous listener wrote to me, *"I think a lot of people get married to fulfill their own needs, but I think you should get married when you're ready to fulfill the needs of your spouse. I think that is real love, to want to give to . . . and make someone else happy."* And making you, dear reader, *happy* in your marriage is my goal with *The Proper Care and Feeding of Marriage.* And make no mistake, marriage *is* the best state for men and women. A new study (Institute for Social Sciences at Cornell University, 12/08/05) shows that people who are married—compared to those shacking up, or seriously or casually dating—report the highest levels of well-being, regardless of whether they are happily married or not. "Even when controlling for relationship happiness, being married is associated with higher self-esteem, greater life satisfaction, greater happiness, and less distress. The finding that people in relatively unhappy marriages appeared to benefit from being married perhaps stemmed from the stability, commitment, and social status of the relationships." I believe that when many people reported themselves as less than happily married, they were complaining about some negative, instead of embracing what is, in the final analysis, the greater number of good things, but "taken for granted."

Researchers (Brandeis University, 2/14/06) also report that "men and women in unhappy marriages suffered from increased stress levels throughout the day at home and at work as well as higher blood pressure . . . stress has been linked to a higher risk of heart disease, stroke, cancer, and many other health problems. . . . When there is marital concern, men and women are equally affected."

So here it is: if you're married you're better off mentally and physically; if you're in a happy marriage, you're even more better off!

A listener sent me the obituary of an eighty-nine-year-old man from Arizona who was a minister, a prisoner of war in Germany during World War II, a professor and president of a college, a fisherman and a hunter ("as a way to build strong relationships, teamwork and family ties"). Where the obituary got to the point of his survivors, this is what was written: "MM is survived by his loving wife of 67 years. He was always quick to point out (accurately so) that his accomplishments and decisions were all shared by her. He was fond of saying that they agreed at marriage that he would make all the major decisions and she would make all the minor ones . . . 'and we haven't had a major decision yet.' "

Another listener, M'Liz, sent me a column published in her local newspaper that does a short job bio on folks.

> *"This gentleman works for a trash company, works long hours, has done it for years, but it is the reason he gives for his motivation that is awesome. It's just like you are always telling us women: our men work hard to take care of their families. It's simple, basic instinct and right. My husband and I just celebrated our 28th anniversary. He is proud to provide enough for us so that I am able to be home with our kids. We all love him for that."*

Here is the bio excerpt of a trash collector who works fifty-five to sixty hours a week:

Q: What motivates you to do your best?

A: My family. I work hard because I want to show my appreciation to Irma, my wife of 22 years. I want her to know how much I love her and appreciate all of the times she has prepared my meals and taken care of our kids. I also want to show my children how to become responsible adults regardless of the job they perform.

This, my friends, is a very good man in a quality marriage. Last, a letter from another listener, Julie:

"This was sent to me and I thought you'd get a chuckle out of it—A man called the government office and requested an estimate of his benefits upon retirement. After he got the information, he went on to inquire about his wife's benefits. 'Has she ever worked?' asked the clerk. 'She has worked all her life making me happy,' the man said. 'That's nice,' commented the clerk, 'but has she ever contributed to a pension plan?' 'No,' he said. 'We made an agreement when we got married. I would make the living and she would make the living worthwhile.' "

The man and the woman in this story have a properly cared-for marriage.

People call me every day on my radio program with minor complaints, resentments, confusions, and bitterness in their marriages. With all the different combinations and permutations of people and problems, there are still **three** points I always try to make:

1. Treat your spouse as if you loved them with your last breath—no matter how contrary to that you might feel at any one moment.

2. Think hard every day about how you can make their life worth living.
3. Be the kind of person you would want to love, hug, come home to, and sacrifice for.

Oh, I know what you're thinking: "But MY situation is just so impossible. (S)he makes it impossible. It is impossible to change my feelings or change the situation." Well, my friends, I believe that you will not feel that way by the time you finish *The Proper Care and Feeding of Marriage.* And if you do I can only conclude that one of two possibilities is operating: you might truly need a good divorce attorney, or you are unbearably stubborn! ☺

Chapter 1

"Me Tarzan. You Jane."

The first and most obvious issue in approaching the glory and angst of marriage is to understand the fundamentals of the two people involved; one is a woman, the other is a man. And that is no small thing! Sometimes it must seem to frustrated spouses that each has more genetics in common with flies and daffodils than each other. Not so; but if one doesn't understand, admire, respect, and at times forgive, the nuances of the opposite sex, then the beauty and satisfaction that can arise from the uniting of man and woman in the most important covenant of marriage will not be discovered and enjoyed.

So much sociopolitical time and effort has been spent trying to eliminate the reality, subtlety, magic, and meaning of masculine and feminine, that men and women are afraid and hostile to acknowledge their own pleasure in being such and in yearning for the complementary gender in their spouse.

I remember some twenty-five years ago working with a middle-aged couple on their marital problems. Frankly it seemed as though they were hopeless, refusing to spend any time at all on their difficulties other than complaining and blaming each other for their unhappiness. I recall closing my eyes for a moment and just listening. I could hear the hurt, loss, and need in their voices. Instead of trying to reconcile their "problems" I decided to get to the root of the plant and stop worrying first about the way the petals looked. I opened my eyes and interrupted their fight by saying, slowly, to each of them, "Sir, what do you do to make her feel like a woman?" and "Ma'am, what do you do to make him feel like a man?"

They both just stared at me, speechless. I insisted that they answer my question, despite their determination to get back into the fight. Finally she began to cry softly, and he looked deflated, when just seconds before, they were both energized, reddened with anger. We had some fifteen minutes left to the session, and they had nothing to say—to me or to each other.

Marriages are not business arrangements of coworkers or co-owners. Marriages are the joining of two minds, bodies, souls, spirits, hopes, dreams, needs, personalities, *and* different genders. Unisex clothing does not erase the fact that men and women are very different creatures, and that they are each at their best in enjoying life and love when they revel in those differences with awe and respect.

I did a number of surveys on my Web site (www.drlaura.com). The first had to do with men's and women's perceptions of the opposite sex. For all my questions about men/women, marriage/divorce, and so forth, I received thousands of responses, usually within an hour of my posting the questions! Presented here are, in no order, the most frequently mentioned answers. This first group of answers are from men, and they are about their perceptions and feelings about women *in general.* So you women need to read these with an open heart and mind, for in these answers are many of the solutions to your marital problems with your husbands. The second group of answers are from women, and they are also about women's perceptions and feelings about men *in general.* You men need to read those with the same open heart and mind, if you wish to move your marriage into a more satisfying place in your life.

PART A—ANSWERS BY MEN

Question 1

What do you, as a man, most admire about women in general?

1. Social skills, nurturing nature, compassion, sensitivity, listening skills, focus on relationships and bonding (friends, family, community)
2. Physical softness, sexy, curvy, beautiful, and graceful bodies
3. They will sacrifice for family, the power of creation of new life, being mothers
4. Better at details (multitasking)
5. They take the rough, hard edges off this world, they bring feelings and emotions and a sense of intimacy to us logical guys
6. They can create a home out of any environment, adding aesthetics (color, grace, beauty) to life, they make a house into a sanctuary . . . a home, homemaking
7. The positive effect a good woman can have on her husband and family
8. In femininity there is gentle power over people

Paul, a listener, added: "*What I admire the most among many things in women generally is the strength, inspiration, love, and support they give men. They are the balance that counterweights all the chaos, hard times, and heartache us men go through.*"

I believe that men yearn for their spiritual and psychological counterbalance to humanize and beautify life. I don't think it matters much to a man if his woman chooses to be an accountant or physician—as long as she is "his woman" and "a woman" to him. That understanding is lost to too many women today. Sadly it is all too typical for women to want to be seen by their men *as* the high-powered position they have at work, instead of *as a woman*, with those special attributes that are natural to her and yearned for by her man.

But the reality is that women today do not think of themselves in the context of helping "their man." Women today have been brainwashed into thinking that efforts in that direction are in the category of oppression, subservience, and catering to frail male egos. It is sad that this is the prevalent point of view, because *interdependence* is what ultimately feeds both the man and the woman what they truly need to be happy.

Generally when people lob the phrase "know your place," the understanding is that they are reminding someone of their subordinate position in a relationship or situation. I look at that quite differently. I believe that when a man knows that he actually has a place with his woman, and she with her man, they bring the best out in the other—and enjoy life more feeling purposeful, needed, wanted, and necessary.

What's in it for a woman? Christine, a listener, can tell you: "*My job is just a place I go to for a couple of hours so I can make money. My home is where I live and love and laugh; and so it's very easy for me to make that my number one priority. I get my good feelings from home, not from work.*"

Of course, the work women do can be very important and very satisfying—mine is to me! But, but, but, but the ultimate meaning of my life comes from my position in my family, not my position on any ratings scale or bestseller list.

Question 2
What do you least admire about women in general?

1. Emotional manipulation, complaining, nagging, controlling through "hurt" or "anger," their ability to verbally rip apart your soul, having always to get their way

2. Moodiness, women initially express anger with slamming doors, pouting, and such, and it takes time to find out the root of the matter, bitchy (bossy, superior) attitude
3. Gossip for sense of superiority, catfight with girl friends and female relatives
4. They want to talk everything to death, often without coming to any conclusion or without the intent to actually solve anything
5. Emotions dominate rationality or truth
6. Constant demand for validation, take everything too personally, obsessed with looks (but not for sake of pleasing husbands)
7. Unable to apologize to a man, stay angry and hold grudges a long time, shrillness and fault-finding
8. Inability or unwillingness to understand what a man is, man-hating tendencies these days, not letting the man in their life be a man, too quickly annoyed with the true nature of a man

I'm a woman, and to all these "complaints," I say, "Ouch!" Frankly, ladies, I can attest to these unpleasant traits as valid complaints since I talk mostly to scores of women for three hours each weekday—and I live in the real world. I spend a lot of time trying to remind women of the necessity for them to realize how they are behaving and what a horrendous impact they're making when the "good qualities" they possess as women are exaggerated. For example, in question one, men applaud our "emotional sensitivity." Well, put that in overdrive and we have "emotional chaos" (moodiness, PMS, etc.) overriding our good sense. Men also applaud our social skills, until they get into the arena of our trying to control everything and everybody by having things our way.

It is the smart woman who learns how to temper her emotions and use them wisely. Glenda, a listener, got to that point:

> *"I have to thank you from the bottom of my heart for your book,* The Proper Care and Feeding of Husbands. *I have to say that reading this book was like looking into a mirror. I realized after 16 years of marriage, I have been a horrible wife. I treated my husband like crap and took out my negativity on him, expecting him to always be loving to me while I was a flat-out bitch to him.*
>
> *"I noticed that after many years of verbally beating him down, he became just like me. I have to say, seeing my behaviors in him was not pretty. That was what motivated me to read your book. As I laughed and cried through the chapters, I realized that I had turned a wonderful relationship into a mess. I recognized that my husband was probably one of those men that was just putting up with me for the sake of our children, and that I was on a collision course for divorce when they turned 18.*
>
> *"So, I took your advice . . . I made myself and my home a place that my husband would WANT to come home to. I am pleasant when he walks in the door. I no longer bombard him with whining and bitching. Instead, if I have something that we need to discuss, I ask him to let me know when a good time for us to talk would be. I smile more. Sounds simple, but he made the comment to me that my smile is contagious—it makes his heart melt—so I definitely do more of that. Overall, my relationships with my husband and children have improved beyond belief! For that, I thank you from the bottom of my heart!"*

Notice, please, that all she did was to stop allowing her sensitive, wonderful, womanly capacity for emotionality to overwhelm the loveliness that is in a woman's smile, touch, and attitude. No biggie, in a way. No five years of marital counseling to work out points of contention; just a *positive* use of feminine blessings, instead of letting those blessings run amok for lack of control.

Question 3
What do you most fear in a relationship with a woman?

1. Rejection, abandonment, to fail in her eyes, that I won't be able to keep her happy—that she'll never be satisfied
2. Modern (feminist) women seem to be able to dump their marriages and take their children away from their daddies on a whim: if they feel like it.
3. That she will take me for granted (common, mundane thing) instead of taking care of me, constant put-downs and disrespect, unwarranted criticism to make me over in her image of man/husband, that I will slip away as not being important in her life
4. The loss of physical and emotional closeness and intimacy (warmth and sex), that she will become cold and aloof, infidelity
5. Lack of support and respect, her inability for forgive and forget
6. That I will not be able to take care of her needs in the way she wants done, that I'm not valued in any way other than fulfilling her needs as she has them
7. The changes women go through when going from girlfriend to wife to mother because with each phase they care less and less about their man and more and more about themselves, withholding sex for control

8. Being open and vulnerable and having her use it against me or paraded in front of her friends and mother when she's mad

Clearly men's worries about their wives distill down into one main concept really: loss. Men fear most losing their woman's love, goodwill, loyalty, affection, respect, value—it is all *very* personal and not at all related to housework or physical beauty. I have said this so many times on my radio program and in *The Proper Care and Feeding of Husbands* and *Woman Power,* but it needs frequent repeating: men are very simple creatures; this doesn't mean they are stupid, but it does mean they aren't really very complex. They yearn for the simple things with their woman: affection, approval, and attention. As macho as any man might be, his true sense of "manness" needs reinforcement by his woman. If your man comes home after a horrible defeat at work, and you look into his eyes and tell him, "Honey, I know you will be able to find a way to take care of this situation because I've seen you conquer problems for us so many times over the years. I believe in you," he *will be able* to conquer. If, instead, you yell, scream, put him down, get all depressed, whiny, and blaming, and threaten him with the loss of his family, you'll see quickly that your response was more destructive to his entire being than whatever happened at work. You, yes, you! have that much power with your man. Use it benevolently, with the compassion men admire so much in us.

It is so sad that feminism demoted that singularly magical ability of women to transform deflated men into heroes and warriors into a notion of massaging the frail, pathetic ego of a weak man. In doing so, feminism robbed women of one of their most blessed abilities in life: the ability to not only create life in their wombs, but to sustain that life force in the husbands.

Dawn and Craig called my radio show when she wanted to know how best to support her man.

Dawn: We both feel that it's very important for me to be a stay-at-home mom. However, my husband's job has become just an absolute nightmare for him. He's working full-time and he goes to school full-time. He's trying to get done with school in two months. His job is just a nightmare for him; however, he makes enough money for me to stay home with our baby.

DrL: Well, Craig, that's what a **man** does. I'm proud of you! A **man** doesn't say, "I'm not going to take care of my woman and my kid because I hate my job." A **man** says, "I hate my job, but hell, I'm taking care of my woman and my kid!" You, Craig, are a **real man!**

Craig laughs.

DrL: No, seriously, there aren't a lot of real men around. There are a lot of males, but you're a real man.

Craig: Thanks.

DrL: And the way you support that, Dawn, is to point out to him that he's a real man, and your hero. He is putting up with crap as a man would, to protect and provide for his family. I respect and admire that. I hope you have some sons so he can raise them to be real men too.

Dawn: I agree.

DrL: That's the answer to your question, Dawn. You put your arms around his neck and say, "You're a real man . . . and you're mine!" Craig, does that truly cover it?

Craig (excitedly): That'll do it!

This was a perfect example of what a man can and will do if his woman lets him know that he's her hero, that she knows she can count on him, and that she respects and loves him. Any woman too high on her horse to understand how important her moral support is to her man's masculinity (and willingness to fight the dragons of life), misses out on real woman power—and also misses out on a happy, motivated husband.

Men praised us in question one, saying that we women can multitask like nobody's business. But we have to be careful that this multitasking does not make us deny Copernicus's discovery (that the earth was *not* the center of the universe—and neither are we!). One listener got jolted back out of the black-hole she was sinking into:

"My hubby is a wonderful man. He works hard so I can stay home with our three-year-old daughter. We are now expecting our second child in July. The other night I was whining about being pregnant, having lots to do, and not feeling great. I was complaining about how WE weren't pregnant, I was! My hubby leaned over, took my hand, and looked lovingly into my eyes. Then he said, 'Don't forget—I'm your financial backer!'

"I haven't laughed so hard in ages. It was so sweet. He is

so much more than a paycheck. We are so lucky to have him as a father and husband!"

This could have been a good example of a marriage going bad with the listener getting into "pissing contests" or "sibling rivalry" about who has more work or more importance, denying the lock-and-key nature of a marriage—neither the lock nor the key is functional by itself. A good marriage is about seeing yourselves as a team, not as competitors or enemies.

It is often true that when we women get challenged we can allow ourselves to get swallowed up by those emotions. Stacey's letter clarifies this:

"I recently lost my father to cancer, and that made me focus entirely on my mother and her needs—and not my husband's needs, or my own. I was denying my husband the things that he deserved the most: a happy, loving home. Listening to your show made me realize that I need to put my feelings of sadness aside and not deny my husband his happiness. This past weekend, I made a point to spend the entire time with my husband doing the things he enjoys doing.

"I was sure to give him a kiss on the cheek or a wink whenever he looked my way. This in turn opened the flood gates of seduction. After spending a wonderful evening with my husband, we made love for the first time in months. Afterward, my husband looked at me and said, 'I missed you.'

"I had finally realized that all this time this wonderful man was understanding and supportive, and here I was not paying attention to his needs. Sure the house was clean and the food was on the table, but he didn't receive the 'love' he so greatly deserved.

> *"So, thank you so much for opening my eyes to seeing how much a little bit of affection can make US BOTH feel better. I started out just wanting him to feel better . . . little did I realize how wonderful it would make me feel in return."*

What scares me to death is what would have happened to this couple had they gone to your typical marital therapy. He would have been cut to ribbons for even having any needs for her, when she is going through mourning. She would have been reinforced in taking care of herself and her mother and leaving him on his own to be "understanding." Their marriage might have been destroyed, or minimally, seriously damaged.

Instead she reinforced her marriage as her first priority, she respected that her husband's needs were not irrelevant simply because she had pain, and she took care of her man, discovering that this fed back to her tenfold. You get by giving—and not by hoarding.

Too often, women look at their husband's needs as a curse and burden, instead of a blessing and oasis from which to derive sustenance.

Question 4

What is the single, most important expectation you have in a wife?

1. A woman who will put family first; create a home/sanctuary for the family; organize household to be a loving mother and raise our children
2. To be understanding and committed—and not easily swayed by external influences on the marriage; loyalty
3. Friend and lover first . . . mother second
4. Trust and faith in me (decisions, actions, etc.); respect

who I am (not try to change me into something she'd like better)

5. That she makes me her knight in shining armor; admire me as a husband and a *man*; appreciates what I do for the family
6. To be trustworthy and loyal; not to see divorce as the simple solution to problems; be committed to working through problems not just complaining about them
7. To be my support/cheerleader; stand by me in tough times; make me feel loved, wanted, and needed; encourage me to be/do my best
8. Make sexual intimacy/love a priority; loving and affectionate even and especially when there is stress

The very day I was compiling this list from the survey responses, I received a call from a dear woman who holds a powerful corporate position in a major company. She told me that her twenty-year relationship was probably coming to an end. She said, "I think some men just have a tough time being comfortable with a powerful woman." I gently replied, "I don't think the problem they have is with her being powerful. I think the problem they have is when that *powerful woman* doesn't know how to be just *his woman* when she comes home." After a moment or so, she softly replied, "Yes . . . that's probably true."

This list from men, about what they most expect from a wife, is not about their *demands*—it shows clearly how much men *need* their women. Real men don't have superiority complexes: "I am the man, therefore I am more important and you should bow to me," is not at all what this list demonstrates. This is a list showing incredible vulnerability because it shows how *dependent* men are on their women for self-esteem, motivation, purpose and acceptance, approval and love.

Real men truly value their women and put them back on the pedestal that feminism knocked down. Reuters (5/3/06) published an article about a "study" that concluded that the yearly value of an at-home mom's work is $134,121. The point of putting a dollar amount on all her duties is presumably to give "value" to homemakers' responsibilities where there is none. I believe it is the feminists, and not the husbands, who don't value homemakers.

The same day this study was published, I received many e-mails like the following:

> *"This morning I heard on the radio that the worth of a woman's work for the family was $134,000. Thinking this was great, I thought I'd call my husband from the car. He was home. Well, I did, and his comment was, 'Oh, yeah,' and not enthused. So I quickly left the subject and continued on home. Well, when I rounded the corner, he was just leaving. I thought, 'Why couldn't he have waited another 30 seconds to see me! Hummmphhh!'*
>
> *"When I walked in, I saw a note for me. This is what it said. 'Cheryl, the study was wrong about how much housewives are worth. They sought to put a price tag on how much your work is worth, but I say you are priceless. There is no amount of money in the world that could replace you. No amount of money could give me the peace of mind you give me knowing that you are taking care of the kids, not just their physical needs—but also being there for their emotional and spiritual needs, and they know they can count on you always.*
>
> *"'You also are always there for me, to love me and to take care of me and to hold me. I want you to know that I love you for all you do and even more, for your desires, because you want to do these things instead of spending your time elsewhere. I am*

blessed by God because you are in my life! I hope you have a great day! I love you, Eric.'

"I will have a great day, Dr. Laura. Thank you for letting me share my blessings."

So the study purports that replacing a homemaker with a professional for each task she does would come up to $134,000? Really? And what about the love . . . what price is love? And what professional could come into the home and create that warmth, love, and glorious family feeling? Financial compensation is not the best compensation for the heart and soul.

I suppose that this listener's husband, Eric, could hire a slew of folks to take on her tasks, but he wouldn't look at them with the awe, respect, admiration, love, appreciation, and passion with which he looks at her.

All husbands, though, should write "Eric letters" to their wives and not do the Archie Bunker routine of thinking that she should know how you feel about her value to you simply because you're still there or not complaining. A letter like Eric's is as elevating to her as her support and love is elevating to you.

Question 5

What is the most important thing you think modern women don't get about being a woman?

1. That chivalry and gentlemanly behavior is a good thing; to enjoy being a woman and let men treat them as such; that men are not the enemy
2. There is value in being wife and mother; they have given up the need to be needed, loved, and cherished
3. They treat men as inferior, yet they spend their lives try-

ing to act like men; women's lib ought not to be about free sex, aborting surprises, and being tough and angry

4. That "it" is not all about her feelings and desires; they are more consumed with "what's in it for me" than concerned about taking care of their man; that it is better to be loved than to be right all the time
5. That there are differences between men and women—and that those differences are complementary—and that's why they need each other; equality does not imply sameness; modern women don't seem to accept their own human, feminine nature and they fight their natural inclinations; femininity is not a disease to be cured; value, morals, and modesty are important
6. Physical attractiveness is only a spark—being cheerful and loving is the flame; being kind, courteous, and respectful; the importance of sex in a relationship
7. They have all the power in a relationship to make or break it; how strongly they can influence a man, make him feel like a man; men are simple creatures and need only sex, food, and appreciation; that being loving to your husband does not make you a slave; you catch more flies with honey than nags
8. They think men and women don't really need each other; they think they can do it all (job, kids, house, and last and least, husband); that being a mother and wife is more important than any job or career

How could it be so that several generations of women don't appreciate the value and power of their femininity? How is it that women would yearn to throw away their magnificent importance as the center of family, community, and life itself? The answer? Feminism! Feminism has been a scourge upon the land and upon women, children, men, and ultimately, families and society.

The true ideal of feminism—that men and women should have the same rights and opportunities—is an obvious positive civil rights issue. But that is not the feminism that has ever dominated. The feminist movement as such was totally co-opted by a mentality that despised femininity, motherhood, wifehood, and men in all forms except castrated.

Michael, a listener, submitted this letter in response to my on-air query, "In what way(s) would you consider yourself a recovered feminist and what parts of the feminist agenda have you dropped and why?"

> *"I am married to a feminist psychology professor—envy me. My life under the feminist Taliban has been a mixture of guilt mingled with hopelessness and despair. I have been less than a plow horse. To be a man was to be blamed for everything, appreciated for nothing. Rescuing her and her sibling's lives, buying her a 4,000 sq. ft., six-bedroom house on a hill with a view earned me a 'performs as expected' as a husband.*
>
> *"I started listening to your show to better understand my wife and her career—and instead, ended up understanding myself. I like me now. I have value. My needs and feelings are not scummy. I am no longer devastated by her displeasure. Although I no longer believe that women can actually have feelings of love and admiration for us men, (with your show) I have hope for my sons. I love your book* The Proper Care and Feeding of Husbands *and appreciate you more than you could ever know. Of course, my wife and daughter hate you, hate your book, and hate me for buying it and 'shoving it in their faces' (their words).*
>
> *"Thank you for the happiness and the possibility of joy."*

Sadly I received hundreds of such letters from sad, lost, unloved, and unappreciated men, who nonetheless worked very hard to try to make their women happy, obviously against great odds.

How and why did the feminist movement create such enmity for men? First it is important to recognize that the enmity was also directed at women—a kind of self-loathing of nurturing breasts, life-producing uterus, and an emotionally sensitive, nurturing spirit.

This is something Erica, another listener, can tell you about:

> *"As an 18-year-old high school student, I participated in my first women's studies class. It made me feel ANGRY and POWERFUL. I suddenly became a militant feminist. In college, I continued with these classes, and fit right into the liberal, left-wing, feminist culture—participating in many feminist marches and rallies, including anti-anti-abortion demonstrations.*
>
> *"Then I met my husband, a Christian and anti-abortion. I found him irresistible—partly because I wanted to convert him to my side. Funny thing is, he changed me to his. Before I knew it, I was in love with him. I wanted to be and do everything for him, if only because he was the MAN I loved. I was happy to cook for him. I'd bring his laundry over and wash/fold while we watched movies on Sunday afternoon. I gave him back rubs after a stressful day. And, do you know what?! He repaid all my kindnesses and more. He'd run out and buy me ice cream in the middle of the night when I was studying for finals; he'd come by my house and drive me to school on rainy mornings; he'd take me to see a 'chick flick' and to a sushi dinner and love every moment of it because he was with me.*

"Now that we're married, we continue putting all our efforts toward taking care of each other's needs. I've never felt myself so fulfilled and happy. I know that as an ANGRY feminist (any other kind?) I would never have experienced the joy of giving fully and having the faith that I will always be safe, loved, and taken care of.

"I still believe that men and women have equal VALUE, but VERY different ROLES. I'm GRATEFUL that I can take such good care of my husband. I am GRATEFUL to be feminine and womanly. I am GRATEFUL that my husband and I don't vie for power in the relationship, but humbly give to each other. I am PROUD that I am my husband's wife, and look forward eagerly to also being my kids' mom.

"I've given up my ANGER towards MEN. I've stopped wanting to FEMINIZE males. I even LIKE it now if a gentleman opens the door for me. I always smile graciously and say, 'Thank you.' I wish there were more gentlemen in this world—I'm so glad I married one. I've given up my hateful 'feminist ideals' and now I live in bliss with a REAL MAN, as a REAL WOMAN."

Of the thousands of responses I received—within twelve hours!—to my question about being a Recovered Feminist, there were a handful of familiar themes:

- *"Everything I want, what makes me happy as a woman (being at home, family, having children, having a knight in shining armor) is spit upon by two groups: chauvinists and feminists. They're one and the same, aren't they? Vile, loathsome, selfish people . . . ironic that they don't like each other either."*

- *"I realize that it is not submissive to let my husband be a man and not expect him to act like my girlfriend. I realize that being feminine is much more powerful than being a feminist."*

- *"I finally realized how self-centered I had become as a feminist. My complete focus was on MY happiness, MY problems, MY agenda, and MY future. I thought his job was to do everything to please ME. Since reading* The Proper Care and Feeding of Husbands, *I have been focusing on HIM more. It is such a delight to me to see how much happier he has become. I continue to enjoy my release from my 'feminist prison.' "*

- *"Feminists can't see power in being a true woman who uses her God-given natural abilities to nurture both children and a husband. I know how marriages can suffer if both spouses are working, exhausted, and too tired to tend to the relationship. I've come full circle on pretty much every feminist issue there is—and I'm no longer arguing with my nature on these issues. I'm no longer fighting to prove that I am not a 'typical woman' and, as a matter of fact, I quite like it."*

- *"Feminists abandoned all the virtues of womanhood (modesty, tact, subtlety, civility) and adopted all the vices of men (promiscuity, vulgarity, aggressiveness). Perhaps this would be less appalling if the feminists adopted at least some of the male virtues (logical thought, adherence to principles, stoicism, reticence), but they have not. Paradoxically, feminism today is about hating men, but at the same time encouraging detestable behavior in men: how, exactly, has abortion on demand improved male/female relationships?"*

- *"How am I a recovered feminist? Let me count the ways:*

  "I no longer: look down on motherhood, open doors when my husband is with me, expect my husband to tolerate my

irrational emotions, think men are pigs, look up to female CEOs who leave their babies to others to raise and love, and I no longer apologize for my conservative and traditional values. In other words, I am much happier being a woman rather than wishing I was a man. God does not make mistakes."

- *"I was raised to believe that I could be all and do all. That philosophy soon crashed into reality. I had a career, a husband, a child, and a home—and I expected to be able to manage it all. With great fatigue, I realized I was doing a pretty poor job of it. Then I realized the feminist movement had robbed us all. Before the feminist brainwash, women stayed home to love their children. Husbands were proud to care for and provide for their families. The woman had time and energy to devote to the pride and care of home and family. Wanting to return to such a life, I ran into the feminist agenda: my husband expected me to have all and do all. He, brought up in feminism, was not prepared to shoulder the responsibility of being the sole financial support for the family. After some problems in day care, that issue was resolved. I am now a stay-at-home mom, and together, my husband and I are raising our children. The feminist lie has been ousted—and we are living the truth."*

Both men and women are confused about the proper source of their self-worth, how to relate to one another, how to find happiness when feeling pulled in too many directions, and how to find peace and security in love with the opposite sex when they don't know how to be or what to expect or what is expected. It is very positive to elevate and celebrate the qualities of men or women—but NOT at the cost of the health of the other, children, relationships, and society.

I have said for quite a while that feminism robbed women of their essence and their ability to find pure joy and happiness. Yes it is a good thing that a woman can run a company; it is a bad thing if she does this while neglecting her husband and children. She will ultimately suffer when she realizes that her life choices have made her a worker drone, and not a full, feminine human being.

As Marla relates:

"I used to be a card-carrying feminist. I've now come to realize that all the power IS ours if we just embrace being a REAL woman. I love my man. I stand behind my man. By making him more important than me and considering his feelings above mine, it actually works out that I get everything I could possibly want. I adore doing things for him because I love him. I don't have anything to prove about so-called equality anymore. I love being my man's woman. I love him opening doors and his heart to me. Being a real, true woman has brought me more happiness than any amount of feminism or liberation ever could. I am a very loved woman and that is because I truly love my man."

Jae, a listener, summarized this all quite beautifully:

"A real woman is someone who has no shame in being a wife and a mother, and puts her career on hold until the kids are grown. A real woman is available emotionally, spiritually, and physically for her man. She is selfless, and in doing so, loves herself because she has so much to offer."

Did you read that? "She is selfless, and in doing so, LOVES HERSELF BECAUSE SHE HAS SO MUCH TO OFFER." Wow!

The simplicity of Jae's letter is stunning. And it speaks to the truth.

As I've mentioned, women are no longer programmed to admire and respect what is masculine and manly. Nonetheless, when asked, it is stunning how "retro" the answers are. That is because what is hard-wired into feminine and masculine DNA and hearts is a need, a yearning for the completion of their beings: the interdependence of masculine and feminine. Part B, women's answers, reveals that truth.

PART B—ANSWERS BY WOMEN

Question 1

What do you, as a woman, most admire about men in general?

1. Hardiness, physical strength, masculinity, mental toughness, protective, courage, self-confident, persevering, emotional strength when facing fear
2. Ability to see the whole picture objectively, think logically, get things done, practicality
3. Honest, straight to the point, backbone, strength of character and opinion, uncomplicated
4. They get over things fast, can be friends with other men who have hurt their feelings (not petty, catty, or gossipy), bond easily, don't make everything a crisis, up front with anger, don't overanalyze everything
5. Provider for family, responsible, driven to fix and help, leadership and devotion
6. Chivalry, gentlemanly behavior, willingness to slay dragons every day, they will sacrifice everything to make their woman happy
7. They are put together nicely and their passion in sex, they are comfortable with their bodies
8. Their simplicity

As I look at this list, I see that the answers were focused on the pragmatic. This is not an accident. I believe that women crave the bedrock characteristics that are "masculine." That is true in spite of cultural pressures working against women appreciating masculinity and having appreciation and respect for what a "man" can offer. In counterpoint to Maureen Dowd's book *Are Men Necessary?* Lori Borgman wrote in a syndicated column, "There are a lot of things I sometimes think I'd like to be, but a man is never one of them. Talk about a group maligned, vilified and marginalized. For the most part—abusers, perverts and slackers aside—most men are stand-up guys. They work hard. They create, tinker, build, engineer and achieve. The take carping, criticizing and complaining on the chin, and rarely get the thanks they deserve."

Liz, a self-proclaimed "recovering feminist" and listener, wrote:

> *"Everywhere one turns today, men are demeaned. After listening to your radio program and reading* The Proper Care and Feeding of Husbands, *I've been appalled at what I now 'notice' in our media: Heating commercial—husband portrayed as the bumbling idiot, who needs the wife's wisdom to choose the right unit; GPS unit commercial—husband portrayed as the idiot who won't ask for directions. Woman saves the day with GPS; insurance commercial—wife talks wisdom with a friend while husband blows up barbecue. . . . I could go on ad-nauseam. Recognizing that many of the above references are 'just to be funny,' I see this as an alarming trend. Feminists would scream if this behavior were directed toward women. It's open season on men in our culture."*

The main problem with these cultural influences is that they result in a constant IV drip of negativity into the veins of women who then treat their men with reflexive, almost unconscious disdain—and then call me nonplussed that their husbands ignore Valentine's Day and anniversaries. I tell them, "Happily married men always remember sentimental holidays." Silence. I add, "So tell me why your husband is unhappily married?" Usual response is, "I don't know." If I nag some more, I can get to the answer, "Well, I guess, maybe . . ." The list I get to includes: no validation, no affection, no sex, lots of complaining, chaotic schedules and lack of warm home atmosphere, arguments about minutia mostly started by dissatisfied, unhappy wife, payback punitive, hurtful behaviors, and so forth. When did we forget that you catch more flies with honey?

With this list, I am happy to announce that at least my female listeners have some appreciation for what is manly, male, and masculine. However when women do acknowledge wanting a man "they can count on," they get grief from the feminists.

For example, the *Los Angeles Times* in February 2006 published an article titled "It Turns Out Money Can Buy Love, After All." The "spin" of this article is obviously obnoxious: "men want a woman with a good sense of humor, while women prefer a guy who has a steady job and pays his bills on time. 'And they say money can't buy you love,' quipped a [female] financial planner."

The truer point is that women are not gold diggers; women want a man who can provide financial security so that she will be able to take care of their children at home! All throughout the animal kingdom, the males have to prove something to the females in order to get one to mate with him; some species have to build acceptable nests, others have to fight competitors; human men need to be able and willing to be sole support.

Every call I have ever gotten from a woman who was the breadwinner was filled with her pain, jealousy, and resentment that she wasn't the one at home with the children. I believe that no matter how financially successful and powerful a woman is, she naturally wants to be protected and provided for by her man—it is what makes her feel more womanly.

Women want a man they can lean on. However feminism has brainwashed women to believe that all men are inconsiderate beasts you can't rely on. Therefore, the threat goes, never give up your independence. This mentality has confused and frightened women into an avoidance of becoming dependent on their men. So to protect themselves, women ferociously parry with their men, while denigrating their own desires to tend the home and raise children. Then they call me all depressed and angry . . . and they think it is because of their husbands.

I recently took a call from a woman who waited until thirty to marry. She quit her job and is at home with their one-year-old son. She called me with exactly this dilemma. Her father had been a loser—at least that is what her mother always told her. And now she's wondering if she did a good thing by marrying a man she sees as so controlling. When I asked her to describe him, what came back was the very definition of a responsible man.

I believe that what has happened is that the healthy part of her picked a man she could count on. The unhealthy part of her won't believe it, is scared of the vulnerability of losing her independence, and comes up with a good reason to avoid turning herself over to him—that's the part of her that is hurt and confused by her childhood experiences. It would seem that there are only two choices: one, guy is loser she can't count on, and two, guy is controller who will consume her. There is a place in between.

She was an extremely intelligent woman and understood the concepts but wasn't quite sure how to put it on the emotional level so that she could think and feel better things. I suggested that the moment he came home from work, she greet him at the door and then ask him to stand still. She was to turn her back to him, tighten up her body, put out her arms like an airplane, and just let herself fall backward toward him. I told her that he would do what a real man does for his woman and family, he would catch her.

The next morning I got this e-mail from Sophie, another listener:

> *"I listened to the caller who was having trouble trusting her man. Your solution was to have her play the 'trust game,' where she would fall into her husband's arms and trust that he would catch her. I played that game last night with my husband. I simply said, 'Do what comes naturally,' as you instructed the woman to do. I turned around, stepped a foot away, fell back . . . and he caught me. He then proceeded to kiss me. He shrugged and said, with smile, 'I did what came naturally. You were in my arms and I had to love you.'*
>
> *"Dr. Laura, I thought you might like to know—it was a good night!"*

Question 2

What do you least admire about men in general?

1. Hard for them to give-and-take in discussion, they want to give the answer, not figure it out together

2. That they can have casual sex; obsession with women's bodies/sex; shallow physical attraction to women
3. Pride (male ego); not good with criticism; won't admit weaknesses; arrogance; emotional neediness
4. Too easily pussy-whipped by intimidating women and/or their mothers
5. Don't wish to do domestic work; expect women do to child-rearing
6. Workaholics; can't multitask; focus on bigger picture, and not on details
7. Crude humor and admiration of violence; sloppy
8. Won't talk about feelings—won't show many feelings besides anger; not sensitive to feelings of woman; won't easily vocalize love and appreciation

It's interesting. These criticisms are largely another way of looking at the compliments. For example, in question one, answers included men are stoic, take charge, protect, don't personalize everything. In question two, all that got turned into not expressing emotions, want to fix things without talking about it, aren't sensitive enough. This must feel to men like a "make up your mind" moment!

One of the criticisms aimed at me since *The Proper Care and Feeding of Husbands* hit the bookstores in 2003 is that I seem to think men are perfect and that women are always at fault for marital problems. I do understand that perspective coming from defensive wives and rabid feminists (sorry for redundancy). For the others who are perplexed at my apparent proman bias, you are seeing the truth! As a woman, I am honest and embarrassed to say that over the last half century, the tide has turned seriously hostile and demeaning toward men and masculinity. As a result, women, in my opinion, behave proportionally more destructively and insensitively in relationships and marriages than have men, and men are less and less behaving like *men*.

However, be very clear that I don't see men as perfect—if that were so, I wouldn't be having daily on-air arguments with some damsel about her ridiculous choice of a scummy, alcoholic, druggie, irresponsible, philandering, violent, self-centered, momma's boy of a boyfriend. But, and it is a big but here so take notice, I think when a damsel picks your basic nice guy, she is generally handicapped in realizing the power she has to turn him from a toad to a prince at a moment's notice with a kiss and a loving compliment. Most women today, I fear, see and treat their men like an accessory in their marriage instead of God's contribution to their happiness.

Yeah, guys in bunches are crude—but your basic decent guy turns it off in front of a lady . . . get it? LADY. Guys have testosterone and a brain wired for appropriate aggression—but your basic guy uses that aggression in sports, business, and war. Issues of guys being interested in the visual with respect to women, or having sex are important—that is built into the wiring of a male, as breast-feeding and bonding are built into the wiring of a female. Would women like to hear as a criticism that they spend much too much time on the interpersonal versus the intellectual?

Men and women are complementary—perfection is created by their union. It does no good to ridicule what is inherent in the male and female; save that for the neurotic.

Men need women to help them be civilized, focused, ambitious, connected, healthy, and happy. Women are men's anchors and connection to the sublime of love, family, and meaning in life.

When women learn to look at a man's nature as something they contribute to instead of eliminating, women will have happier selves, men, and marriages.

Instead most women want their men to be just like them. Look at the list again: it contains descriptions of what a woman is! This is why I believe this book is so important; women and men must learn to have a sense of humor about, and a respect for, what is not themselves.

Lisa, a divorced listener, who hopes to meet a good man after her youngest graduates, wrote:

> *"I lost my father early in the year and admired him greatly, as well as other men of his age. He was 83, grew up in poverty, had a broken home with a mother who married several men, all of whom were less than gracious to my father.*
>
> *"Yet, he grew up to be the kind of man that stood up for his convictions, he told you like it was, pretty matter of fact. He worked hard and was proud. He raised me to be a competent woman, yet he expected me to be treated like a lady.*
>
> *"I do not care that Dad wasn't in touch with 'his feminine side.' These men demonstrated for the most part accountability for their actions. The best men I know today all have said their fathers were more than a little hard on them—it's because they were raising them to be the men they are today."*

Your basic decent guy, ladies, is a guy! So don't expect him to talk in paragraphs when men deal with pointed sentences; don't expect him to sniffle over a chick flick or your girl friend's problems or the sixth rendition of your hurt feelings—men handle things and get on with it; don't expect him to not want your body in rapturous passion—men show and receive love through that very tight connection . . . without flowers.

Question 3

What do you most fear in a relationship with a man?

1. Rejection; infidelity; he will get tired of me sexually; I will disappoint him (poor housekeeping, bad mother, not good with money, too independent, get old and wrinkled, etc.)
2. I won't understand him; coming across as a nag; take him for granted so he falls out of love with me
3. Being controlled; lose getting my own way; lose myself to make him happy
4. Physical and/or mental abuse
5. Not being "happily ever after"
6. "I'm nervous about meeting my husband's sexual needs. I know this is how he likes love to be expressed, and it has taken me a long time to realize that this is just as important to him as loving and talking and hugging is to me."
7. Involvement with pornography

The overwhelming response was number one. Over 95 percent of the women who answered this question were most in fear of being rejected and abandoned. This is an issue I deal with a lot on my program—and not because it is a typical male behavior. Of course it is sometimes true that some women select a husband poorly, picking an immature guy because they think they can fix him, or a narcissistic guy because they are charmed by him; this results in a man they cannot count on.

For the most part the insecurity that is expressed by my female callers has to do more with their underlying recognition that they are not behaving in a way that bonds their men to them. It usually takes severe badgering on my part to get them to look at and accept this truth. One recent female caller was telling me about her problems with "rage attacks." It turns out that he installs kitchens, and she is concerned that some babelike single woman client of his will seduce him away from her. I asked her if she thought screaming at a man would make him feel more loved, connected, and happy in his marriage. "No," she said, "but I don't know what else to do. I get scared." Another woman called to complain that her husband ignored their thirtieth anniversary. I told her, "No happily married man forgets his anniversary; for him it is a monument to his joy!" Not surprisingly she couldn't/wouldn't deal with his unhappiness—just about how hurt and disappointed she was.

The very next morning I received this e-mail from John, a listener, who has the answer for both these wives:

> *"The other day my wife and I had the good fortune to catch part of your show while driving home from work early. We heard the caller who was complaining about how her husband had completely ignored her 30th wedding anniversary. I find that hard to believe, and thought you may appreciate a man's point-of-view.*
>
> *"How could her husband possibly ignore the fresh cut flowers in the living room when he got home from work? How could he ignore the perfume she was wearing, or the outfit she had on? Or that she had cooked his favorite meal, or in the least made reservations at their favorite restaurant. How could her husband possibly ignore the candles, or the bath that she had drawn for them to share, or the lovemaking that followed such a wonderful evening? Or even the hotel reservations that she had booked for them.*
>
> *"Oh . . . I know . . . none of those things happened. She*

simply sat there and expected their anniversary to be another birthday party for her. She forgot that an anniversary is about celebrating their lives together, not an opportunity to get another piece of jewelry she had her eyes on. It isn't about things. It's about each other.

"I guess her husband didn't have much to celebrate."

It is typical of most marital therapy to spend months going over every harsh word said and every stupid deed done—this immerses folks in the negative. Instead go right ahead and create the positive. If you wish to stay together, commit to being your best dream, not your worst nightmare. It's the people who relish hanging on to the hurts and the power that gives them over their spouse, that never salvage nor create beauty in their marriages.

Question 4

What is the single most important expectation you have for a husband?

1. Listening and remembering what I say
2. To make me feel loved and cherished
3. To be a loving husband and father; that he is primarily committed to family; faithful and loyal; a kind heart; be spiritual
4. To be my superfan; be my best friend
5. Financial security
6. To be appreciative and not just expect
7. Leader in the household and make family-wise decisions; comfortable with being head of the family without being cruel, bossy, controlling, or overbearing; a positive role model; to slay dragons

8. Faithful—no affairs (emotional or physical) and no pornography

Unless it was included under answer 2, not one woman mentioned sexual intimacy. I recently received this e-mail from Michelle:

> *"It seems like your book* The Proper Care and Feeding of Husbands *should have been titled* Have Sex With Your Husband . . . *so he won't leave you; so he'll pay attention to the kids; so he'll fix the bathtub; so he'll buy you something nice. I've heard it all on your show. It makes me very sad. It sounds like marriage is a lot like prostitution, using sex to get something to have power. No woman should have to get it on all the time so her husband will participate in the family. There is so much more to life than getting naked and doin' it."*

I e-mailed her back: "Prostitution is receiving money for anonymous sex. Marital sex is about love and bonding."

Some women *expect* to be cherished, protected, and provided for by a man without that man enjoying the depth of passion that makes him feel loved, needed, wanted, adored, and ultimately accepted; that doesn't work for long. A man *needs* the physical to feel connected emotionally to his woman, and by extension, the family. Any woman who dismisses that truth about her man will lose her man—even if he doesn't walk out the door until the children are in college.

Question 5
What is the most important thing you think modern men don't get about being a man?

1. Vulnerability is okay (at least with your woman)
2. The need to be a good provider; not expect wife to be just another paycheck
3. To be old-fashioned gentlemen; chivalry is still in demand
4. We still need you to be our heroes
5. Being kind, gentle, and considerate doesn't mean they are "whipped"
6. No "metro-sexuality"—good old masculinity!
7. Responsibility to wives and children versus own personal needs
8. Mothers should be home with their children

This list just goes to prove a point I keep on making: the "times" are irrelevant to the true needs of men and women to be true to their own natures. Please stop making politically correct social agendas out of the simple needs of a woman for a man and a man for a woman. Please stop trying to understand the opposite sex as though they were a bug to dissect. It is important to accept and respect what is masculine and feminine without envy or negativity. And, it is essential to support what is the ultimate truth in each other: you both are a blessing to each other—SHOW IT!

Toni, a listener, wrote this e-mail to me:

> *"I just want to thank you, Dr. Laura, for your program and for what you do—but more specifically, for what your program does for my marriage. This may sound strange, but I have actually never heard your program, but my husband has. His job requires him to travel frequently, so he listens to the radio quite a bit. Many times he has come home and held me tight and*

spoke genuine words of appreciation for me as his wife and the mother of his children.

"He then proceeded to explain to me how he has been listening to Dr. Laura and realized how blessed he truly is. So, I don't know what you're doing or exactly how you're impacting my husband, but please, keep it up!!"

And another e-mail from Nicole, who took my on-air advice and can't believe how much happier she is in her marriage. Her husband is a gun enthusiast, and like most women, she wasn't at all interested in going to a shooting range for entertainment. After listening to my program she decided one day to offer to him a day at the range with her! Turns out they had an excellent time and his enthusiasm for teaching her made her smile.

The very next day she received this e-mail from him:

"Hey, I just wanted to tell you thanks for being such a great wife and companion. I don't know any guy who has such a beautiful, funny, caring, intelligent, sexy, loving wife as I do and one who will not only get involved in the things I like, but be truly interested. I am truly the luckiest man alive. I'm sorry I don't always reciprocate, and I'll work harder to do better. You mean everything to me and I will try harder to be worthy of you. Thanks for everything you do and everything you are. Love, your husband."

And all because she went to the shooting range with him. Nicole feels *"like the luckiest woman alive!"*

Your assignment, dear friends, is to reread this chapter, paying primary attention to the lists made out by the opposite sex. Without arguments, lengthy discussions, endless hours of therapy airing complaints, pains, disappointments, threats, and demands—JUST DO what you know your spouse needs and wants to feel important to you—what you know any woman or man would appreciate. It will, as these last two letters have shown, be lovingly reciprocated.

Or you can dig in your heels, pout, and plan "payback," and, I'm sorry, to what end? Oh yes, "end" may sadly be the correct term.

Chapter 2

"I've Met the Enemy . . . and It's ME!"

Through all the years I was in private practice as a marriage, family, and child therapist, I never once had folks walk in and point to *themselves* as a/the problem with the marriage; not once. When couples or individuals call in to my radio program to address their marital issues, one of the very first things I do is to ask, "What do *you* do to hurt your spouse personally and/or the marriage in general?" It is amazing how capable people are to place blame anywhere else but with themselves. This is not to say that the other person is not contributory; this is to say that it is easier to get your spouse to take responsibility if you role model doing such! Also the only control each one of us has in our relationships is over ourselves.

What I tell callers is, "Look at it this way—if you are causing some problems in your marriage, it is good news and bad news. The bad news is obvious: you're being a pain. The good news is not so obvious: you have the power to change, and in doing so, bring happiness and pleasure to yourself and your family faster than if it is your spouse who is the problem since we can't force anyone to change!"

Why do people so quickly see the other as the enemy when once they saw the other as *the* antidote to all life's negativities and the ultimate source of happiness? The answer lies in the question. When people come together, there is a romantic, albeit somewhat naïve, immature, or desperate notion that this joining will fill holes in their souls and psyche. Actually that is ultimately true, but *only* when each is aware of and understands the meaning of their own emotional "issues" and is similarly aware and sensitive to the same in their spouse.

My three decades of experience dealing with people struggling with intimacy tells me that too much of marital therapy is dealing with marital structure, disappointments, and disenchantments with one's spouse, and not enough on understanding the dueling inner dynamics of spouses. By "inner dynamics" I mean the complex web of the impact of their earlier family experiences tangled up with their repetitive, and largely unproductive, ways of handling real and/or imagined fear and hurt.

In this regard, it is most interesting that many people wonder about their ability to change! Do they truly think personal change is impossible? Of course not. I believe that what they are really worried about is whether they will be *safe* and *loved* if they change. Most people behave "badly" because they are struggling with those core concerns. They are concerned that if they change they might not be loved and won't be safe from hurt . . . like they were in their pasts.

Phillip, a caller to my program, was confused about just these issues.

Phillip: I don't know where to start. I'm trying to save my marriage. I'm trying to find out whether or not it's possible for me to change. I want to change so badly.

DrL: What is it you'd like to change?

Phillip: My outlook and my attitude and how I treat my wife and my child. I am so demeaning to them and I don't give them the respect they deserve. I see what I'm doing but I still do it.

DrL: Explain to me how at the very moment you know you're being a snotty, nasty bastard, that you don't go, "Oh my God, I'm sorry!" I just want to know what's going on in your head at that very moment when you see and hear yourself and you don't stop.

Phillip: Wow! That's a good question. Maybe I realize that I've lost control of the situation.

DrL: Okay, so what I learned from you is that when you're at a point in which you're making a choice between feeling in control or being a good man—you're choosing being in control. That means being in control is the most overwhelming concern. That's an anxiety reaction. Where do you think that comes from?

Phillip: My parents were separated twice during my childhood and then finally when I was twelve it was over between them. My mother was an alcoholic. I could ramble on forever . . . my life was out of control during my childhood.

DrL: What do your daughter and wife do that makes you feel out of control as a parent and husband?

Phillip: Lazy and messy.

DrL: So you need order in your life because you're still trying to survive your childhood even though you're not in your childhood any longer?

At this time I took a commercial break and suggested to Phillip that he think about how he is living *for* yesterday instead of *in* today. When we came back, Phillip started out with an embarrassed admission that the lazy and messy issues were really small things.

DrL: No, they aren't small because they *mean* something very big to you which is why you become a bastard. You're a sensitive, aware guy who can't control being a bastard. So they mean something very big for you—don't minimize them because what they mean is huge! Close your eyes, Phillip, and tell me . . . "When the house is messy, it means my wife———"

Phillip: Doesn't care how I feel.

DrL: "When your daughter is not busy at something, seeming lazy, it means she———"

Phillip: She doesn't respect me as a father figure.

DrL: You're looking in the wrong place to get verification and proof that you're a man and that you're your wife's man. When the house is neat you feel less anxious, but you really don't feel more loved—you can't convince me of that, Phillip.

Phillip: How do I feel more loved?

DrL: Close your eyes right now and imagine her looking up at you with adoration—you know that look from her—you've seen it. Can you see that look?

Phillip: Okay, I see it.

DrL: Do you like it? Does it make you feel good? Does it bring the anxiety level down?

Phillip: Yeah.

DrL: Then when your anxiety level is up and you're needing that "fix," do what you know will bring that look to her face and then bathe in it! Neat house; anxiety down and love down. Adoring look on wife's face; anxiety down and love up. Win—win. Stop looking at the order of the house and start looking at her face. When your house is a mess and you walk in and get the anxious feeling—GASP!—walk over, lift your wife off the ground, and give her big smoochies; tell her how gorgeous she looks and that she's a hot babe and you will get the look that you need. That's what you do instead of saying something about the mess. Your mother's house is in that mess. Your house is in your wife's face. Do you understand that?

The very next day, Jolene, identifying with Phillip's situation, wrote an incredible letter to me. I am sure she represents many who saw themselves in Phillip's struggles and gained the strength to go after their needs in more constructive and productive ways.

"I was listening to your last caller who treats his wife and daughter badly when the house is a mess. I had to stop what I was doing to hear what you had to say because I treat my family the same.

"When you told him to search for the love and respect in his wife's face, the faces of my husband and loving boys came to me and brought me to tears. I have four wonderful men in my life who adore me and I treat them poorly when things are not done my way.

"When you told Phillip about the house no longer being his mother's, but his wife's, you made me realize what valuable

time I have wasted on being a control freak, and how I have made myself viewed as the 'jerk' in my home. How could my family love and adore me after the way I have treated them?

"I will go home tonight, and if my house is a mess and the kids are being lazy, my reaction will be that of hugs and kisses, knowing how lucky I am to have such a wonderful family who still adore me after my bad, bad, bad behaviors.

"You made me see something that I had no idea I was doing and I thank you for that. I now have a chance to make things right.

"I'm going to change starting today and I'm going to tell my husband what a sexy stud he is and pull out a chair and have a glass of wine and look at his face, not the house."

Controlling behaviors really have nothing to do with maintaining order. Controlling behaviors are about trying to feel lovable. Unfortunately as beautifully illustrated by Phillip, controlling behaviors only empower yesterday's pain, rage, and fears to push aside today's love; ironically, the opposite is created.

Katie called me because she constantly asks her husband if/how much he loves her. She'd like to stop this behavior and offered up her own self-analysis of why she is stuck in this annoying habit of nagging her husband to give her the feedback she needs.

She began the call by telling me that she grew up feeling that her dad hated her.

Katie: My mother, even from the time I was six months old, thought that my dad hated me and that it had something to do with jealousy over me taking her time away from him . . . whatever. My relationship with my dad is a lot better now and we talk occasionally.

I've grown up feeling that I'm just inadequate, like I have issues with self-esteem that I've been working on my entire life.

She describes being married for two years to a wonderful man and that most of the time everything is fine, but sometimes, usually close to "that time of the month," she just has a hard time believing how much he loves her and just accepting what he has to say. So she badgers him with "Do you love me?" and "How much do you love me?"

What I didn't bring up at the time, but will discuss here and now, is that her father was probably never "hateful" of her; he more likely was resentful that his wife paid him no attention once she gave birth. I was frankly angrier in my mind about her mother asserting that the object of his anger was her own child and not herself! This was most likely a marital issue and not a rejection of a daughter by her father.

I did not want to bring this up during her call as I was concerned about orphaning her by yanking her illusions of her mother out from under her. Plus I don't believe that needed to be dealt with in order to make progress!

DrL: Well, Katie, nobody in the world but you can control your mouth. There is no trick. There is no magic. There is only you saying, "I choose not to drive my man nuts!"

Truth is, he's not going to love you because you're needy; he's going to love you if you're loving. So every time you feel concerned that you're not loved, act in a loving manner and create that love feeling in the other person. In other words, if you're suddenly going into your "poor me, I'm not lovable and you have to prove to me I am and make me feel good and I have to be the center of the universe and none of your feelings matter because you're just here to make me feel good" behaviors, he's bound to get very tired of it and you.

If in his mind coming home means there's an irritating little girl who is demanding and pouty, he's not even going to want to come home at some point.

If you want to know that you're loved, love the hell out of him and you'll see that love reflected back multifold.

Katie: But how do I stop needing so much?

DrL: You probably won't ever be free of those anxiety-driven impulses to squeeze instant adoration out of him. However take that impulse as narcissistic as it is, and turn it into loving generosity. You will find that two things will happen: first, giving feels good and makes one feel special to be able to bring happiness to another, and second, his response of appreciation and affection will be true and real—not extorted.

We don't ever truly *get* by grabbing, demanding, and manipulating. When we "get" that way, we know it's synthetic and we're never satisfied with a fake meal. When we see our efforts being genuinely and spontaneously rewarded, well, plan to get fat on that!

Some people sadly find it extremely difficult to get out of themselves, their neurotic, self-centered drives,

> and be giving. These people stay frustrated and bitter and they cause a lot of pain.

I had such a caller. This woman called to tell me that her forty-something-year-old husband is under a lot of stress because his father is going on trial for his sexual abuse of him when he was a boy. I thought she was going to ask me about how she could help him; WRONG! She called because she was miffed that he wasn't being sexual and affectionate with her, they weren't "connecting" and she needed that to feel loved. When I tried to point out that this was not the time for "getting," she tried to bury me in sad stories about her childhood and how much she needed, needed, needed . . . well, you get it.

DrL: Well, there are times in our lives that we can't indulge ourselves in our own pain because WE ARE NEEDED. It is a blessing to be needed and a special kind of obligation that saves us from our own inner demons and turns us into a force for benevolence.

The attitude I am trying to convey to you is that your needs don't matter right now. Just be sensitive and not demanding. Touch his face, shoulder, and arms with understanding affection. Listen without comment. Take walks. Connecting to you seems to mean that he does something to you. How 'bout you connect to him by becoming his support.

Well, that very night I got an e-mail from her expressing her disappointment in my not helping her and a long dissertation about her ugly childhood.

I couldn't get her to see, understand, and accept that sometimes we just put ourselves in a pocket in order to give our beloved air to breathe.

Barbara, another listener, wrote me the next day:

> *"Prior to becoming a Dr. Laura listener a few years ago, I sounded just like that caller. My husband was rarely interested in sex and never instigated physical contact, and like the caller's husband he'd been sexually abused as a child.*
>
> *"I knew this entering into our marriage, yet I still pouted and moped and behaved passive-aggressively because I wasn't getting what I wanted. Also, like the caller, I felt I had ISSUES with sex because I wanted to be found attractive and validated and inundated with intimacy . . . wah . . . wah . . . wah! After listing to your program and evaluating my own behaviors, I was able to realize what a selfish baby I had been. I expected my husband to put aside all those feelings of pain and hurt which are unimaginable just because I didn't feel 'pretty.'*
>
> *"Needless to say, I gave myself a swift kick in the pants (not easy to do, I might add) and started to love my husband and love my family more than I love my ISSUES.*
>
> *"In return for this, I've been rewarded with a generous, forgiving, supportive husband. I've discovered the closeness of back rubs and cuddling and welcome-home hugs. Because my husband loves me, he has sex more often than he'd like, and because I love him, I have sex less often than I'd like—and that's okay. I wouldn't give the rest of it up for all the gigolos in Europe!*
>
> *"Thanks for helping me enjoy what I have. With my new outlook I won't waste any more of our years together."*

"Enjoy what I have." That concept is the basis of the Tenth Commandment against coveting. When we envy others for what they have, when we spend time on regrets and disappointments for what we don't have, we ensure a lack of pleasure in life. Postponing happiness until "all your ducks are in order" means never because life is not that clean, fair, or predictable. It isn't what happens to you that defines your life, it is what you do with it that does.

And if what you do with the "slings and arrows of outrageous fortune" is to pout or lash out, happiness will elude you. Leslie, a listener, wrote in response to a call she heard on my program in which a couple were fighting over the fact that the wife puttied in some holes in the wall when the husband said he would do it but didn't get to it. Leslie wrote that early in her marriage she was just like that. She and her husband would argue at the drop of a hat.

> *"In retrospect, it was never the subject, just the ability to get mad at each other over something. One day I talked to my mom about it. She and my dad had a marriage of 45 years and going strong. She said, 'Let the little things go. Let it roll off you and be grateful for your love and friendship.'*
>
> *"It seemed like such simple advice. I wasn't very good at first, but then I started realizing that I wasn't being grateful for our marriage—I was using it as a punching bag to get out a lot of stress from work, commuting, and taking care of children."*

It was insightful of Leslie to realize she was "kicking the dog," in other words, using the blessing of the intimacy and its promised safety to unleash her frustrations; frustrations she wouldn't dare take out on anyone but her dear husband for fear of being judged and dumped.

We all have those moments of "losing it," because that too is a part of real life. However if this behavior is continuous and not overwhelmed by feelings and actions of gratitude, a disaster called divorce or affair may likely result.

Pounding on your spouse because of inner frustrations does seem to be a familiar behavior, doesn't it? Annie called my program whining and complaining about how her husband doesn't realize and appreciate *how much she gave up and sacrificed*.

Annie: I got pregnant at eighteen and two years later is when I married the baby's father and now we have a two-year-old. The problem is that we've been arguing a lot lately. It's just that I stay at home and because I was so young when I had our first son sometimes I don't think my husband realizes how much I gave up and how much I sacrificed.

DrL: Didn't he sacrifice also? I don't know that you realize how much he gave up and sacrificed to be sole support of four people. Maybe he's at work thinking, "She doesn't appreciate all I'm doing for the whole family!"

When one or both in a marriage starts thinking like that I know the marriage is in serious trouble. Because then it isn't about a team with different positions on that team with each taking responsibility for their own position and appreciating the other's work.

And whatever you sacrificed is not his responsibility—it's yours! You had a choice: "Let's see, I'll be a brain surgeon or I'll have unprotected sex with my boyfriend. Surgeon, out-of-wedlock sex, surgeon, out-of-wedlock sex . . ." And you picked sex! You did that—you weren't raped, right? Marriage is where you love and adore someone; you sacrifice for them, and you do everything you can to make them happy.

Annie then went immediately into a litany of the "small stuff" like "he doesn't pick up his plate from the table and he relaxes with computer poker a while after work." I reminded her that her job is the home, his job is the support. Frankly—and I know this gets people worked up—women need to stop denigrating their own roles as homemakers. When a woman cleans up the dinner dishes, it is not slavery, it is being responsible and good at "her obligations." I often ask women who complain about their men not doing the laundry if they drop everything and rush to their husband's work during the day to do the filing or take the meetings. Of course they say, "No." "Then," I follow up, "why do you expect him to do your work?"

Husbands generally do the lawns, fix the cars, and work on the heavy jobs in the home. This argument that a husband should be doing his own dishes emanates from a mentality that disrespects domesticity. No one, husband included, should disrespect domesticity. Without a home running smoothly, lives within it don't run smoothly.

And as far as his doing computer poker, everyone needs brain candy time. Annie's husband's brain candy time would probably be lessened by his being greeted with more loving enthusiasm when he comes home.

Jenny, another listener, wrote that she learned the value of plain everyday loving seduction "after reading *The Proper Care and Feeding of Husbands.*" Her complaint was that she cried and begged for him to be like he was when they were dating—to woo and court her. He would always say that he'd try to do better but Mother's Day was just a store-bought card. She wrote him a three-page letter once again bemoaning her sad state. Included in this letter was her admission that she felt in competition with their three-and-a-half-year-old daughter. When on a recent business trip he mailed his daughter a toy of a father and daughter and sent

Jenny a card. When they went out to dinner, he suggested purchasing some little gift for their oldest daughter.

> *"From this suggestion of his I knew that my husband was capable of thinking of others and doing things to demonstrate his love. While reading your book, it dawned on me. Sarah has been demonstrating for me what I, as a wife, needed to be doing. The moment he walks in the door after work, she runs to him yelling, 'Daddy!!' and nothing else matters to her but that he is home.*
>
> *"I on the other hand, am too busy getting dinner ready and am irritated that he would actually expect me to drop what I am doing to give him a king's welcome. I shed many tears thinking about this, knowing it was not too late to start."*

She made some simple rules for herself:

1. *Stop whatever it is that I am doing and greet him.*
2. *Do my laundry, dishes, etc., during the day, and put everything away. It doesn't have to be perfect, like I want it to be—he just wants a comfy home to come to with a loving wife and children.*
3. *Just love and appreciate him without nagging and criticisms for the way the baby's diaper is on, or that he picked out the wrong pajamas.*

Evidently this worked very well. Let's hear it for priming the pump. If you want water out of a pump, you have to prime it *with* water to make it work!

Sometimes in addition to priming, the pump needs a smack aside the spout! Amy's husband got such a smack while listening to my radio program. Amy generally comes home from work and hops into the shower to calm down and relax and think about her day. She often asked him to join her, but his typical response was "But I already took a shower this morning." Perhaps he didn't fully understand the invitation or he's the type who tends to be a bit too pragmatic and thought only of hygiene.

> *"Anyways, when I came home yesterday from work, I gave him a kiss and went to take my shower when he stopped me and said, 'Can I take a shower with you . . . and would you like a glass of wine?' My eyes gleamed and then he told me about what he heard on your show, about how taking a shower together creates a good moment to talk about the day and relax TOGETHER. It was wonderful . . . and I will assume you can guess what happened next! ☺"*

I work very hard trying to give people what they deeply want, and that is to be happy. The main reason feelings of happiness are so elusive to many is that they don't really know what it is, and usually try to go about it backward. So of course when a husband or wife isn't happy the typical assumption is that it's *because* of some (imagined or exaggerated) fault of their spouse; this justifies leaving because, after all, isn't everybody entitled to be happy? But at what expense?

I had a caller, Michelle, who called to get validation for dumping her husband of three years. One hitch though—she's just discovered she's pregnant.

Michelle: I'm thirty-six. The pregnancy actually took place completely by surprise. Due to some reasons I wasn't quite happy with the marriage and I was thinking about leaving.

DrL: Well, you've got to rethink that because you now have a child who dearly needs a family structure with mom and dad. What's so bad in your marriage that you gave a though to leaving . . . considering it's been good enough to have repeated unprotected sex and create new life.

Michelle: Right (laughs). I guess two things. One is that my husband is much older than I am.

DrL: You already knew that one when you married.

Michelle: From the financial perspective I have concerns because he's probably into getting retirement pretty soon.

DrL: Well then you might have to live modestly, but at least your child will live in a home with a mom and a dad modestly. Those are not reasons to leave and those are not reasons to destroy a child's home.

Michelle: (laughing) I guess so (pause). Yeah, um, I guess, um, another thing is I'd like to see if you have any insights into what's the best thing I can do to make the most out of the pregnancy and being happy and enjoy the whole process.

DrL: It's your moral obligation to be happy.

Michelle: Okay.

DrL: Don't you think that's everybody's moral obligation? To work as hard as they can to be happy? Or do you think everybody should be free to walk around mopey and ticked off, depressed and negative? What kind of families, communities, and societies would we have if people allowed themselves the privilege of sinking into every negative emotion they have rather than believing that they have a moral obligation to be their best selves?

I don't care if you wanted a daddy so you married an old dude. You married him and you made a kid with him. I don't care if you're not going to live in the lap of luxury because the most important thing to the child is not how much money you have, it's how loving the home is. You're bringing forth new life into the world and you're having an opportunity to live for somebody besides yourself. One of the positive reasons to have children is to learn not to be selfish anymore.

I was frankly pretty sure that I didn't reach her at all. A number of folks responded with e-mails, having identified with that caller's issue. JoAnne wrote:

"The caller sounded shocked to hear that she had a moral obligation to be happy. I currently suffer from depression and several doctors want to put me on medication. Listening to your program, having a wonderful husband and good friends has given me the strength to do it on my own.

"My prescription to myself is to get more exercise and watch what I eat. I have also started volunteering for special needs kids. I do not deny that there are days where I just want to give up—but by stepping outside of myself and doing for others, it has helped me. Not only have I been happier, but my husband has been happier. He comes with me when I exercise and cheers me on! What a wonderful MAN!

"I hope more people will take more responsibility with their attitude and do as you suggest: exercise, eat right, volunteer, and always show respect and love for those around you."

For way too many married people, their spouse is to be the antidote for all their present and past emotional aches and pains, disappointments, fears, confusions, and rage. There are at least two categories of this misplaced responsibility: one is taking past frustrations out on one's spouse as a safer and present target, the second is to try to have a second chance at a childhood by re-creating in actuality and in your mind the same circumstances as your childhood; in this way you hope to redo and then rewrite your past—and then be healed, or get revenge, or have it work out in your favor, and so forth.

Mary was raped when she was a virgin at twenty years of age. Her father did not let her prosecute the rapist. Here she is a married adult woman who "doesn't have a healthy attitude toward sex" even after seventeen years of marriage. In the first of two calls I had with Mary, I told her that she was actually quite angry with her dad for not letting her get justice.

Mary: And that really upset me because I've always thought very highly of my father. I've always felt he was the only one in my family that loved me—and to hear something like that . . . and to acknowledge the truth of that . . . it hurts.

DrL: Of course it does. That was what we call denial. You didn't have many supportive, loving family members in your life so you didn't want to lose your dad; which you would have had to do if you looked at the truth of the matter.

Mary: Well, you told me that I should think about justice, justifiable anger, justice with the wrong man and then also about me not being able to enjoy, as you said, my God-given sensuality. And then also this past weekend I allowed myself to enjoy sex with my husband for the first time. It was very pleasant. However I just feel angry still. Like you said I would. I still feel angry.

DrL: I want you to continue to feel anger where anger is due; but it isn't due to your husband and it isn't due to your sex life. You can stay angry for the rest of your life, it's okay—it is valid anger. Picture having a coat with two pockets. You need to have anger in one pocket—anger toward your dad not permitting justice—and your marriage and sensuality in another pocket. Right now you have them commingled. I'm just asking you to separate them out.

You are not getting justice with respect to the guy who raped you or your dad who wanted to keep it quiet. You're certainly not getting justice by spending the rest of your life not enjoying your sensuality. You're not getting justice by punishing your husband for the rapist and your dad!

So since you're failing at your task of getting justice by denying yourself pleasure with your husband and by whitewashing good ole dad, it all seems like that's something you ought to stop doing.

You'll never get justice for what happened. You have to accept that. There will never be justice. So keep the anger in your left pocket, and put your sensuality and your love for your husband in your right pocket. It's going to be a while before your attitude switches over. Keep your rage if you wish, but keep it in the left pocket . . . and don't visit it often.

What we can learn from Mary's situation is that the past has tentacles that squeeze the life out of today when we have *unresolved* passionate hurts and disappointments. One of the toughest things to do is look at the past *objectively* when there are simply truths we don't want to know. In Mary's case, the truths were that it was too late to get justice for the rape, and that her father didn't want to be embarrassed and therefore was not her protector. Since she hid herself from these truths, the tentacles followed her into her marriage. Her "resolution" to these problems was to punish her husband for the sins of her father and rapist. What she gained by slicing those tentacles was the freedom to be a woman in love *in spite* of losing the fantasies of a perfect father and justice.

Probably the primary childhood issue, whether or not there was abuse or outright negligence, is the feeling of not having been important to your parents, and not getting the attention and tender loving care all children crave and require. The end result of all this loss is sometimes an overfocus on being sad. What does "sad" create? It creates lots of attention and caretaking coming *in* with minimal responsibility going *out* to others. This is like being the squeaky wheel or the noisy kid who gets all the attention.

Obviously this kind of behavior from a spouse is draining to the marriage and the family. Recently a caller talked about how she could not stop bad memories from her childhood from filling her every minute and she was just wrecking her life. By the end of the call, I made it clear to her that she was not letting go of the bad memories because being *in pain* all the time gave her control over her family; she forced them into showing her attention, taking care of her, and, like any child, she was not responsible for giving.

The result of this call was a virtual avalanche of e-mail and faxes as so many people recognized themselves in the caller, or recognized themselves as the victim of such a spouse.

Rachel, a listener, wrote:

"You had a call on Monday that changed my life. I have tears in my eyes as I write this—tears of relief at finally understanding a certain behavior and tears of relief because now I know how to fix it.

"I was born into a chaotic household where the adults looked to the children to have their needs met (emotional and otherwise) and burdened the children with adult matters (money woes, in-law problems, job stress).

"I was the oldest girl and was assigned the mommy/caretaking role from a very young age. I never in my life felt like someone cared for me the way a parent should care for a child.

"Your caller got anxious and worried about her life, and then allowed her anxiety to debilitate and paralyze her so that she felt unable to do something as simple as housework or cook dinner, much less give her children and husband some emotional support, help with homework, or spare a kind word for them at the end of the day.

"She never had anyone really take care of her as a child either, and whenever she got anxious, she shut down so that someone else (her husband) would be forced to take over her responsibilities.

"Hearing you tell her that this was why she acted as she did changed my life. For the first time I have an inkling of what drives my anxiety. I use anxiety as a time machine to try and go back to the past, turn into a child, and have someone else take care of me and my problems! WOW. WOW.

"The long-term challenge for me will be to reset my thinking so that when I feel that old worry and anxiety stirring up in me, I don't take it as a signal to shut down and see if I can get my husband to parent me. Now when I feel worry and anxiety,

that will be a signal to take a positive ADULT action: kiss and hug someone I love, clip some coupons, take a walk, clean out a closet—do something productive that HELPS my life in some small way."

How incredible that Rachel and so many other listeners were willing to embrace such a truth without shame, defensiveness, and denial. To realize and own that you're wasting precious adult time, when you could finally enjoy loving and being loved, needing and being needed, focusing only on the getting because you didn't get enough when you were a child is of course sad—but truth sets you free, if you embrace it.

If you don't, then this letter will be about you! Greg, a listener, also responded to that call:

"I was listening to your radio show recently and heard the caller who kept dwelling on her past in order to get attention and care from her husband. I recently ended a relationship with a woman who also had a troubled past. For the first thirteen years of her life she had a father who was a drug dealer and a mother who abused her. Eventually she ended up in foster care until she was eighteen.

"Throughout our relationship whatever I did for her was never enough. I was constantly accused of being selfish and uncaring. For the first year I believed these accusations and continually tried harder to please her, comfort her, and make her happy.

"I then began listening to your show and began to recognize what was really going on. I was trying to rescue a damsel in distress—only to end up with a distressed damsel! The more I gave, the more she wanted and the worse the manipulations, such as crying and putting me down, became.

"I continually hoped that one day she would realize what she was doing and recognize that I really do care about her. That never happened."

Fortunately many callers and listeners get it, embrace it, and change. Interestingly, some spouses don't turn to their spouse for the parent replacement job. Sometimes they go straight elsewhere.

Steve called ostensibly about him not living up to his full potential because he did "bad things" to protect his brother from his mother's wrath. Rumor had it that Steve's brother may have been the product of some affair of his mother's.

DrL: So your mother may have had a child by some other guy, your father stayed, but then she was unkind to the child.

Steve: Yeah, kind of punishing him for some problems. At the time, of course, growing up and even as teenagers, we had no idea why one of us might be treated bad and the other one not.

DrL: What can I help you with today?

Steve: Well, as kids, he was treated badly and I think I've kind of slipped into a pattern of being a huge trial to my parents to try to get some of the negative off of him and focused on me maybe.

DrL: So you're thinking that you sacrificed some well-being in order to protect him?

Steve: Yeah, I did just about everything wrong I could think of.

I then asked Steve to close his eyes and revisit his childhood without his brother in the picture at all. I directed him to give me some other reason he might want to stick it to his mother by driving her nutsy with bad things he'd done. Steve's response was an incredibly heavy sigh, after which he described her as very emotionally unavailable and distant. His teachers all the way through school had informed Steve's parents that he was gifted.

DrL: So you were mad at her and didn't fulfill your potential. Is that what you're saying? Keep your eyes closed . . .

Steve: Yeah. I mean she expected everything . . .

DrL: How did your brother benefit?

Steve: In the long run, a lot; he's been hugely successful because she gave him nothing and so he bent over backward to prove that he could do what she said he couldn't.

DrL: Perhaps some of your actions were intended to protect your brother by taking the heat off him—but I think it's more that since your mother's love seemed so conditional you didn't give her the conditions!

Steve: That makes sense.

DrL: How does that relate to what you're doing today? Do you love your children? Do they know it? Do you love your wife? Does she know it?

Steve (holding back tears): It's just hard to be close.

I told Steve that it was sad that he was just like his mother. I asked him to tell me about the future when his kids were going to call and tell me how they're struggling with life because their dad was so cold and distant. Interestingly, he offered up immediately that it would be one over the other who would make that call.

DrL: How does your boy, Ben, make you feel better about yourself? In one sentence, "He makes me feel better about myself because he———"

Steve: Because he's bubbly and always happy no matter what I do. He's always excited when I come home.

DrL: So—you've made him your mother!!

Steve: I guess I look to him for emotional support.

DrL: You don't get close to your wife or kids, and you have one kid living to please you and make you feel good. Meanwhile, you give nothing to them. Isn't it amazing that the thing you wanted the most from your mother—

Steve: Is the thing I'm withholding from everyone else.

DrL: And you won't let yourself have. That which you are squeezing from your boy, you need to get from your woman. Your woman's got to be the one human being on the face of the earth you feel safe being vulnerable with.

He went on to describe being afraid to go to his wife for loving, attentive affection because, like his mother, she won't give it. I told him that he's really going to have to force himself to be Steve and not Stevie, a child.

"No man is going to enjoy life when he's still scrambling after his mommy or protecting himself from his mommy. You got starved by your mommy for half your life and the other half of your life you're planning to starve yourself?"

At this point I gave him his assignment before making an appointment to talk with him some two weeks later. I told him to go home, walk over to his wife, lift her off the ground, swing her around, give her a big huggy smooch, and then later when the kids are in bed to say to her, "Can I put my head in your lap and can you just pet my head because I need peace and joy?" The first part of the assignment was to tap into the Steve part; the second part was to then receive the loving support of a wife while still being a man.

Two weeks later Steve called back and told me that he did the assignment and it was fabulous.

DrL: Did you give her a big, slurpy kiss on the face?

Steve: Oh yeah—and then later in the evening she was more than willing to sit there and give me that other kind of attention. It was great and it changed my attitude about my relationship and it's really, really improved things. I'm not so concerned that she's going to reject me somehow and not give me what I didn't get when I was kid so I'm more focused on accepting what she can give me now and not accepting less than that.

DrL: Do you realize you went from zero to one hundred?

Steve: In one day pretty much. Because it's been good and much better with her that I'm sharing more and

> being more emotional and close with both of my kids and everything has been good.

You may sniff your nose and say that people can't change that much that fast—but you'd be wrong because a shift in attitude that opens you up to letting your husband/wife in close and personal lets the love through. When people feel loved and appreciated, the bad old stuff just doesn't seem that important. Steve, and so many men and women, are stuck because they fear that *if* they're vulnerable to their spouses, the results will be negative and there will be no hope ever for happiness. That's a risk you have to be willing to take—and most of you will have a success as warm as Steve's. Keeping on track gets easier and easier.

Jeff and Wendy called in to my program because he and Wendy had gotten into a dispute, after which she called him on the cell phone screaming that he was mean to her. Jeff said he was calling for an opinion about whether or not he's mean or if it is a communication problem.

I love that term "communication problem." Whenever I ask people to clarify that . . . they can't. I don't think that many marriages are stuck on communication problems, whatever they are. I think that most marriages are stuck on people needing or hurting so much (from their childhoods, primarily) that they forget to or resist giving love. Jeff and Wendy were no exception to that rule.

You may be interested in knowing that I was inundated with critical e-mails for two weeks after my two calls with Steve and Wendy. Everybody—save one—said I was totally wrong.

What happened was that I asked Wendy to describe one or two situations where Jeff was clearly mean. She talked about his very angry expressions, very loud voice, angry tone, and angry delivery. I wondered why expressing anger had to look friendly? She said that he would get angry too quickly at little things and that this had gotten worse over the years.

I then went to Jeff and asked him why his fuse was so short. He said that he's not getting respect from Wendy—and that this was getting worse over the years.

Chick or egg?

I asked Jeff for two examples of Wendy's disrespect. The first was when Wendy asked him to put air in the van's tires. He went and did that and after coming back, Wendy went out to look at the tires and saw that there was a screw in the tire and asked him if he'd checked for the screw and he replied that he hadn't checked the tires—he just put air in them and came home. He then goes to put the spare on and she tells him to forget it and take it to the gas station for repairs because she doesn't believe he's going to do it right. Jeff blows up.

Second example: Jeff teaches sixth grade math and science. Their son took his little volcano experiment to school and needed to bring the ingredients for it, baking soda and vinegar. Even though he himself had gone out the day before to get fresh baking soda, he grabbed the old baking soda and took it to school with his son and the volcano. Wendy was mad because he took the old baking soda. Jeff blows up.

I had Wendy hang up so that I could talk to Jeff alone. I told Jeff, in the nicest way possible, that he's just not paying attention to things that actually most guys pay a lot of attention to. I described Wendy's behaviors as a reaction to his not paying attention and not a display of disrespect. I gave him the assignment to call me back the next day without Wendy and to tell me why he chose not to pay attention and aggravate her on purpose.

The sky opened up with men e-mailing me all afternoon

and all night saying Wendy was a bitch, Jeff was within his rights to be angry, and that I was dead wrong.

When Jeff called the next day, he still fought me about following through on his assignment, which was to "think about why you *chose* to irritate her." His comeback was a repeat of yesterday's, "I can accept constructive criticism, if it is in fact constructive, and if there's something that I'm doing wrong. I know you said my examples from yesterday were poor examples."

DrL: No, they were very good examples—not of Wendy being disrespectful—but of the passive-aggressive behavior that exists when a person feels tremendous hostility but has difficulty being up front about it. She called you mean; I don't think you're mean at all. But it was interesting that you gave two very good passive-aggressive examples: taking the wrong baking soda when you knew better and not bothering to check a deflating tire for a nail.

I then asked him to take me back to when he was eight (yes, I just pulled that one out of a hat).

DrL: Who's in the house, and what are they doing?

Jeff: Nobody is in the house and I'm not at the house either. I'm at a babysitter. A very strict lady who made us play board games. We were eight kids stuck in a fifteen-by-fifteen room.

DrL: I see, so that was how she controlled a large number of children; you played board games and stayed put. This is tougher on boys than on girls.

From there Jeff, with much prodding from me, painted a picture of parents not only uninvolved with his interests, but actually negative about the things he liked. He had gotten into wrestling and his parents didn't like that because of the violence . . . the aggression. Financially they were supportive, but not emotionally.

Basically the picture I got from our lengthy discussion was that women were a big disappointment to him in particular. First, a mother who was uninvolved and freaked out about aggression in sports, and the control of a strict babysitter who kept him caged up. I suggested to Jeff that he was an angry man; anger is the final by-product of hurt. And since aggression was squelched, his hurt/anger came out as passive-aggressive. His pattern of dealing with Wendy reflects his reaction to his early upbringing. If Wendy is not lovingly supportive of something, doesn't make him feel good about himself, or seems to control him, he strikes back with passive-aggressive behaviors. It is when he is "called" on this behavior that he loses it more directly.

So-called communication problems are generally that we're not talking about the current moment; the current moment is just a trigger for a memory. And Jeff's memory, as I told his wife, Wendy, the next day, is filled with not being supported, being abandoned, being controlled in terms of his natural male-child energy and aggression, instead of hearing a lot of hoorays and "You're terrific—we think you're great," and "We love you," and "We're here."

Wendy responded with, "And she continues to do that to this day."

I left Jeff with a deeper understanding that he was overreacting to perceived slights from Wendy because he was already primed to believe that she was "just another controlling, emotionally uninvolved, and nonsupportive woman." Interestingly, when I posed that to him, he responded by telling me how wonderful she was. And, from my discussions with her, she was indeed wonderful and loving. I suggested to Jeff that he behave toward Wendy as though he actually believed that instead of trying to punish her. I suggested to Wendy that she be aware of opportunities to support his ego by compliments and by giving him the respect of expecting him to do the right thing—without motherly follow-through.

It is not an unusual concept to imagine that a man might be unpleasant with his wife because he had problems with a mom; it is a little less obvious to imagine he wouldn't have sex with his wife because he had problems with a father.

Kenny and Lynn, married four years (her third, his first) called because Lynn felt very rejected sexually. She expressed loving him because he was a good and honest man for whom she has great admiration and respect. Kenny described himself as never feeling he had the competence that he could take care of a wife and children and give them the life they deserved.

DrL: What do you think drove you to that conclusion about yourself?

Kenny: From my father and my mother. My father was an alcoholic and terrorized our house. I was always just a coward in the corner and had fear of him and everything. My mother didn't protect me.

DrL: When did you stop having fear?

Kenny: I still have fear. I just deal with it a lot better now.

After interviewing Lynn a bit more, I learned that they didn't have sexual intimacy before marriage either.

DrL: Kenny, you didn't marry to have a man-woman relationship. You really married to not be alone and have some womanly-motherly companionship. Isn't that right? Lynn married to have a husband and you married to have a mom.

Kenny (wistfully): A mom I never had. Well, what do we do now?

DrL: I guess you're at a crossroads. Here you are almost half a century old and the rest of your life is going to be a shorter amount of time than what you've had up till now. So, Kenny, you need to decide whether you're going to continue being the damaged little boy or a man with his own woman. You have a decision to make, sir. Do you want to be a man for the rest of your life or do you want to continue being the hungry little boy?

Kenny: I want to be a man.

DrL: Then say in a loud, firm, grown-man voice—instead of that little boy whisper—"I can be a MAN!"

Kenny: I CAN BE A MAN!

DrL: Right! Your parents robbed you of a childhood. Don't let how they were rob you of your manhood.

I asked them to call back in one week. When they did, the transformation was amazing for both of them.

Kenny: Last week you helped me learn that I was a child of an abusive drunk and that I was robbed of a normal childhood. I continued to rob myself of a normal adulthood. It's true. I believe within myself there's been a shy, scared little boy for a long time. Your assignment was for me to think about what it means to be a married man. This was difficult for me. The first thing that came to mind is that I can't live within myself as a married man because there's someone who depends on me to give of myself. Even though I feel the fear and self-doubt, I can't live within myself and be a married man. I have to intellectually or somehow come out of that and understand that even through the fear I have to act otherwise.

You pointed out some little things, that I spoke like a child, for example. So I've been trying to speak more clearly and firmly and let her know that I'm a confident man and that she's safe with me as her man. That's one thing. I've been trying to show her that I love her and that she is the only woman for me; that I adore her. I'm trying to come out of myself a little at a time. It's really hard to do.

Lynn opened up to explain her feelings too.

Lynn: My reaction to all of this since yesterday is a lot of hurt. I know that sounds bad, but I had never considered that he had married me for a mother. Although it explained a lot of our past before and during marriage because he is always telling me what a wonderful mother I am [she has four adult children from one of her marriages]. I love to be told I'm a good mother, but I'd rather be told that I'm a beautiful woman by Kenny.

Lynn wrote to me several days after our second conversation:

"I saw a tremendous change in him throughout the week you gave him to think about what it means to be a married man and I continue to see great changes. I have no doubt anymore that he is MY MAN as I am HIS WOMAN. I would like to thank you from the very depths of my soul for your help and guidance in Kenny's life as well as my own. One man and his woman—my dream as well as his—came true.

This sad scenario, marrying for a parent and not a spouse, is not unusual, but is usually the last thing either imagines. Jan, a listener, wrote:

"Your comments to the woman who wanted her husband to be her daddy haunted me. When you asked her to say something great about her husband, and she said only that he was incredibly supportive, you interpreted that to mean that she was looking only to be taken care of and that she wasn't treating her husband like HER MAN. Wow, did that ever hit home.

"I never realized that I was doing that to my husband, but after hearing your comments, I began to list in my mind all of the ways that I try to make my husband my dad instead of my man.

"This insight led me further down that road, and I realized that if I wanted him to parent me, then I must want to stay a little girl. Then I began to think of all the ways I act like a girl instead of a grown woman. In spite of all my degrees, children, and 23-year marriage, I feel like a scared little girl inside—always fearing that someday someone will find me out for the imposter that I am. I don't take care of myself physically like I

should, my house is disorganized, I feel out of control 99% of the time—like I could fall apart any minute from the weight of acting like an adult.

"I decided that whenever I want to act like that little girl and feel entitled, fearful, stubborn, or demanding, I am going to choose to act like a mature woman instead. What that is exactly, I don't always know—but I'm going to try to find out."

It is not always that being "starved" emotionally as a child results in demanding good parenting from a spouse. Sometimes it means that the hungry adult-child starves out their spouse because their unfamiliarity and discomfort with affection scares them. They've spent all their lives surviving without it—opening up to affection becomes a very frightening risk.

I told one such caller, Maria, to "sit down with your husband, hold his hand, look straight into his eyes and say, 'You are a wonderful and loving man and I'm scared of love because I never had it. Sometimes I push it away only because I'm scared of it and I'm not comfortable. So please understand that I'm not rejecting you—I love you and you're wonderful. I want to kiss you, I want to hug you, and I want to feel comfortable about it.' "

I went on to give her an assignment I described as one that would make her think I'm nuts or hate me altogether. "Maria, for one month I have an assignment for you. For one month, every day, you hug him, you kiss him, and you have sex. Every day. But *you* do it. You're in control. You're going to like this after a while. But the first week or so you're going to hate me . . . then you'll discover something—and when you discover it, call me back."

Maria called back a month later sounding, frankly, like a different woman. She admitted that I was right, she hated me for two weeks. After two weeks, she actually began looking forward to the affection and sex. She loved feeling good about him, about sex, about hugging, and about feeling close. She sounded giggly, strong, and happy.

What she discovered is that she actually had a choice to live as though today were only an extension of yesterday, or its own promise and opportunity. She discovered that talking about something is not as powerful as living it to change one's perspective. She discovered that she could be happy if she put in the determined effort. She discovered that happiness is always possible.

It's your turn to discover you no longer have to be the enemy of your current opportunity to be happy and make someone else happy.

Chapter 3

The Good, the Bad, and the Ugly

I don't know how many times I've tried to explain to callers that marriage is not advanced dating. Somebody fun to date is not necessarily someone you will be able to count on when the "going gets tough." An all too familiar caller problem has been that they partied well while dating, but after having a child, bills, and mundane, repetitive responsibilities, being married to someone who continues to party is . . . well . . . no party at all. Another typical caller complaint is that their spouse has an unacceptable point of view or behavior which they accepted while dating but is now too huge to suffer any longer.

Somehow many folks have a notion about marriage that it will automatically change everything to the positive and "their way." Disappointments occur when expectations don't meet reality; and the reality is that dating, even shacking up, are nothing like marriage at all. In "shacking up," two ambivalent people stay "two," while in marriage, two committed people become "one." This makes shacking up a bad warm-up for marriage, as statistics of higher breakup rates, domestic violence, affairs, and emotional problems demonstrate.

The question does linger in people's minds these days as to whether or not marriage truly has anything to offer them that being single or shacking up doesn't already satisfy. In one of my many surveys in preparation for this book, I asked listeners (male and female separately) a number of questions in order to answer that question.

MARRIAGE

1. What was your biggest surprise to learn about marriage?
2. In what way(s) has marriage made you a better person?
3. What are the benefits of being married vs. single?

Below are *typical* answers from women:

1. What was your biggest surprise to learn about marriage?

- "Having to let go of the notion that everything can be compromised—sometimes on an issue either me or my husband will not get their own way, and I've learned that's okay because we can't be satisfied all of the time."
- "That I have this immense power to either ruin my husband's and children's lives, or enrich them. If I decide to disrespect my husband, then my children will disrespect their father as well. My mood, and to what degree I allow that mood to dictate my behavior, has a direct result on everyone else's mood, and therefore, their daily lives. Amazing! And scary! And so very humbling."

- "After I said my vows on my wedding day I felt even more committed and bound to my husband, even though we had dated monogamously and felt committed for a long courtship."
- "That marriage didn't solve all of my problems and it didn't make me feel complete. What a letdown."
- "Because my parents were divorced, the biggest surprise I had was how harmonious marriage could be. I expected that fighting and acrimony were just part of marriage . . . but that's not so!"
- "That I couldn't just think about 'me' anymore; there was another human being to consider in every single decision. Sounds obvious, but it's not!"
- "That there is always more learning and maturing to do."
- "I never really knew how much work (bills, meals, cleaning, kids, family stuff, emotions, problems to solve) it took to have a happy, well-working marriage. It takes responsibility and accountability." "It takes more than love to get through this life together." "That marriage is a business partnership as much as it is a romance. You have to manage your life together—your money, children, home, work, relatives, etc."
- "I was most surprised to learn how dull and exciting marriage actually is. We have basically been doing the same thing every day for the past twenty-one years—but each day still seems exciting while we're living it . . . marriage has a way of making life more fun, in an ordinary way."
- "That you could love someone so strongly one minute and want to kill them the next minute." "That people are like coins; there are two sides to a coin and you cannot

separate them. The side of the coin you love, is linked to a side you do not love and can drive you crazy."

- "I was surprised to vividly experience the difference between men and women. My husband is a wonderful man, but he is not concerned about housekeeping or making social plans. I think to make marriage work, men and women need to respect their gender differences and personality differences."
- "How amazing it is to *belong* to somebody."
- "Was learning that the 'in love' feelings fade. But an even bigger surprise was finding out that if you stay faithful, honor your commitment, and keep doing the right thing, those feelings are replaced with something far deeper and precious than the dating feelings ever could be."

The single most common response had to do with every day not being full of butterflies and passionate kisses. This means that an obvious motivation to be giving, patient, and loyal, those lovey-dovey feelings, come and go. This means that it takes work to stay committed.

Jake, a recent caller, has been married only four years, and has two children, three and one. He told me that about a year ago their "closeness was unraveling." He began an affair some nine months ago, which ended recently because the "honey" was angry about him not spending enough time with her. (Sidebar: I couldn't stop laughing when he said this because it seems odd that a woman who wants a lot of "intimacy" would pick a man with a wife and two very small children!) I resisted giving him hell about his affair because he already presented himself as truly remorseful; additionally, with the time I have available for a call, I wanted to focus more on keeping this family together.

I asked him what "unraveling" meant and he responded that daily life just got repetitive and boring and this affair put excitement into his life again. I told him that when one spouse is bor*ed* it is usually because they are bor*ing*. Expecting some automatic magic to transform you from the tired and stressed human being you are at the end of a workday (homemaking or employee status) into a happy and carefree individual is going to result in disappointment and resentment.

Consider coming together with your spouse at the end of the day as an opportunity to drink from a well. The water doesn't come up out of the well by its own force; *you* actually have *to do* something active to get the water to soothe your parched lips. The same goes for psyches. When at the end of the day you yearn for some relief from the day, prepare your mind and heart the same way you'd prepare for anything else:

- Start thinking positively about it (think *good* thoughts about your spouse and warm thoughts about the family together at day's end).

- Get ready in your mind something you're going to say to be fresh water to your spouse's parched being.

- Package up your problems and day's annoyances and put them on the floor in the back of your basement closet; don't compete with each other's day by having the worst story of the day's problems.

- Be affectionate in small ways; a touch, a kiss on the cheek, an offering of a flower (and this all goes *two* ways), a suggestion that the other relax while you do something nice for them like get an ice tea, etc.

- Find something special about that day to compliment him/her on.
- Invite your spouse to have an opinion on something you're dealing with . . . and *do not* criticize their response—instead, be gracious and grateful.
- Ask him/her something specific concerning something you know they had to deal with today . . . and look interested even if you're not!

The key is to give, give, and give some more. Coming out of me, me, me is the sure way to reduce your own tension and to get the best from your spouse; their appreciation will turn into loving, considerate behavior toward you, and the well will gush and satisfy you more than any nagging or demanding could ever.

When you are planning for making someone else happy, and when you are using your beloved's mere existence to enrich you, you can *never* be bored!

2. In what way(s) has marriage made you a better person?

- "By showing me that putting someone else's needs *before* my own is the true definition of happiness."
- "More honest, because I have someone who holds me accountable; more responsible, because my actions affect him; more relaxed because I know I have someone who cares; more confident, because I know he loves me as I am—and that alone gives me strength."
- "Being with him makes me want to be a better person."
- "I have felt accepted and loved for exactly who I am, the good and the bad, and therefore have been able to accept

my husband and our kids in the same way. I used to seek an impossible goal of perfection for myself and others and I was miserable, always falling short."

- "He is the logical one, and if I actually sit long enough and listen to and follow his counsel, it is actually good advice. We complement each other; I am the emotional one. So where I lack, he makes up for and vice versa."
- "Together we make an awesome team."
- "Learning to share, care, and love another person makes me a better person."
- "I like myself more because I see that my husband loves me."
- "My marriage taught me to be less touchy. I had to survive as a child and young adult. Now I let my husband scratch my soft underbelly and I LOVE IT!"
- "Marriage has made me a better person because my husband has taught me a whole new way to look at life. I tend to be an anxious person who gives up at the slightest frustration. My husband has brought in stability and peace, as well as teaching me perseverance. He has a great sense of humor too—so he makes me laugh."
- "I really feel like I have been given a dream partner to share life with and while that is a gift, it is also a huge responsibility. The desire I have to see my husband happy was surprisingly overwhelming for me, considering that I have always been a self-focused, depressed person (childhood scars). My problem was a need to have him parent me with daily reassurance. However I could see in his eyes from time to time, a longing for ME to truly KNOW that I was okay so that I could be his peaceful woman and not his anxious little girl. When he was tired and emotionally drained from his workday, I know the last

thing he needed was for me to drain whatever drop was left in his emotional tap. That is when the accountability part kicked in: I LOVED HIM SO MUCH THAT I WOULD CHANGE. I started practicing not being in a slump all day and now it is becoming almost natural!"

I was most touched that the majority of the women's answers had to do with (1) learning not to be selfish, self-centered, and focusing on primarily "what's in it for me," and, (2) that a man and a woman *complement* each other *and* become "one." The becoming "one" issue is a controversial one in the feminist community since it implies a woman is owned or oppressed by a man and can't be her own person.

Carey, a listener, wrote that her husband of eighteen years spontaneously surprised her with a gift. Out of the blue he ordered her a new personalized license plate for the truck she uses. Her husband has an unusual name: Brud. Her new license plate says BRUDSWF (Brud's wife). Did she throw a fit and yell that she is not a possession? Nope!

"I felt so honored and loved when he presented me with this gift. He knows how hard I work to be a good wife to him and a good mother to our four children. He appreciates what I do and values my contribution to our satisfying marriage. I know that he is a good man and I am so proud to be known as his wife.

"Women usually look at me with scorn and distaste when I explain what the letters mean, but men usually love it and tell me that their wives would never go for it. What a shame because I am sooo proud to be known as the wife of a kind, considerate, loving husband. Sign me: appreciative and appreciated in California."

Tausha, another listener, had a great story to tell. For her husband's birthday she drew him a picture of a knight decked out in shiny armor, with a long, sharp sword in one hand, and a large, decorated shield in the other. The knight in her picture is actively fighting a big, ugly, fiery dragon. Overlooking this scene is a fair maiden in a tower. *"I tried to make the maiden look like me so that my husband would recognize that it was me up in the tower, and that I was anxiously watching and waiting for him, with his strength and courage, to slay that dragon and come climbing up the tower for me."*

Enclosed with her sketch was a note that read: "*You are my knight in shining armor. Thank you for putting on that heaving, binding armor each day and going out and slaying those dragons. Your bravery in defense of me and the kids is more than I could have ever hoped for. I will forever be your maiden.*"

Whew! What an incredible sentiment to express. There are many out there in our society, and those reading this now, who would mock her sketch, suggesting that it implies the fair maiden was too weak, and should have just woven a ladder of her own hair, climbed down that tower on her own, and then either run far away from the violent scene, or taken the sword from the knight and accuse him of slaying the dragon the wrong way as she slayed the dragon herself. But, as Tausha continued,

> *"I am proud to be the maiden who works hard at home taking care of our three children, the dog, the cooking, and the cleaning. I am proud to be able to make a warm meal and a comfortable place for my husband to lie. Thank you, Dr. Laura, for instilling in me a 'maiden' attitude where I can encourage my knight to get out and fight, and then welcome him home to heal from*

his battles. Words cannot express my gratitude to you for your service to women like me, who are doing their best to create peaceful palaces."

I don't know, folks, do these women really sound oppressed and depressed?

3. What are the benefits of being married vs. single?

- "I always have my best friend here with me. Sometimes we can sit and say nothing for hours, but know the love and comfort are there. We can say absolutely anything to each other without fear of being judged or unloved."
- "I have the benefit of knowing that someone loves me enough to commit himself legally to me. We're forever responsible to each other under the law and in God's eyes."
- "Knowing that no matter what difficulties life throws at us there is always someone in your corner to help you through it."
- "The benefit I have gained in being married is that there isn't a single joy or burden that I carry alone. Sharing all this makes the joys sweeter and the burdens lighter."
- "Just not having to date anymore is a big benefit—it's scary out there. The world keeps filling up with amoral, liberal morons who want sex on the first date because the women available now don't think twice about giving it to them. With the exception of church, where the heck can a decent girl go to meet a decent guy?"
- "Sharing a home and a life is amazing. I am never lonely. I never eat alone. I don't sleep alone. I always have some-one to talk to, even when that talking is picking a fight—I

have someone to make up with. I have someone who respects, supports, and loves me every day."

- "Safe, happy, and fulfilling sex."
- "Being with someone who understands what I am thinking and saying."
- "Making memories with someone."
- "Married life is more secure, stable, and comfortable. Having an intimate relationship in which I can be completely vulnerable, playful, passionate, and seductive is more than I ever dreamed of having."
- "When you have someone who is willing to lay their life on the line for you AND make love to you until you are beyond satisfied . . . well, there is nothing greater than that!"
- "I get to sleep next to this adorable, loving, amazing, generous, caring, soulful, handsome, giving father to our children man for the rest of my life. If I were single, my bed would be empty—as well as my life."

Actually, I don't think I have to add anything to this selection, do I?

I am convinced, as I have said earlier and will keep repeating (!), that attitude is everything. I know from the feedback I received from the folks who contributed to these surveys, that many of them felt revitalized in their sentiments about their spouses and their marriages just by filling out the survey and massaging their thoughts around these positive marital issues/ questions. There's good and bad in every situation, however the more you review the bad, the worse you feel; the more you review the good, the better you feel. When you think more positively about life, love, and marriage, you instantly become more patient, compassionate, forgiving of the small stuff, and very grateful for what you have. This attitude shift immediately changes the marriage from a chore and a cross to bear, to a pleasure and a blessing to embrace.

Below are *typical* answers from men:

1. *What was your biggest surprise to learn about marriage?*

- "Your free time is cut by 80 percent."
- "The problems of my wife (with her family, etc.) become our problems."
- "I was surprised how quickly the frequency of having sex diminished."
- "That the bad times and the pain would be so remarkably awful: the agony over a sick spouse or child or the times our relationship got bad."
- "I was amazed how little my outside friends and activities mattered. I would much rather and still do rather be with my wife and do things with her."
- "How feelings fluctuate during the years; but in a solid marriage, one thing remains the same and that is that you love your spouse."
- "How destructive extended family can be."
- "Married women do not compromise much; it is left up to the man to compromise to his wife's perceived problem."
- "Keeping track of schedules, paying bills, spending money on girl things I never thought about because all I was thinking about was the sex. That was a huge adjustment for me."
- "Marriage, I learned, was an opportunity for character building. Letting go of one's opinions, desires for the good of the whole."
- "It was surprising how many decisions she makes tied into emotions rather than sound, logical basis."

- "The struggle to make needed sacrifices and having to support a family. I can't just walk away when times get tough, I need to stick through it all. Giving up of hobbies to support the family and toning down sexual drives and desires to fit more to her liking."
- "It's not just about me and I must have her approval when I am to do something."
- "How many times I'm requested to go shopping."
- "It's not easy and requires work. My parents always made it look so easy."
- "Women are more complicated than I first thought."
- "How much children impact a marriage . . . disciplining, etc."
- "The biggest surprise was how much a woman misleads her man until the ring is in place. Once the ring was set, she figured she would set the record straight as to how the structure of the relationship will be built, and it was nothing like the relationship we had talked about before we were married. It took me months to convince her that there was no master/slave clause in our vows and I would not be held hostage to emotional or sexual blackmail. Thirty-five years later and we're still going strong."
- "How different women see marriage as opposed to dating. The women's attitude to please, to meet her man's requirements seem to sag after marriage even with the best, most loyal woman. It is as though her objective as a couple changes overnight; 'We must now start building a home and family in lieu of concentrating on each other.' "
- "Sex did not become a free and easy, fun activity. It became and remains a power struggle."
- "That two *can* live as cheaply as one!"

- "My biggest surprise would have to be how my happiness is directly connected to my wife's happiness . . . and when she's not happy, I'm not happy, and I try very hard to 'fix it.' "

What stands out the most in comparing the answers from the women to these from the men, as well as reflecting on phone calls and e-mails to my program, is how dominant, in general, women are in setting the tone and style of the relationship of marriage. Men aim to please, and acquiesce to feminine direct and indirect pressure to do so, while women aim to be pleased, and generally consider this imbalance reasonable.

Women in particular like to talk about the necessity for good and open communication. Unfortunately, when a guileless man communicates simple facts, that is often enough to set off a woman's insecurities. For example, a recent female caller complained to me that her husband, a kitchen contractor, came home from a job in a private home and told her, "My goodness! The guy's wife came to the door in skimpy clothes and was acting flirtatiously." My caller was furious that he said that to her!

DrL: Let me understand the source of your anger. Was he responsible for how this woman behaved?

Caller: Well, no.

DrL: Did he take advantage of the situation and have a fling?

Caller: No, of course not.

DrL: "Of course not" means you trust him and his fidelity to you?

Caller: Yes . . . but . . .

DrL: Please, don't "but" me; you either recognize his loyalty or you don't. He can't control her behavior but he controlled his own. If that doesn't please you, what would? Furthermore, why don't you greet him at the bedroom door the same way you imagine she greeted him at her front door? Or are you going to give me the "I hate my body so he can't have some" typical female nonsense?

Caller: Okay, okay—I got it.

DrL: You only had something to fear if he didn't tell you. That would likely mean one of two things: he's taking her up on it, or he can't talk to you because of your insecurities and hypersensitivities.

As I have said probably too many times before, it is the woman who rules the relationship and the home when she's married to your typical fellow (omitting, of course, narcissists, psychopaths, and addicts). That is the natural order of things in a home—"mother" and "wife" is dominant. So when you ladies use that power well, you end up with a husband who could write this:

"The biggest surprise of marriage was that it could be a very wonderful experience and an exciting journey. I am also grateful for my spouse and neither of us ever engages in the spouse bashing that seems so prevalent in recent years among my peers. I just simply smile and think how it bites to be them. I consider myself a very lucky man with the woman I am married to . . . very blessed is a better term for it. She never nags, she is

confident in herself, and she doesn't buy into any of the 'typical' female emotional traps that us fellers cringe at—nor does she ever play emotional/mind games. So . . . don't wake me just yet . . . I wish to enjoy this dream a bit longer."

2. *In what way(s) has marriage made you a better person?*

- "I am a better person because of the sacrifices. I have greater patience, reliability, stability and happiness.
- "I've learned how to love with all my heart and to trust because I feel like a man, a wanted and desired being, and a complete man. I love it and how it fits."
- "I have learned to give in advance of receiving, and in some cases give without receiving. Furthermore, I can give almost without limit, given my wife's nurturing love."
- "Marriage has made me better by forcing me out of myself and living for others. In fact, I am called to do no less than lay down my life for my spouse. Some days I can say, 'Well done.' And other days I'm less than stellar. Always being called to this total giving of self saved me from total destruction."
- "I was very selfish and self-centered. She opened me up to sharing and caring about others."
- "Before marriage, my idea of a good time was going out to the bars with my friends. Now that I am married, I enjoy spending more time at home with my wife and kids than I do out at the bars. My wife has made me mature more than I ever would have imagined."
- "It has pushed me to my emotional limits and allowed me to control my emotions better!"
- "Focus on a purpose in life—taking care of family."

- "Made me responsible and kept me from doing foolish things."
- "Marriage made me a more responsible person and made me focus more clearly on obtainable goals. I could see myself as a beer-drinking, pot-smoking lout being forever twenty-one and stupid."
- "Taught me that love is not a feeling, but an action."
- "My life is more complete having a wife and kids."

Research studies have always demonstrated that men are generally medically, emotionally, physically, psychologically, and financially more well off when married. Marriage settles men down, which probably protects them from excessively risky behaviors, gives them feminine, loving caretaking, and gives them something—the family—to live for. That sense of purpose and importance is the very essence of the elixir that keeps a male yearning to be more of a man as well as making him happy.

An e-mail from Michael caps this off nicely:

> *"One day I was helping a friend build a fence. It was hot and he was down on his knees pouring concrete for the fence post. Our wives were both there. His wife could see that he was hot, she began to fan him with her hand and then she bent over and began to blow on his neck. I was astounded! Where do you find such a woman? Hell would freeze over before my wife would blow on my neck. My wife said that she was doing that just for effect. But I can tell you this—her husband would die for her. And all of his friends wish they could trade him places."*

A well-treated husband will definitely become the best man possible.

3. What are the benefits of being married vs. single?

- "To love someone else and help serve their needs brings deeper happiness than simple hedonistic pleasure. Having someone doing the same for me gives me a trusting, happy place in the world."
- "My life is very fulfilling now. When I was single, it was filled with temporary happiness through things I could buy. This side of the coin is much better and I wish everyone could experience having such a blessing."
- "In marriage, two people can establish a virtual endless highway of giving, sharing, and love. When I was single, with each girl I dated it was like I constantly lived on a one-way street, either mine or hers. When I found my wife, all of a sudden it seemed that the road went two ways—and then things grew and developed from there into a highway of respect, love, and communication."
- "Married I always have someone on my side and someone to talk to about anything."
- "I realized a most wonderful benefit of being in a happy marriage when my wife went out of town and I came home after work to an empty house—no wife or little boy to greet me. My only thought was, 'Oh yeah, this is what it was like to be single—that bites!' I love having someone who cares and has a real interest in me to share my life with. We can talk about the trials of the day and I am able to find peace."
- "Always having someone to share your day with. Having someone there to help you through the bad times, and share the good times. Knowing that no matter what happens in life, she will always be there by your side. We can tackle life as a team—rather than alone."

- "I eat better."
- "The screaming sex drive actually can have a regular outlet with someone who loves you." "I think sex is more enjoyable because it is safer and easier to obtain." "A constant loving companion, someone who is 'in it' with you, good sex, frequent sex, good sex . . . did I say frequent sex?"
- "Raising kids."
- "You have someone to build a history with."
- "To have someone there to share with. From the **good,** to the **bad,** to the **ugly.** A partner who can help with the troubles and share in the successes; someone to laugh with, cry with, and to hug and say nothing."

The kind of call that makes me saddest is when a caller tells me a story of a husband and wife pulling apart when the bad and the ugly are pounding on their door, and their response is to turn on each other, or turn away from each other, when that is the very time they should entwine arms and defend against the bad/ugly together. I have to remind many callers of their vows concerning for better or worse, in sickness and in health, as well as not allowing anyone to turn them asunder. I often think that the vows should be on the refrigerator door and bedpost, reminding people that these issues are usually temporary if they cling to each other rather than the alternative.

Please, before you turn your back on your spouse and your marriage, consider how much you'd lose from the lists of this chapter. Perhaps this letter from Sally will help.

"For years I have been listening to your show, reading your books, and trying to walk the walk. There was a problem however in my marriage that I was having trouble facing—and as a result I was doing nothing about it. Nothing, that is, except

grieving silently inside. Then on Friday you had a caller whose problem mirrored mine. The intimacy had been lost in her marriage and she was afraid if she made the first move her husband would push her away. This is a fear that I could easily identify with. You advised her to seduce her husband and that she had to do it by the weekend.

"Okay, I said out loud to myself, 'This now applies to you too!' So, to get to the point, Dr. Laura, mission accomplished. I am writing to you with a huge smile on my face and a thank you to you for giving me the courage to physically love my wonderful man again as in my heart I always have.

"We women do have the power to make things right again. He even volunteered to fix a sink. An orgasm and a sink fixed all in one morning. Can life get any better?"

I don't think so.

Chapter 4

Dos and Don'ts

Through all the different marital mistakes that will be described in this chapter, keep three things in mind: (1) if you make changes, not *try*, but actually *make* and stay with more positive behaviors, your marriage will improve in your head (attitude is everything) and in your spouse's head, heart, and actions (unless you married a seriously disturbed individual), and (2) the difficulties, discomfort, and embarrassment involved in acknowledging your mistakes and developing new patterns of actions and reactions is worth it!

The third lesson of this chapter requires a bit more explanation. I recently received a letter from a listener who described "getting it" when my advice seems inconsistent from call to call. The example he gave was my telling a grandmother to follow the daughter-in-law's wishes about the kids' bedtime when they visit her. Another call had me telling a daughter-in-law to loosen up and let Grandma do grandparent things even when they seem to spoil the kids—that's what kids throughout the ages have enjoyed about going to Grandma's house! The listener wrote that although my advice seemed inconsistent, it wasn't if you consider my true goal: peace in the family.

To have peace, everyone's got to give a gift to the other. There is a biblical story about Aaron, the brother of Moses, dealing with two feuding neighbors who were no longer talking. Aaron met one in the public square and told him an absolute lie: "I was talking to your old friend the other day and he said nice things about you," is a reasonable paraphrase. Aaron did the same thing to the other fellow when he saw him later. Now when the two accidentally met in the square, they greeted each other warmly, in spite of the fact that their dispute was not negotiated, arbitrated, litigated, compromised, or argued out.

There are a few lessons to be gained from that story. However the most important one, and the third lesson of this chapter, is the incredible power of making the other feel cared about, special, important, valued, admired, loved, and appreciated as a real woman or a real man. That is more important than typical marital dispute resolution techniques, even compromise, making deals, and so forth; without that important sense of being adored, there will be no compromise.

Daniel, a listener, sent me a copy of a letter he gave to his wife:

> *"I want my wife back. I don't know who you are. You are not the person I married 27 years ago. It seems I am marginalized and relegated to the point of insignificance in your life. For you it seems there is always something more important than being my wife. This has been going on for a long time. My hope was that 'some day' things would be different.*
>
> *"Your priorities have been: your mother and father, the children, work, your aunt, a friend's needs, some task that has to be finished before bed, or whatever . . . The list goes on and on. All of these are noble causes, but it leaves you with having nothing left over for me.*

"I do have needs and have told you this numerous times. Your response is typically that I am some selfish, unreasonable, irrational SOB—and then anger that I keep bringing this up. You cry about it, but don't do anything to change. You just want to be angry about it and then act like you are the victim."

This is the plaintive cry of a lonely man who is losing hope. It isn't a midlife crisis that will send him into the arms of a woman who behaves excited to see him and appreciative of his company—it is too many years of emotionally devastating neglect, which is a form of spousal abuse, emotional domestic violence.

The loneliness situation in life is not actually being *alone*—it is being married to somebody to whom you appear to be invisible or have the importance of a wilted house plant. Being ignored, marginalized, disrespected, and then belittled for expressing your pain is a level of pain that is unbearable.

One of the biggest mistakes spouses make is not making much of an effort at all. If it isn't fun or easy then it isn't worth doing? Obligations and responsibilities don't require "feeling like it," they require honor and compassion. Whether it is sex and affection, showing interest in the activities and passions of your spouse, giving up something important to you because it would make family peace and/or a happy spouse, you are required by your vows to function out of commitment, rather than running on *your* immediate needs or feelings.

I know it is no longer a popular notion to give when "ya' don't feel like it," but this is the best route to a wonderful closeness and the most intimate feelings that are unimaginable if you focus in on only what suits you.

What follows is a list of dos and don'ts to help you avoid and/or repair some of the common mistakes in marriage.

TAKING EACH OTHER FOR GRANTED

"*Guys take good wives for granted and don't see them as the crown jewel of their lives,*" wrote another listener, John. T.J., a listener, admits that "*Men take a lot for granted, especially if our wives are good cooks, good mothers, etc. These characteristics aren't 'sexy' when compared to a pretty single woman that you could be with, but they are so important.*"

When a husband treats his wife's attention to the home, meals, laundry, child care, and so forth with quiet acceptance, he begins to relegate her to being his mother instead of his woman. I have told many a husband who has called my radio program to frequently express gratitude to his wife for "making the home a beautiful garden with the sights and smells of heaven." Sounds corny? Then use your own words!

Don't think that you are *entitled* to all the responsibilities and loving actions of your spouse; **Do** behave as though every mundane gesture of your beloved is a direct *gift* from heaven.

Don't think you don't need to make pleasing your beloved a priority because he/she is already yours; **Do** think that every day is an opportunity to forge a stronger bond between you.

Don't assume that all or even most of the problems of the marriage are his/hers; **Do** come up with changes you *know* you need to make to be a better husband/wife . . . and do them!

Don't wait for your spouse to make changes before you make the ones you know you should make; **Do** make an offering of your part even though you feel hurt, angry, or embarrassed, because that change in your actions/attitude will likely have two wonderful effects: (1) you will discover that you can create more of your own happiness with your own change in behavior and attitude and (2) your spouse will be motivated by your actions . . . and around it goes!

Mindy discovered the power of this last **Don't/Do,** when after complaining repetitively and bitterly to her husband about being unhappy with the role of an at-home mom, wife, and homemaker.

"For some reason I wasn't happy. I spent weeks telling him how bad our marriage was and that if we didn't get help soon, we would fall apart. After many fights about how he did not ever do the little things for me, and how much more I needed from him, he told me that I would not get anything until I started to keep up my end of the deal. I protested that this is a marriage and not a deal. He agreed, then told me to do my part of the marriage.

"I decided that I would 'do my part' for a few weeks—and do it better than ever. After a few weeks, I would then bring up the issue and finish it! I would prove that I deserved more. After only one week of doing my part everything changed. He was doing more than I had ever asked him to do. All of the little things were being taken care of as well as the big ones—and some I didn't even know about.

"I had started treating him as though he was number one on my list. As soon as I did that he helped me to realize that I have always been number one on his list—but I was just too busy (complaining and pouting). I forgot my role. I am truly sorry for doing this to my husband. He is the best man I have ever known. He loves me with all of his heart, and I will spend the rest of my life trying to love him better."

Love Alert! To paraphrase an e-mail from a repentant spouse: treat your spouse like the catch they are, do not let careers and hobbies get in the way of time together, don't let debt and possessions possess you and bring turmoil and blame, don't use your spouse when you need what you need and then ignore them and their needs, leaving them to fend for themselves until you get lonely and need something for yourself again; don't be haughty and lazy about the priority of love in marriage and your responsibility to make them feel loved and important to you and the family.

Your Tip: Write a letter to your husband/wife today, telling them specific and general things they do/are that are spectacular; cover everything from their sacrifices, activities, manliness/femininity, successes, character, being great role models for your children, sexiness and sensuality, compassion, and so forth. For example: "Thank you for showing our sons how to use a drill, chop firewood, change a tire, do income taxes, and all the other things that tend to fall under 'Dad's Duties,' " or "Thank you for homeschooling our children so they can be guided and educated to their full potential."

As you write your letter, you will find immediately that you will begin to feel happier in your marriage simply by focusing in on the good and the great instead of how your attention is generally drawn toward the negative and annoying trivialities. The second thing that will happen is that you will ignite a loving reaction from your spouse that will keep your marriage warm for a long time.

"ME" VERSUS "WE"

A good start to not taking a marital partner for granted is to think in *we* terms more often than *me* terms. Don't take this to the extreme, of course. It is good and even necessary for each of you to have some different interests, hobbies, friends, buddy time, free time, and so forth; your individuality needs to be nurtured and respected. Now here's the big HOWEVER: it is a bad mistake to selfishly guard your right to do and be what you want without respect for your duties as a spouse.

I had a woman caller recently whose husband was not coming to their three-and-a-half-year-old son's rodeo appearance where the kids, led by a parent, all dressed up cowboy/girl style and paraded around the arena. My caller wondered what she could do about this.

DrL: Well, the first obvious question is why won't he be there?

Valerie: He says he'll have folks there with whom he does business and one shouldn't mix business and pleasure.

DrL (long hesitation): That's not the truth. I don't know what the truth is, but that ain't it. You know your man—I don't—why would he not show up? (Repetitive nagging on my part ensued.)

Valerie: I don't know.

DrL: Come on, Valerie, tell me, is he typically neglectful or self-centered?

Valerie: Yes. That's been an ongoing problem.

DrL: So you know the real reason then?

Valerie: Yeah, I think he wanted that time to practice for himself and didn't want to give it up for our son.

DrL: My dear, you've got to sit him down tonight and get him refocused on what makes him a man in your eyes.

Valerie: Okay.

I got an e-mail the very next day from Valerie, happily letting me know that her husband had heard our call and had gone to his son's event and had taken tons of pictures.

> *"I'm pretty sure my phone call to you was the straw that broke the camel's back. He knew he was in the wrong which is why we couldn't get him on the air with you but he really struggled with postponing* his *time with his horses. Plus he really values your show and I have seen such a difference in our relationship since he has started listening to you. But he still resorts to his old 'selfish' habits from time to time—but I'm right there, gently nudging him in the right direction! And, our son won third place in his first little junior rodeo—and I could tell my husband was proud!"*

"Gently nudging," as opposed to screaming, ranting, and threatening, is what helps a spouse grow in the "us/we" department. Selfishness is generally a lifelong characteristic and requires gentle nudging before—and enthusiastic kudos after—to help someone grow into being joyous about giving without feeling as though they are giving up something more important . . . themselves.

Basically it comes down to this: if you don't think about *we/us* (spouse and children) you will lose track of each other, feel disconnected and alone. The simple act of a wedding ceremony or childbirth does not ensure ongoing bliss and bonding—that's where the work comes in. I'm sorry to even use the word "work," because it is often used synonymously with burden; well, maybe sometimes our obligations do feel like burdens, and when that's so, we call forging ahead honoring one's commitment. When each of you makes those efforts to honor the commitment, you will each have more respect and deeper love and sense of loyalty to one another.

Chasing career and personal goals with little regard to the impact it is having on your spouse and family is a map where all roads dead-end. Men who do this usually end up with heart attacks; women who do this end up with out-of-control families (as the parenting and home atmosphere are sidelined) and Valium drips.

I'm convinced that *most* affairs are due to two things: a spouse feeling ignored or a spouse feeling overwhelmed. In both those situations, flirting and sexual affairs are considered "medicinal." When these affairs are followed up with divorces, children's lives are destroyed, and the remaining husband/wife is left with defensive anger, confusion, regret, and profound loss.

Don't think first about what you're getting or losing at any one moment; **Do** think about how putting your spouse before yourself makes your spouse feel cherished.

Don't insist on your opinion or way of looking at things as the only way; **Do** check with your spouse about his/her way of handling a particular issue to see if there might be a solution that incorporates the wisdom you both have, as in "two heads are better than one."

Don't focus so much on making sure "my needs are met"; **Do** prioritize the needs of the union—you are now "us/we," and not primarily "me."

It is important that spouses pay attention to staying connected. Have date nights, to flirt and chatter—so you can remember why you married in the first place.

Love Alert! "It's my way or the highway," works when you are the boss, but it is not a sentiment that endears lovers to each other. Never assume that your way of thinking and doing things is the only possible way. Don't assume that your spouse will automatically have or absorb your attitudes about sex, communication, housework, lawn mowing, budgeting and spending, and so forth. Instead of feeling threatened by difference or possible change, look at it as a way of expanding your universe.

When there is a difference in opinion or desire, a good rule is to allow the person with the most invested or the most passion about that issue to make the decision. Two things come from that: (1) you make them happy and when they're happy, they're more likely to be motivated to make you happy, and (2) when people are given power, rather than having to arm wrestle for it, they tend to use that power more benevolently. Over the span of sixty or so great marital years together, it will go back and forth many times; don't get stuck on one moment in six decades!

IT WAS OKAY, NOW IT'S NOT OKAY

"When listening to you talk to some men and women, I hear them complain how bad their marriages are and how difficult their spouses are. I also know that every marriage reaches a time that I call 'The Honeymoon is Over Time (THIOT).' As much as the beloved was idealized early on—their faults are seen with as much intensity," writes Dorothy.

THIOT is a universal phenomenon. Why? Because when people yearn to bond and be loved and secure within a relationship they are highly motivated, of course, to succeed. That means that when gargoyles present themselves, that is imperfect habits, behavior patterns, preferences and interests, the beholder of these gargoyles, wanting a "happy ending" (marriage), will ignore them, rationalize them, deny being negatively impacted, manipulate to make them (temporarily) disappear, or have the fantasy that it'll all magically work out and get better if we just keep talking and talking and talking about it or just get married.

Valerie called about this very issue. She is twenty-seven, married four years to a man in whom she imagined great potential. He recently went on a trip to visit his folks, and when he came back he announced he was going to quit his umpteenth job/career and wanted to postpone having children for at least a decade. He also expressed how tired he was feeling like a lump of clay for her to punch, pinch, and mold, and wanted her to be satisfied with him as he was—albeit not mature, stable, or responsible as yet. This was a boy.

Valerie, being a decent and kindly young woman, felt compassion for the pain he was expressing; that impressed me about her. Valerie was also devastated—her gamble did not pay off. I urged her to live in the land of "what is," and permanently vacate her condo in the land of "wish it were."

Most of the time, however, the situation is not this entirely out of focus. Most of these disappointments with reality are smaller, like, for instance, Mike's case.

> *"Being absentminded is my problem. When we were dating, it happened as well, and for a time, she thought it was cute. I clearly remember telling her at the time that absentmindedness was a big fault of mine and that after we were married she wouldn't think it to be cute or funny at all. Boy, was I right!*
>
> *"Anyway, I have to write things down all the time as I am living proof of Mark Twain's theory that mental notes are not worth the paper they're written on."*

Women do have more of a tendency to label annoying behaviors and characteristics as cute or funny before marriage.

Men have more of a tendency to simply ignore them. Mark admits that his wife's dislike of anything to do with sports is annoying. He knew about this mismatch issue when they were dating. *"During our dating, I should have focused less on the sexual and more on how we fit together in the other ways. I see no solution for this. I've tried many times and in different ways to even understand it. We share many things together and I would like nothing more than to share these awesome recreational experiences with her."*

What is the saving grace in Mark's situation? It is that he has to embrace and celebrate the other "many things together," and realize that those "awesome recreational experiences" can be with buddies; with his woman, he has the rest of his being to share.

I typically beseech people calling my show ready to marry someone of another religion to rethink that decision. Usually, the scenario takes one of three forms: (1) "Religion doesn't matter to me, anyway," or (2) "We'll just have a two-religion family and bring the children up knowing both," or (3) "He/she is going to let me raise the children my way in my church."

Big mistakes. Generally as one gets older and children enter the equation, one's religion (roots) gets more important. The dissension between spouses who wish to pull the other one their way is often very destructive to the marriage and family functioning. The two-religion concept doesn't work because neither spouse has someone to share with and the children end up painting matzo for Easter; the family is fragmented in a most meaningful arena. "*My mistake is that I did not marry a girl who shared my religion. My wife converted when we married, but within a few years decided it was not for her and has not practiced since. I have missed out on sharing my religion with someone I care about. This mistake is not fixable because her religion is her choice, not mine,*" explained Daniel, a listener.

It is not unusual for people to underestimate the importance of *common* values, goals, and ideals because they're swept away by sexual pleasures; this has been a strong argument against unmarried sex which virtually eradicates rational, objective thinking and assessment. When people have great, exciting sex and a lot of fun together, they often imagine marriage a simple extension of those pleasures throughout all eternity.

When there is a basis of trust, honor, and devotion, people can weather the storms of incompatibility in matters of lesser importance, but on the big ones "*there remains a wall that prevents true intimacy, which on my part at least, is a constant source of loneliness and frustration,*" admits Tom, another listener.

Some things cannot be fixed; they must be endured. When some things cannot be endured, honorably and positively, they usually have to be terminated. It is amazing, though, how many people of past generations have chosen "to endure" and, over time, when they've treated each other not with disdain, but with respect, have come to embrace more issues together.

I have always found that the key to frustration with one's spouse is the difference between *expectation* and *reality*. Other than psychosis or coma, I know no way to escape reality! This then leaves expectation as the adjustable quality. If you expect your spouse to change, and you are frustrated because they don't, try dropping the expectation altogether, or changing it to the opposite. If your spouse, for example, tends to be messy, expect the messy and don't fight about it anymore. If a lack of clutter is important to you, more important than it is to them, neaten it up yourself! If you expect them to be sloppy and they do something to neaten up, well, won't that be a delightful hoot! Be sure to tell 'em how much you appreciated the thought!

Many a time when you're frustrated by their annoying

trait, there might just be a logical explanation for things gone wrong. Please don't jump immediately to assuming they set out to hurt you. One absolute necessity in any marriage is the inherent belief that the other has your best interest at heart. So, please, always leave room for benefit of the doubt!

Don't imagine you're going to change your spouse by complaining, hating, punishing, demeaning, threatening, or manipulating; **Do** know that you can change your view of your spouse and your marriage by finding something each day about your spouse that brings you pleasure, pride, or gratitude.

Don't choose to dwell on the annoying qualities of your spouse; **Do** remind yourself each time you're annoyed with him/her of at least three qualities you admire and enjoy.

Don't believe for a moment that you aren't annoying too!; **Do** acknowledge to yourself and to him/her that you both brought a lot of baggage into the marriage to unpack and that you promise to be more aware and considerate of your impact on him/her.

> ***Love Alert!*** "*I think that husbands and wives forget why they picked one another. They think there is something magic that happens when they marry that erases the irritating things and automatically brings people closer . . . the reality is that marriage is a magnifying glass for irritations, but it also helps if you remember what drew you to one another in the first place. I think also that gratitude is way underused in marriages,*" explained Kris. Kris went on to say that marriage is a daily dose of humble pie. Her husband is patient, calm, and good-spirited, while she describes herself as volatile, reactionary, and somewhat snooty. *"My husband is a daily*

reminder of the joy that comes from living with grace, and I try to take that lesson in each and every day."

Kris is an example of an essential aspect of marriage; instead of glomming onto the bad, which admittedly can be annoying stuff, use each day to learn something about yourself from your spouse's role-modeling of quality characteristics.

PRIVACY BETRAYAL

Part A: Let's imagine for a moment that you did something reasonably stupid, bad, self-centered, thoughtless . . . you get the idea . . . to your spouse. Part B: You then have remorse, take responsibility, attempt to repair the problem, and make efforts to never repeat it. You think that "it's over," until you realize that his/her parents and family and most of your common friends know all about it. How do you feel? Humiliated? Betrayed?

This is a common mistake that married folks make because they either want folks to side with them, so they can feel superior to their spouse or more justified in their rage of victimhood, or they want the attention that complaining and public suffering brings.

When we truly want help with a problem, we don't present it to friends and relatives as, "Woe is me—look what he/she did to ME!" When we truly want help we humbly go to clergy, counselor, close friend, or trusted family member who will focus in on *ourselves;* how we may be distorting things, how we may be overreacting, how we may have contributed to the problem, how our perception might be off, and so forth.

"*The biggest mistake I see my friends make,*" writes Pete, "*is telling their friends about their problems instead of going to each other within the marriage. It only builds resentment and if the information is leaked—which it usually is—then the trust is gone, making the problem even worse.*"

Meredith offered that whenever she feels annoyed, "*I remind myself that I'm sure I'm at least twice as annoying as whatever he is doing. I also NEVER EVER discuss 'issues' with anyone. If it's important enough for me to want to tell other people, that's my signal I should consider discussing the topic with my husband—or just let it go. But NEVER go outside the marriage to discuss disagreements.*"

Another form of "going outside the marriage" when there are problems is becoming available to listen to someone else's problems. When a husband or wife starts tending to the emotions of someone else, kidding themselves that this is all about friendly compassion, it is the beginning of an emotional affair—which could lead to adultery. Putting yourself in the position of being special to a member of the opposite sex is another form of "medicine" for what's ailing you: your relationship. It's funny, in a sad way, that folks will choose to be more compassionate, listening supportively to a stranger, when they resentfully withhold this behavior from the so-called "love of their lives."

Spending an inordinate amount of time with your buddies, friends, or mommy is another form of rejection of your spouse. Granted, some of you might find more peace outside your own homes, but abdicating and gravitating away from home will not offer much in the way of repair or growth.

The straw that broke the camel's back in my listener Margaret's first marriage ("in my twenties, no children—except maybe 'us.' ") was when she suggested to her husband that they repaint the apartment together and hang new curtains. This was her attempt to have them work together on their nest as a positive move in a troubled situation. He told her that he'd have to ask his mother. Camel died right there. Letting family influence decisions whether big or small in your marriage is to be a child playing grown-up.

Don't use discussions about how bad your spouse is as entertainment with your friends; **Do** take every opportunity you can to build up your spouse in your mind by relating wonderful, positive stories.

Don't escape from contentious issues with your spouse by avoiding home and hanging with family or friends or at the local bar . . . and don't even think of an affair; **Do** walk into your home with something generous to say and kind to do and watch the immediate change in your home environment.

Don't let your family or friends determine or influence what happens in your home and marital relationship—do not take polls with them to decide anything about your home life; **Do** have the courage of your own opinions and the respect for those of your beloved to make your own joint decisions.

Love Alert! "*Husbands and wives forget to maintain the boundaries of their marriage and this causes so many problems. My husband and I do not share our arguments with others; we do not speak poorly of each other, we don't call each other names or swear at each other; we are always loyal to each other first. I don't keep things from my husband or tell my girlfriends secrets that my husband doesn't know. We don't allow other people to interfere in our marriage. If we have a problem that we can't handle, we have agreed that we will go seek the advice of a professional,*" commented Jacquilyne.

TALKING ABOUT . . . WHATEVER

Women often complain that their husbands never talk about their feelings and the relationship, and that they won't listen without giving advice. Men often complain that their wives talk incessantly about their feelings, are defensive when they try to give their opinion, and repeat themselves over and over and don't seem to want to actually do anything about the problem—just talk about it.

Both are correct. There are inherent difficulties in communication between men and women; most difficulties are surmountable—as long as each is willing to understand, accept, and somewhat cater to the characteristics of masculinity and femininity.

Paul, a listener, wrote that a typical woman mistake in a marriage is to believe that the husband's silence is solid evidence that he is happy and satisfied in the marriage.

> *"Far from it. I wholeheartedly agree with Dr. Laura when she explains to women callers on her radio show that men are not their girl friends. Men are stoic, and women are gabby. Men survive by enduring, while women must have been born to converse.*
>
> *"If a woman expects her husband to express his dissatisfaction with some part of a marriage, she is sorely mistaken. I believe a man would rather walk naked on hot burning coals than express a concern about his marriage to his wife. He doesn't have the skills to converse at her level, and why complain when he is likely to generate only denial, anger, tears, or (worst of all) denial of sex?*
>
> *"So we endure silently . . ."*

Even assuming that a man and woman love and care for one another, a lack of a sense of freedom to express oneself to one's beloved without fireworks or punishment is profoundly deadly to a relationship. "*If one hesitates to speak for fear of the other's reaction, that person will close down and not only will the couple not solve whatever problem they have, but resentment will build. Few things hurt worse than the thought that your loved one does not care about your concerns. Even if an answer does not readily present itself, just the thought that your spouse cares enough to listen, and not immediately get defensive or judge, can make all the difference,*" explained Randy, a male listener.

Lori, another listener, wrote that she believes the best thing she and her husband did for their relationship while dating was to agree to be brutally honest with each other. Neither has to wonder or guess what is going on with the other, nor do they get confronted two years after the fact with ancient hurts that they cannot remember, much less defend. Once a problem is addressed and it is over, she explained, it *is* over. This makes for a relationship with a lot of security *if* each is mature, emotionally healthy, and generous enough to be willing and able to sustain themselves through the uncomfortable and unpleasant part of working something out.

Bradley admitted to having trouble with communication because he takes it all so personally: "*It's hard for me to listen to her problems, issues, or whatever, and just listen. I feel like because she is with me that she has issues or problems, and I take it personally—like I am not a good enough husband. I think I am overly sensitive sometimes and I get frustrated, which is only counterproductive.*"

I get a large number of calls from people who wonder why their spouses haven't told them things. Generally, as evolves during the call, it is because the spouse is afraid of the repercussions—and by repercussions I don't mean appropriate consequences for inappropriate activities. The repercussions mostly have to do with the communication being filtered through one's own insecurities, assumptions, and perceptions, without truly hearing the message of the other person.

What is the solution to this hypersensitivity? Manual override. That means you work very hard to keep your fears out of the way of your ears. If your beloved is telling you that someone came on to them at work or the grocery store, your first reaction *should* be to be pleased that they are open with you about what happened. People having affairs or flirting their brains out usually don't share this information, do they? Besides, as I often have to remind callers/listeners, no one can yank a happy spouse from your arms, so keep your spouse feeling loved and valued; this is more powerful than screaming paranoid nasty comments!

When your spouse has done something stupid or wrong with finances, home electronics, the car—whatever—the one person in the universe they should be able to come to is you. And when they do come to you first, be there for them. If the two of you can't talk about everything without one of you behaving like a ferocious parent, how can you expect them to ever come to you again or feel safe with you and loving toward you?

It is sadly typical for spouses to say, "I want you to be able to come to me and talk about anything," but when the spouse takes you up on it you break down, get hysterical and punitive, and then manipulate the situation so that you're the poor victim and they have to take back everything they tried to work out with you.

One woman, for example, called my show to complain to me that her husband complained to her that he's tired of her gaining weight and not taking care of her appearance or health. My question to her was, "Well, is it true? Are you fat and sloppy or not? If you are, why can't he express dismay over something that *is* under your control and is an obligation of yours?" She had been trying to turn it around to make him insensitive and hurtful for simply expressing his unhappiness that "his woman" wasn't doing her best to stay his woman.

For women it is usually weight, sex, and her intrusive family that they don't want to converse about; for men it is more typically their overworking, drinking, and finances. Where there are taboo areas because of sensitivity, where no conversation is permitted without defensive hostility, recrimination, and payback, those areas become the assassins of intimacy and love.

Merritt, a listener, had this general advice concerning bad things to avoid in communicating: "*Don't expect your spouse to read your mind and then get bent out of shape when it doesn't happen. Saying one thing, meaning another, and then punishing your spouse when words are taken at face value is another no-no. Pick your battles carefully. Never name-call and don't dredge up old, dead, and should-be-buried stuff to throw in a spouse's face.*"

Some people communicate only to win, dominate, and protect their own self-image and ego. To that end, they attack viciously and say things that cannot ever be taken back. Watch your words, for if you leave deep enough wounds, your beloved will not ever be able to share his/her heart with you again. Some things are too terrible to be forgiven or forgotten.

Nobody really enjoys hearing that their spouse is dissatisfied with something about them or the relationship; fears of judgment and rejection rise up. However if you stuff your childlike insecurities, and rise to the occasion of hearing whatever it is he/she has to say to you, you actually increase their respect for you as well as have the opportunity to make life better for them. This is how you build that feeling in them of cherishing you and grateful that they chose you in the first place.

Jenny learned that lesson mainly because her husband was so understanding:

> *"I learned to bottle up all my feelings and to never speak about anything that was bothering me because my mother raised me to believe that my problems had no merit because hers were always worse. Until I was married I didn't even realize I had this defensive behavior. Then when I had concerns with my husband, I would hold it all in until some random event would push me over the edge and I would cry and whine about things that were months past.*
>
> *"Luckily I married a wonderful man, and he always asked me why I hadn't told him anything earlier, and asked why I was afraid to talk to him. I was afraid he would become angry because that was the reaction my mother always gave me.*
>
> *"I had to find the strength within myself to break through the barrier I had created within myself and force myself to communicate. It's been amazing and has had such a wonderful impact on my marriage."*

Sometimes you'll need to curb your anger and help each other along.

Timing is also important. Calling each other at work or in the middle of child care to express hurt, anger, upset or concern about some issue, may not be the best choice if you want your spouse's calm attention. A more typical mistake in the timing issue is dumping on each other the minute you come back together at the end of the day. I usually suggest people hug, kiss, flirt, play with the kids, and have dinner before they get into the unpleasant stuff.

What is supremely difficult is to be kind and respectful when you're mad or hurt. In this regard, please remember, marriage is not about unconditional love. You can definitely cause your spouse to love you less if you're continuously hurtful, disrespectful, and generally not cautious about their feelings. Make sure you're thinking about longevity in the marriage before you open your mouth.

Before I go on with more communication tips, let me reinforce a key concept: **communication is not just about complaints!** If more than 20 percent of your "communications" are about problems, even neutral ones like about the dishwasher, you are cruising for a bruising. Most of your communications should be about telling your spouse how happy he/she makes you, cute things the kids did, compliments, and so forth. Forgetting to keep love fresh is the worst communication mistake of all.

If you are aware that the two of you bicker constantly, the fastest way to stop this is for you, unilaterally, to stop. When folks call me complaining that their marriage is one long argument, I ask them immediately why *they* choose to argue or fight. An argument takes two; you can decide to be calm, nondefensive, reasonable, understanding, and compassionate without ever discussing new styles of communication with your spouse! You alone can change the destiny of your marriage.

Dedicate yourself to not getting sucked into the fray. You will find that no matter the subject, no matter how high the emotions, you will be able to help create a better environment for working out problems. When your spouse is no longer confronted with another angry spouse, he/she will tone down and you will be amazed at how dramatically different your relationship will become.

Don't speak out of anger; **Do** remind yourself that you love him/her just before you express yourself.

Don't make your spouse have to keep secrets from you; **Do** become the safest place to discuss everything and anything by listening without dismissing or attacking.

Don't think that all communication is with words; **Do** realize, accept, and enjoy that there are little things you're both doing for each other that say, "I love you," just as loudly.

In Summary:
For You Men: You have probably spent too much energy trying to solve all your wife's problems or complaints, only to find out she isn't bringing you a problem to fix, she just wanted to vent. Perhaps you might ask her, "Darling face, before you go on, do you want me to be the 'problem-solving husband' or the "just be quiet and listen husband'?"

Glenn, another listener, has another solution for the reality that women love to talk about "tragedies" and "issues" not only once, but again and again. He and his wife have instituted The Ten Minute Rule.

"When my woman comes home from work, she has ten minutes to unload the day's tragedies. Whatever the tragedy, I will sit and listen. It's her time and she needs to use it wisely. When the long pause comes, I simply ask, 'What's my role? Are you asking for a solution or am I just listening?' Most of the time I'm just listening.

"The whole theory behind The Ten Minute Rule is that women have a man that listens to what's serious to her. The rest of the night is left to live life: biking, hiking, golf, sex, movies, dinner, planning a trip, playing with the kids, watching the sunset—all the things that make the memories of a good life."

For You Women: Please remember that if you want to just talk and talk about something, turn to your girl friends, sisters, and mother before you imagine that your husband will make a good girl friend. Men fix things; it is in their nature. Men are not insensitive or inconsiderate by birth—they are just geared for action. As I tell my women callers, explain yourself to your man in such a way as to give him an assignment—they're great at that!

Also remember if you communicate with your man as a mother would talk to an errant teenager, you're probably not going to get the best results. Approach your man as though you see him as such and you will get great results. Men do best with crystal clear clarity as to what you mean and want—they're not terrific at interpreting what you mean so mean what you say.

SEX

Good marital sex is when both are sensitive to the needs of the other. Sex is a very important part of a marriage because it creates a physical and emotional bond. As David, a listener, added: "*Sex is like oil to an engine. It can be the thing that helps to cool the friction and stress that will naturally arise.*"

Dan commented: "*Good marital sex is all about giving . . . giving your partner what they want and desire. An unwillingness to give indicates a selfishness that will ruin things both in and out of the marital bed. The gifts that couples give to one another in the marital sexual relationship have to be among the most cherished gifts of all. You open yourself completely to your spouse; you are completely vulnerable. It is a time when you trust the most. It is that giving of oneself and the receiving by their spouse that makes the sex so great.*"

Yet with all this tender, spiritual, and loving sensitivity about the meaning of passionate marital sexuality, the typical letter or call I get from a husband sounds like the following letter from Dallas:

> *"My wife informed me earlier this year that she just doesn't have any interest in sex anymore (she is 36 and I am 40). I can't remember a time of intimacy in the last 5 years that she didn't make me feel that she was 'allowing' me to have 'make it quick' sex with her, and without making me feel pathetic about the urge. Her refusal to do anything at all that she doesn't 'feel like' doing has robbed me of all the joy in my life, both in my marriage and motivation for work. It is affecting my children in that they don't get the chance to see love and affection between their parents.*
>
> *"What an amazing blessing it must be for men who have wives that actually contemplate their husband's feelings and happiness and think about doing the simple things that make a man feel like a man.*
>
> *"I am drudging through a day at a time, hoping that when my daughters are grown and out, that I will still have the energy and desire to go out and find someone who I might share my joy, achievements, and affection. That's the only hope for a man who will never spend a single day away from my girls as they grow, and who has a wife that says, 'get over it, you're married . . . go take care of yourself in the shower.' "*

Frankly I have been amazed at how blatant and cruel so many wives have become over the issue of their marital intimacy. Women call me to complain about their husband's desire for them all the time. Complain! As if being desired were some kind of intrusion or insult. These women excuse themselves from intimacy with their husbands because:

- I was molested and I'm turned off to sex.
- I don't like my body.
- I'm busy and tired with work, school, kids, relatives, and household things.
- I have too much on my mind.
- It's disgusting that all he wants is sex, sex, sex.
- He should just accept and understand I'm just not interested.
- I just don't feel like it.
- I'm bored sexually.

Get over yourselves and get under your men (although most men enjoy their women on top too)! If you don't, when the kids are up and out, he'll likely go with them.

These would likely also be the first wives to complain that their husbands don't do enough around the house, that they have virtual sex while looking at pictures of naked women online, and can't seem to remember Valentine's Day. No kidding.

Sex for men is like talking is for women with respect to feeling loved, cared about, and special.

Nancy, a listener, wrote that she always wondered and questioned why God blessed men with a greater sex drive than women.

"I felt my husband's needs were really unnecessary and that he merely just needed to curb his appetite.

"Fortunately I did marry a man and not a 'guy' and he patiently put up with me in this area of our marriage for 30 years. However, after listening to your show and your detailed explanations of man's needs vs. woman's, and that men really do need the intimacy and all that goes along with it, just this simple attitude change has made all the difference for me and opened up a whole new world of intimacy between me and my sweet, dear husband."

I am often challenged by an angry woman with the question "Am I obligated to have sex with my husband? Even when I don't feel like it?" My answer has always been the same. "Yes, the same way he is obligated to go to work and support the family even when he doesn't feel like it." Sexuality is a very important part of the covenant of marriage.

My next answers are: "Do you remember ever having an orgasm? Wasn't it fun? Didn't it feel good? Doesn't a great orgasm just melt all the cares and troubles of the day away? Don't you feel happier you're married, and to him? Don't you love the feeling of being a sensual woman? Don't you sleep better afterward? Why would you want to give that up?"

Most women have to get it into their heads that enjoying their own sexuality and sensuality is not slave labor to a husband, but a beautiful, meaningful way to lead their own lives.

Even the most resistant women discover that when they "do it anyway," they do get turned on and have a great time.

And that's where you guys come in: you have to know how to "light her fire," with sensual talk, gestures, and pleasures. In other words, make sure she gets the payoff!

Julie discovered, after listening to me explaining all of this again and again on my radio program, that being sexual with her husband has led to her appreciating him more and more each day. Without this element, people become crass roommates.

"Our sex life has become a wonderful way of building our bond, relieving the day-to-day stress, and just having a good ol' time. Today I discovered one more of the many side benefits from actually ENJOYING my husband and our sex life. He's so mellow and forgiving of my (occasional) stupidity. I wrecked a pipe on our property. Once I made the call to get the cost of fixing it, I owned up to it today to my husband. His response? We are going to have some hot and heavy 'bonding' tonight so that I can make it up to him. What a deal! Life is good and my husband is wonderful."

And for you women who think marital sex is repetitive and boring . . . it is all in your attitude:

"I have never watched Desperate Housewives; *however, I have heard about it. I must admit I am one. I am a married woman who sleeps with a married man who is a devoted husband and loved Dad. I also have sex with our landscape maintenance man, the plumber, and the electrician. I wear my purple satin baby-doll pajamas for a former Marine and a computer geek who fixes what I mess up on our home system. If we had a pool, I am sure I would sleep with the pool guy too.*

"The teenager I sleep with is a real cutie! Well, he is not really a teenager but he sometimes acts like one and it is a real

> *turn-on! Oh, don't let me forget that I sleep with my golf and bowling buddy too.*
>
> *"Just eighteen months into my marriage I slept with the chauffeur who taxied me to the hospital and held my hand before and after my radical mastectomy. This chauffeur also accompanied me to, and sat with me through all of my chemotherapy. Afterward, he would massage my back while I was throwing up and cursing the world. That same chauffeur tells me I am his 'Babe-a-licious' when we shower together.*
>
> *"I guess I must be a desperate housewife because I am desperately in love with my husband who has played all of these roles throughout our marriage. He is always full of surprises and every day I ask myself, 'Who will be my next lover?' "*

You cannot tell me this letter from Penny doesn't grab you where you live.

The husbands who refuse sexual intimacy are generally exceptions: ones married but homosexual, severely emotionally damaged and unable to be intimate with their woman as they don't perceive of themselves as men, have medical issues that interfere with performance, serious depression, addictions, feeling emasculated by wife, and so forth.

Don't ever (unless desperately ill) reject an amorous approach by your beloved; **Do** make your beloved feel such by some degree of physicality combined with words of love and praise.

Don't complain that your beloved is a lousy lover and not making you "happy"; **Do** compliment them when they're "getting warmer" (it is so motivating) and actually show them what would turn on your ignition switch.

Don't let your day or your history rob you of your right to marital ecstasy; **Do** make at least as much time for your "love" life with your spouse as you do for all the other stuff you consider important.

Love Alert! There is plenty of easily available information about sex. One woman listener gave this list of "suggestions" for a good and smart wife to follow:

1. Go to your local sexual products store: lubricants, toys, etc. Purchase some. Take them home and use them.
2. Remember that men are visual creatures. Purchase some naughty lingerie. Take it home and wear it for your husband. Don't worry about it being uncomfortable—it won't be on long.
3. Go to a salon and get a Brazilian wax. It will hurt something fierce, but he will really appreciate the effort. Keep yourself groomed down there—that shows you have an interest in sex. Oh, and keep your legs shaved.
4. Send the kids to Grandma's. Make love on the couch and kitchen table.
5. Go get a book on the Kama Sutra . . . they publish them with drawings and they have them nonpornographic. There are about five hundred different positions. Try them all, then you won't get bored with the same old thing.
6. Say YES more than NO. Be generous and affectionate. Read *The Proper Care and Feeding of Husbands*—understand it and put it in practice.
7. Call your husband at work. Verify you are not on the speaker phone and proceed to tell him just what you will do to him when he gets

home . . . or what you want him to do for you.
Leave naughty notes in his briefcase.

Yes, this takes effort—but it is effort that will make both your lives more worth living . . . together!

MARITAL SIBLING RIVALRY

I was still recovering from feminism when we had Deryk. I told my husband, not discussed—told!—that he'd better be doing 50 percent of everything from diapers to hands-on time with the baby. I wanted to make sure I wasn't used and abused because I was the woman. Horrifying, actually, to remember thinking in this bizarre way. Anyway, once Deryk was here, I would sneak to change his diapers over 90 percent of the time! Why? Because it was so much darn fun! He would laugh through the whole adventure and I so loved that joyous, happy, and loving bonding time. Having Deryk cured me finally from feminism. I learned that domesticity was not a put-down at all; it was the power to set the tone for the whole family experience, starting with the ambiance of the home. Houses become homes when women make them so.

As Scott, one of my listeners, wrote: "*The biggest mistake in a marriage is looking too much at the 'weight and balance' scale of who is doing what for whom and measuring responses accordingly. Giving your all, acting correctly regardless of circumstance, should be the goal.*"

One of the best descriptions and explanations of this destructive "keeping score" mentality came from a listener. To paraphrase: Both sexes make this mistake. And what makes the score-keeping double trouble is that men and women score things differently.

For a woman, her man going to work and bringing home a paycheck gets one point. To her, laundry, floors, child care, shopping, cooking, and maybe even sex? is one point every time she does it. So when she measures her day against his, she has accumulated fifty points (probably minus the sex point . . . 'cause she's mad) and he only has one. That means when he comes through the door she jumps on him to "pull his weight" at home, and that leads to resentment on both sides.

From a man's point of view, his going through traffic to work, dealing with bosses and coworkers and clients, meetings, paperwork, stress, and so forth is worth thousands of points. Compared to his bringing home the "bread," he sees what she's doing as comfortable, convenient, arbitrary, and relatively simple—so he gives it all maybe five points. After having done that math, he doesn't understand why she gets angry because he doesn't want to do anything when he comes in the door.

Our culture has made two things perfectly clear: anything she does that benefits her husband points out her oppression; if he doesn't do at least half her work once he comes home from his work, he's a heartless, lazy, selfish bastard who doesn't care about her or the family.

Karen describes rescuing herself from this typical and destructive mind-set:

> *"I'm married to a wonderful man, and our marriage is as close to perfect as I could dream of . . . but in the beginning I was guilty of keeping score and being mad at him when he didn't meet what I felt were obvious and righteous expectations. And if I'm honest, this came from feelings of shame and jealousy. I*

felt shame because I wasn't out working, and I felt as though nothing I did at home was important; and jealousy because he got to go out and DO something with his day instead of being STUCK at home with children.

"Because I started listening to you, Dr. Laura, I changed that mind-set and the keeping score stopped. And we are both happier for that. I was making myself crazy with it. Although my marriage wasn't in trouble, had I not changed my thinking—it would have been."

When confronted by a score-keeping spouse, either being hard on themselves as inadequate—or puffing themselves up as superior—I try to help them eliminate that destructive thinking by asking the following question: "Who is more important? The pilot of a fighter jet, or the person whose sole job it is to put that last screw into the wing?"

Believe it or not, the typical answer is "The fighter pilot!" I tell them, "WRONG!" They are aghast and argumentative. "Look at the training, talent, education, responsibility . . . how could the pilot not be the most important?"

"Simple," I say, "the pilot can't get the plane off the ground to run his mission without that one screw being properly placed and secured." A quiet "Oh" is usually the reply.

The romantic notion of marriage meaning you become ONE is more than just a platitude. All the many things that must be done to support you both so that you can function as a person is TEAMWORK. And no part is more important than any other part because all the small parts add up to the UNION which should be the most important concept in your mind and heart.

Let's just say that you both want to go to the movies after you have dinner at home. Who should put the dishes in the dishwasher? Do you wait to see if the other will do it? Do you do it in anger? Do you nag or threaten your beloved to do it?

If the goal *is* the movies together, then the goal is *not* who is subservient and who is superior by virtue of who takes care of the dishes. Maybe one of you says, "I'll get the dishes cleared away, how about you warm up the car?" or "Which do you want, rinsing or dishwasher?" or "You've had a tough day. Let me get the dishes while you take a warm shower before we go out." See? This changes everything from competition to collaboration. Which do you believe is more loving?

Some of you are going to have a hard time with this because, frankly, you are control freaks. Debbie has something to say about that!

> *"I went into my second marriage wanting him to cater to me and to make my happy. My husband just gave and gave and I took and took until it became real clear to me how horrid I was being.*
>
> *"I was a control freak used to doing everything my way. I was always pointing out some way in which he had let me down—much to my shame. Now I consider him first and try to give more than I get. Marriage has made me a better person in that it has made me WAY less selfish and argumentative than I was when we married.*
>
> *"Being married means someone's always got my back, having my best friend around all the time, great sex, and more personal growth than I could have imagined or admitted I needed! The biggest mistake most couples make is not understanding that the most important thing isn't 'me,' it's 'us.' "*

The most important concept in Debbie's letter is the understanding that your spouse is not your enemy. I think that needs repeating: your spouse is not your enemy. Yet so many people treat their spouses as though they were really their reincarnated mean parent or competitive sibling and they lie in wait for the assault to begin.

Another listener wrote that he treated his wife as though she were his sibling with whom he had to compete for an imagined lack of resources and seek validation through "being right." He feared that if he was found to be flawed, wrong, or imperfect, that his wife wouldn't love him, so he got really defensive when criticized or when he imagined he'd done something wrong. When they had an agreement, instead of being her partner and working to find a common ground toward a resolution, he got defensive and gave tit-for-tat arguments to prove that he was more long suffering and more hard working and more important than she.

Sound familiar?

His parents divorced when he and his sibling were very young. His parents got into their own love lives with various partners and his dad, between girlfriends and work, was never around. His sibling had learning disorder issues and got a lot of attention. Add all of this up and instead of his becoming a grown man, taking care of his woman, he was a little boy hungry for love and validation, and hypersensitive to even the thought of losing it at any particular moment.

"Yes, I believe that these behaviors are fixable. Usually when I act out inappropriately, I figure it out later and get embarrassed and apologize to my spouse. More and more I am getting better at being able to stop myself. I use some of the things you've said on your program as a chant to keep me from following my knee-jerk response, such as, 'She is not the enemy,' and 'No one is loved because they're perfect.'"

When you walk into a room and are introduced to a new

person, you put out your hand immediately to shake hands, don't you? Sure you do, it's just polite. It is amazing, though, how many of you spouse-types don't put out your hand to your spouse unless he/she does it first.

Elizabeth wrote that she and her husband have been married almost two decades and are more in love than ever because ten years ago she realized that she was responsible for the chasm between them—a chasm getting wider and wider every day. She admitted to mirroring his behavior toward her, meaning that she behaved lovingly only when she *perceived* he was behaving lovingly toward her. She did things for him only when she *perceived* he was doing things for her. She complimented him only when she *perceived* he was doing things for her.

"As soon as I behaved AS IF . . . and took the lead in loving him—the change in his attitude and behaviors toward me was almost overnight!"

The emphasis on "perceived" is because the mix between reality and our sensitivities often cancels out the good we could be enjoying. One woman called me to complain that her husband never said loving things to her. However she did recount in passing that he went out at five A.M. to scrape the ice off her windshield and warm up her car so she would be comfortable going to work. I asked her, "Isn't that the loudest 'I love you!' a woman has ever heard?"

Don't even think about keeping score with who does what; **Do** keep in sight of what the goal in your marriage is: peace and happiness.

Don't compete with your beloved for who is more important; **Do** spend every possible moment telling your spouse he/she is the most important part of your life.

Don't withhold love or affection because of some perceived slight—or even an actual slight; **Do** remember that a cherished spouse will "slight" you less.

Love Alert! When I take a shower, I love the bathroom to be totally dark so I can just relax and luxuriate in the hot water. One night my husband came in to use his sink and he turned the light on over that area. I opened the shower door and asked him to turn off the light because I needed this quiet time. He was momentarily bugged because he was trying to find something. He turned off the light and left the bathroom.

Now this could have turned into an "I have my stuff to do and don't interfere with me" competitive moment. But it didn't 'cause he's a good guy.

The next night, while I was again in the shower, I had left one of the lights on and just didn't want to leave the warm shower to turn it off. Humpff. Then I noticed that my husband came into the bathroom, saw/heard the shower, went and turned off the light, and silently left. That is an "I love you" moment. Learn to hear/see these!

SHOW ME THE MONEY!

They say that money and sex are the two biggest causes of divorce. I don't think so. I believe that they are merely more obvious symptoms of the lack of ability and willingness to desire to make your spouse's, your beloved's, your woman's/man's life worth living. Instead your focus is your fears and immature/neurotic needs that result in a desperate attempt to control in order to keep safe from imagined dangers from your childhood.

Consequently some of you are cheap and miserly and some of you spend like crazy. Money becomes a means by which you attempt to solve your emotional problems from your childhood. Perhaps you spend over the budget because that is how you deal with anxieties about your own value or depression over your self-obsession with looks, smarts, happiness, or whatever. Perhaps you hoard money and control expenditures because that is how you deal with anxieties about loss, loneliness, and failure.

You may point a finger at your spouse, condemning them for not being as responsible or generous as you, and you may be absolutely right! However it is interesting that you made the choice to marry and form a household with them in spite of knowing about their financial behaviors and perspectives. Once done it is important to work *with* them on compromise, instead of *against* them with anger.

One recent example from my radio program might help in this regard. A woman called very upset because she has built up a lot of credit card debt with spending on household things and stuff for the kids. She didn't know what to do at this point, and was obviously too scared of the consequences and reaction to tell her husband.

Her husband is very organized and meticulous about bills and budgets and hasn't at all respected her as a partner in these areas as she is such a "free spirit" about money. Basically it made her feel like she's the teenager and he's the parent, doling out an allowance totally at his whim.

I told her to go to him that very night and present the bills with an apology. She was to tell him that she was treated as a child and sank to the occasion and behaved like a rebellious child and spent behind his back. She was to clarify that she did not spend frivolously on "stupid girl stuff," but instead on reasonable things for the home and family. She was not to yell, cry, attack, or argue. When she finished her story, she was to stay quiet until his reaction was over. At that point she was to say, "I appreciate that you are more experienced and knowledgeable about family budgets, but I feel left out of our life in this area and you must feel like you don't have a partner you can trust and count on. This is sad for both of us. Here is my suggestion: I will work up a weekly/monthly budget for all those things I need for us all and after we agree on this, you can place that amount in a checking account. I will then work from that. Each month we'll go over what has transpired—maybe even savings!—and we'll discuss any changes we think ought to be made."

She was to then hug and kiss him, and say that she's looking forward to reducing this source of tension between them so that they both could feel more safe and affectionate with each other.

She called back several days later to say that she "blew his mind" with how grown-up, responsible, brave, complimentary, and sensitive he saw her being and that things were working out well so far.

What I worried about was how emotionally constipated he might be, which would clearly get in the way of his being open to sharing responsibility and control. Obviously she approached him with enough sensitivity to his sensitivities that he came out of himself.

The aforementioned "constipation" reference is generally a result of "starvation" as a child: emotional and/or virtual. "*I was OBSESSED with not being poor,*" wrote Douglas. *"I grew up in a difficult situation."* Sometimes folks who, as children, were not treated with open love and affection, or whose families suffered great financial hardships (due to circumstance or irresponsibility) will find themselves hoarding money and affection/attention. The cure to deficits in one's childhood is *not* hoarding; the cure is to become a virtual wellspring of what you missed. That's where the relief comes from.

Please, you must remember your ultimate goal: **peace and happiness.** And that doesn't mean you repair your childhood struggles and dramas by dragging your spouse into a reenactment of your upbringing that you will make damn sure "goes your way" better than your childhood did!

Repeat after me: peace and happiness, peace and happiness, peace and happiness! Good. Now keep in mind that peace and happiness cannot be arm-wrestled, demanded, bullied, or threatened into being. Peace and happiness are the results of **loving and giving.**

Rick discovered the blessings accrued by giving. He and his wife adopted a two-month-old. He hadn't wanted to have children because his wife was working and he believed he couldn't afford to have her stay home—which he knew was best for the child. He loved his life the way it was because they did whatever they wanted without worrying about money. But once this beautiful child came into their home, Rick realized that there was more to life than his selfish desires.

> *"Every time I looked at my son I would think of my second mom, Dr. Laura, telling me to have my wife stay home. I would tell my wife about Dr. Laura's haunting voice in my head all the time.*
>
> *"I had this investment account set aside with enough money to pay off both cars and our credit cards. This would enable my*

wife to stay home while I would still have to work some overtime to make it work. At first I fought tooth and nail to keep my wife working.

"My wife kept telling me to call Dr. Laura to ask what she would say about cashing in the account to afford her to stay home. I dreaded making the call because I knew the answer Dr. Laura would give me and I didn't want to sound like all those other callers, saying, 'Yeah, I know, I know.'

"I bit the bullet and cashed in the account. I know it was the right decision but that doesn't make it any less scary. I have faith in God and I know things will be fine. I really appreciate all your motherly advice!"

I have been growing in my dismay at the number of women who don't value the magnificent gift of motherly attention to a child and the number of men who don't value the magnificent gift of fatherly support. It seems we've grown a few generations of males, not men. A man does what it takes to protect and provide for his woman and children. Too many males today sound more like Rick used to sound: "I like my things! We both need to work so I can enjoy my things!"

Lately I've gotten calls from a large number of women curious as to my take on whether their husbands should hold out for a job they love and are "happy" with, or a job that takes care of business for the family. These wives feel guilty that their husbands might not be "happy," as though happiness were the greatest good, and that it could only be obtained through "having."

I tell them all that *real men* are happy to be able to take care of their families no matter what they have to suffer to do it. Most of the time, these women callers are astonished at that answer. I refer them to history, when men sustained themselves through terrible hardships but retained the pride of knowing that their sacrifices were the strength of the family's survival.

One such woman, Bridgitte, wrote:

> *"The first mistake I made in my marriage was not anticipating and implementing a financial plan to stay at home with my children. Before marriage, I never expected to want to stay at home, and while dating I never voiced this possibility.*
>
> *"Now that I have been home for almost three years, dealing with monumental resentment from my husband and him feeling unloved because I've let him have all financial responsibility, my husband is asking on a daily basis if my daughter is worth all of the strain."*

Frankly if Bridgitte puts her daughter in day care and goes to work full-time, she will definitely solve the money problem—but the marriage will be lost because her respect for her man will be gone, and her guilt at sacrificing her daughter will eat at her heart.

It is not unusual for educated women such as Bridgitte to come to realize that a more traditional marital approach (one parent nurturing children; other parent slaying dragons) is superior to dueling careers and neglected children; exhausted, frazzled wives and alienated/emasculated husbands. As I tell women ambivalent about this issue: "You can work outside the home when your child is in kindergarten—as long as you leave for work after the child goes to school and are home when your child hits the front door for a mommy hug!"

Bridgitte continued:

> *"My problem was thinking that most aspects of a traditional marriage were absurd (i.e., the man as the primary breadwinner)*

but now I find myself in the . . . position of being educated and wondering if parenting is a significant enough contribution—yearning for most aspects of a traditional marriage. I know it's not too late to make some changes!"

There is another side to this issue. Ervin had listened intently to my many provocative lectures on a "real man," and reflected on a "real woman":

"You keep saying a real man brings home the money so the mother can stay home with the children. What you fail to say is it takes a real woman to take the money and use it responsibly to take care of the family. Without her working to manage the money wisely your concept will not work.

"The mom needs to be conservative or it will be a lost cause. Please stop blaming it on the man for mom working. For me and others I know mom wants more and more and decides on her own to get a job to buy her luxuries and the man still spends his money on the family bills."

Fair enough and well said!

Nonetheless research shows that women still tend to prefer men who are breadwinners, whom they can consider intellectually superior, and who can physically protect them. Women tend to respect more and be sexually attracted to men who can take care of them.

Don't ever make money the measure of the importance of either one of you; **Do** think of money as the joint air you breathe . . . use it wisely and enjoy it.

Don't allow your insecurities to rule how money is saved and spent; **Do** remember that having your spouse know that you are joined as a team, struggling together, reaping the rewards together is, for you, a wonderful blessing.

Don't use spending or hoarding money as a means of punishment or control; **Do** try to balance your whims, desires, and needs with a responsible sense of awareness that you both benefit from or are hurt by money problems.

Love Alert! How money is earned and spent is a subject that needs calm, frank, and constant attention. I think a good rule is that for the big things (and each marriage at different times must determine the dividing line for "big") there ought to be a conference and a mutual decision. If an agreement cannot be made the "NO" wins. It behooves spouses to realize that when you thwart the reasonable desires of the other too often, you win the battle but lose the peace and happiness.

An important part of every budget is "swing" money, that is, money that each can splurge or save without the big discussion. It is gratifying for each to feel some freedom for the silly things.

CHILDREN IN THE PICTURE

How is it that something that can't walk or talk, much less roll over on its own or even use the channel changer, can RULE the universe? A child changes everything. The biggest mistakes that spouses make when children arrive are (1) getting themselves all consumed and emotionally spent with the children, (2) having dueling parenting styles, and (3) abdication of parental leadership responsibilities because they want to be liked.

The first problem results in the spouse and the marriage being abandoned and neglected, which is sad and foolish because if children are your main concern, then keeping their home safe, secure, warm, and functional should be your first motivation.

The second mistake results in parents not working as a team by becoming combatants, which lets the children rule the household; did you ever read *Lord of the Flies*?

The third mistake results in out-of-control children, causing problems and bringing a tremendous amount of unhappiness to a marriage that cannot be endured because the marriage has ceased being a partnership in child-rearing.

One specific area with built-in aggravation is a stepfamily situation. Generally the stepparent has no power with stepchildren and is saddled with the animus of the prior marriage, especially on issues of discipline, planning, privacy, money, expectations, and so forth. Second marriages with children have a higher divorce rate than first marriages—I always beg people to wait until their kids are grown before dating and remarrying. Of course, even when kids are grown, one has to find a prospective mate who isn't hostile about sharing time with the reality of extended nonbiological family.

The central point though is that spouses not lose each other, swallowed up by the reality of the needs of children. Michel admitted,

> *"After we had kids and they were doing sports, dance, and piano, my wife gave me zero time. I noticed women at work and starting giving them compliments, spending more time talking to them and looking at every girl that caught my eye. I was starting to think about other women more than my wife and it scared me. I sat my wife down and told her about this and how I felt. My wife is a good woman and she agreed that the kids had come first—and said she was going to change. And she did!*

"Our marriage changed and was awesome! A month after this, I remember thinking that there is not a woman more beautiful than my wife. I don't even look anymore because I am so satisfied with her. It's easy to keep a man that worships you—just make him feel like a man."

Many women call me to complain that their husbands need to understand that they now share their attention with the children. What I reflect back in most of these calls is that the term "sharing" suggests that there is attention for them; that's often not the case. Many woman callers, when presented by me with their virtual elimination of any recognition, respect, or attention to their husband's needs and desires for them, say, "Yeah, I know . . . BUT . . ." "But" has no place in that sentence if a marriage is going to thrive. There is not a woman alive who would tolerate a man paying all his attention to his child and telling his wife, "Sorry, you'll just have to fend for yourself because I'm tired and have nothing left over for you."

And that brings me perhaps to one central issue: TIME. You can't do and have it all simultaneously. You can't even have it all sequentially—unless of course you're immortal. I can't tell you how many men and women call and tell me that they *know* they should spend more time together, but what with feeding the kids dinner and putting them to bed (after the children have had a full day of day care or day care and school), a full-time job and full-time work . . . there's nothing left. NO KIDDING!? I usually ask these people, "Why did you bother to marry? Why bother having kids?" Their answer is, "Because I wanted to have a family." My response? "HAVE a family, like a possession, or actually BE family, by sacrificing for their sake . . . and ultimately, yours?" This usually engenders pure quiet.

Don't overbook children's activities—it isn't good for them and it eliminates family and intimate time; **Do** make sure that you take time every day to make your beloved feel beloved and special.

Don't assume you are always right about every issue of parenting; your spouse's experiences and ideas may be different, but different is not automatically wrong or bad; **Do** defer to your spouse on discipline or decision making with respect to the kids—it shows the children that you are a team and it'll make your spouse feel respected. Remember, there are many roads to Rome.

Don't try to make your child your best friend or put your child in the position of having to choose between the two of you; **Do** make every attempt possible to engage your spouse in decision making so that when you present something to your kids (punishment, rules, etc.), it is from US.

Love Alert! Even if you didn't discuss the particulars of raising children before you married (tsk tsk)—it is never too late. How 'bout the two of you sit down and talk about the blessings and problems of your respective childhoods. Then openly and courageously reveal how you think your own brand of parenting is more about your own early childhood pain, and less about the best interests of the family. When each of you is being open, the other needs to be physically (hold hands) and emotionally supportive. In this way you will both get rid of baggage and free yourselves up to enjoy and improve in your parenting skills with the *help* instead of the *argument* of each other. Parenting classes taken together will be a big help. Get out of yourself and into each other! Think of the peace and happiness of knowing that even at your worst (admitting failures and weaknesses) your beloved loves you even more and feels that much closer.

Don't abuse your children by using them as a safety spacer between you and what you're not comfortable with in your spouse. Yes, that's right, that is child abuse. For the sake of the children, as well as your own peace and happiness, your marriage must come first—NO EXCUSES. When it is time to give your adult child the pink slip on his/her life, do it and fill that empty nest with marital love and new adventures.

Chapter 5

To Hell and Back

To Hell: "*We never used the word divorce, but one day we sat on either side of the bed with our backs to each other. We were, for lack of a better word, tired,*" wrote Benjamin, a listener.

They each asked each other, "What are we going to do?" They each responded, "I'm not going anywhere."

And Back: "*We faced each other, lay on the bed and began talking about all of our fears, frustrations and hurts. We found that we had the same concerns about one another. We cried, we talked, we kissed, and we held each other all night.*

"That was ten years ago and here we are approaching our 25th anniversary in December."

I believe the folks who know the most and the best about how to stay married *well*, are those who have gone to hell and found a way to come back. Platitudes and lovely stories are inspiring and educational, but when a marriage has gotten to the point of hate and terminal hurt and the man and woman find a way back to each other, past all that, that is some kind of miracle we all have to know more about. It is these marriages that demonstrate above all others how sacred and special the marital covenant is, for only those things that are deeply meaningful are worth fighting for.

I am impressed that anyone fights for their marriage at all. The liberal mentality supporting a total lack of structure for people (hooking up, shacking up, out-of-wedlock children by choice, abortions for convenience, promiscuity no longer a dirty word) certainly works against especially younger people discovering and appreciating the blessings of having someone in your life as part of a covenant. With so many of their parents divorcing—often multiple times—young people are afraid of hurt and loss so they "play" with intimacy without really risking much in the hope that they can create "safe love," only to discover that such a situation doesn't exist and that they feel desperately lonely.

There isn't much in our culture (media and neighborhood) that portrays traditional love and marriage in hopeful ways, nor is their much support for those who attempt to venture into a committed relationship. Largely people are left floundering or using personal fantasies.

Carrie, another listener, described her two-year marriage as very unhappy and she thought it was time to get out rather than prolong the misery. She had had dreams and fantasies about the "perfect life," an expectation that wasn't being met in spite of the fact that they were such good friends. He didn't want a divorce but she just "*wanted it to be done so I could move on—so I filed for divorce.*"

Their basic friendship kept them talking and discussing their thoughts and feelings. He even helped her move into her new apartment so she could be on her own—for the first time in her life! They discovered that they were having a better time together separated than when they were married. They became better friends and better communicators as they shared their thoughts and feelings without the rancor of their ill-conceived notions about marriage being perfect all on its own; two people, just add water and stir.

"*Ultimately we realized* [all we suffered] *was something we had to go through to get where we needed to be—to understand what we had been blind to before. We will be celebrating our ten-year anniversary this year. It is not that life has been easy, but we certainly have a greater appreciation for marriage, the commitment and savoring the good, bad, and in between times of a relationship.*"

Of course it is instant disaster, not instant happiness, when two people come together, each with their own notions of how it is going to be—almost on its own—when they marry. Many people perceive marriage as a kind of sauna, you go in and the heat does something to you while you are passive. What Carrie and her husband happily discovered was that a good marriage all about "doing" something, instead of expecting something. When both spouses understand that—it is a beautiful thing.

Lori wrote that she had filed for divorce five years ago after a sixteen-year marriage. She related not being able to bear another day of being treated as the least important person in the universe. She described her husband as self-centered, chauvinistic, disconnected from her and everyone else to the point that all that mattered to him was his work and the accolades everyone gave him for being so technically smart and valuable to his company. She described how he often volunteered to be told how great he was.

"He left me alone to deal with anything difficult like my mother's and two brothers' untimely deaths. What was important to me just didn't matter to him. The home repairs were neglected to the point of embarrassment. I was married but very alone. I became an angry wife with much resentment toward him."

She went to a marriage counselor, who affirmed that she

had a right to be angry and a right to be happy. She thought that to be happy she had to leave that mess and start anew with a person who was willing to grow with her and share her values—and this marriage seemed hopeless.

They spent $5,000 each for divorce attorneys and the real fighting began, with depositions and court appearances. They were still under one roof and the tensions were unbearable. And then . . .

> *"My husband came to me in tears one day during this time and said that he came to the realization that this was it, everything we built together would be gone, our four sons at the time—between 11 and 16 years of age—would be crushed and broken just like the homes we were both raised in. He promised to do whatever it took to repair and rebuild our relationship.*
>
> *"I told him that we'd have to live in a cared-for home that I could be proud of and that I'd have to be treated like I WAS IMPORTANT! HE WANTED TO BE ACCEPTED and have a loving wife and a peaceful home. We both promised to do our best.*
>
> *"Today, and each day, we work on bringing our best selves into this family, and we have, for the most part, succeeded. I decided that no matter what transpired, I would not lose control over my emotions anymore. Our home is peaceful and I'm happy (by choice) and our boys are secure and loved by us both each day.*
>
> *"I know we are doing the right thing for our children. Once they're raised, I'll look at our relationship closer and see if we can extend our commitment to stay true to our vows. He still has issues that he doesn't address, but I have accepted them for now. As you say, Dr. Laura, I've stopped fighting them. A*

two-parent home where the adults demonstrate love, respect, and compassion and show the value of family are what's most important to me. I'm very thankful we both found the strength to keep it together."

Lori's story brings up an important point—which is difficult for most people: when you know the other person's core drive, main issue, biggest need—don't fight it or criticize it . . . work with it. Lori needed to feel important. Lori's husband needed to be approved of, and be seen as special. As they both came from broken homes where parents had their own problems, their biggest "need" derived from their biggest "loss" as children. When we spend our adult years trying to fill the space that should have been filled as a child, we end up ignoring our spouses and being in competition with their needs.

Lori finally recognized and toned down her angry responses, and that made her husband turn less to work and volunteering to get attention and approval. When Lori's husband realized that Lori leaving him was his ultimate worst nightmare—withdrawal of approval—he fought to do what she needed (to feel important to him) in order to regain her approval. Instead of fighting each other's core need, they turned to feeding that need; in doing so, they both became better people and better spouses. Funny how that works out!

Chris and his wife were also at the brink of divorce. He'd discovered his wife's affair and had told her from the beginning of their relationship that that was the one thing he definitely would not tolerate. They had two children, thirteen and fifteen, and a twenty-year marriage. He was planning his exit strategy when he met three men who had divorced in the last one to five years.

"Not one of them was better off now than before. All had bad times with the split family hurting the kids. All were financially worse off than before. Not one of them had anything good to say about their life post-divorce. Bitterness, loneliness, emptiness, and loss were evident in their conversations—besides, I calculated that the divorce would cost me about $60,000!"

Chris brought up a very important point: most people look at divorce as the saving grace without examining it more deeply. When I was in training as a marriage and family therapist, I remember reading a research paper stating that upward of 75 percent of divorces were unnecessary and that most people did not report being happier after their divorce. The reasons are obvious: loneliness, financial problems, children's pain and acting out, visitation issues, dealing with the ex's new relationships and children, greater daily burdens not shared, and so forth.

Chris's wife went into intensive therapy to deal with her personal problems with a "bad-dad" hangover (controlling, unloving, put-downs, etc.) and followed through on trust through verification (cell phone bills, e-blaster computer reports, lots of touching base during the day, etc.). *"It is now 1.5 years after the explosion and we are more in love now than in many years. It was hard to grow back the trust but the decision to put 150% back into making this thing work was hard and painful—but oh so worth it!"*

One of the best descriptions of surviving hell and coming back in a marriage was sent to me by a firefighter, Thomas. He wrote that he had a revelation about marriage and divorce one day while actually fighting a fire. He talked about the claustrophobic feeling a firefighter gets from being hot because of the fire and the heavy protective gear they wear.

"It's the same feeling we get when we're standing in the sun on a hot summer day when you're wearing a hot, heavy sweater. Intolerable! The only reason wearing heavy clothing in the summer becomes intolerable is because we have the choice not to. If the choice is not there, it somehow becomes bearable—because you endure.

"In firefighting, I have to wear a heavy turnout coat and pants in the heat. I never get the TEAR THIS STUFF OFF NOW OR I'M GONNA DIE *feeling. That fact that I'm baking never even occurs to me because there's nothing I can do about it—taking the stuff off is not an option.*

"Marriage and divorce is the same way. So many people are getting divorces because they consider it an option. Even if it's a last option, they will still turn to it when things get too 'hot.' Marriage is very tolerable when you don't keep your eye on the EXIT door.

"In my marriage we don't even consider divorce as an option, so there is no temptation to take that route, and things we experience become tolerable. There are times divorce has entered my head, but I just throw it out and know I have to work on making things 'cooler,' not just running from the heat.

"Life is hot. Heat is everywhere."

Life *is* hot and heat *is* everywhere, so think ahead when divorce seems the only solution for right now.

One day Kory's wife dropped the "divorce" bomb on him and he was even more stunned to realize that he wasn't too disappointed with her decision. After about seven hours of discussing what their living and custody arrangements were going to be, they came to the realization that neither of them really wanted to be apart, but had just forgotten to put in the effort needed to keep a marriage strong. *"How easily we do forget."*

It is four years since that day, and their marriage is still going strong. He compares his sometimes "distant from her feelings" to his truck's gas gauge; the feelings are letting him know that his tank is getting low, "*and only I can fill it. The way that I fill it is to show my wife how much she really means to me. The more I give the more I get. As time goes by I feel that empty feeling less and less. If I remember any advice that my dad gave me, it was to never let your gas light come on. It is just as easy to fill the top half of your tank as it is to fill the bottom.*"

And smarter, don't you think?

"THE BRINK OF DIVORCE" . . . A BLESSING IN DISGUISE?

Patricia and her husband had a long history of infertility problems. After years of treatments and surgeries for both of them, she had three consecutive miscarriages. The fertility problems and the miscarriages strained their marriage to the brink of divorce.

> *"I was wrapped up in my own self-pity and neglected to love and nurture my marriage through this hellish time in our lives. I know that most of my feelings were a result of my wacky post-pregnancy hormones, and my own grief over the death of our babies. I have always wanted children and I thought I should set my husband free so he could marry a woman who could give him what I could not. Yes, this was very childish and stupid on my part. This was a miserable time in our lives, and I did not think our marriage would survive the immense heartache we were both experiencing.*
>
> *"Then, after much prayer, we were finally able to scrape ourselves out of our grief and get back to living the life God meant*

us to live. We finally realized our commitment to each other, and happiness in our marriage took precedence over the heartache trying to conceive children brought us. We simply decided that having children naturally was not worth our marriage. We do hope to adopt some day."

She went on to say that she believes this very dark time in their lives was a **blessing in disguise,** because they now feel that if they could work through this, they can work through anything. It has made a bond between them that would never had been there if they had taken the easier way out and called it quits. It taught them how to work out their problems instead of pulling inside themselves and away from each other. No matter what challenge confronts them in the future, this experience taught them, promised them, that they could get through it . . . together.

DON'T WANT TO HURT THE KIDS

Conventional wisdom has it that having children generally puts a strain on a marriage. That is true. However there is another side to that story.

Harrison and his wife were newly married. She was an airline attendant with a solid financial base and had even purchased a home with a female colleague; she was used to security. Harrison was an entrepreneur who had just sold a business and was revving up to start a new one having found an opportunity in another state. They moved states, had the financial strain of starting a new business, and then she became pregnant. Things were getting out of hand since she was pregnant, not used to debt, and uncomfortable with the prospect of purchasing a business with debt. It was getting bad.

After she gave birth, something incredible happened.

> *"With the addition of our new family member, we both dedicated our life to her. The pressures of the proposed business purchase seemed to melt away as we concentrated on our daughter. For my wife it was the 'best' experience ever, even for a girl that never aspired to have children.*
>
> *"Now in our late 50s we are closer than ever and the reason is the joy of our now two children. It has given us the* ***direction*** *and* ***purpose*** *that otherwise would have been lacking in our relationship."*

I believe that people mature with marriage (or at least have the opportunity to) and become unselfish with parenting (or lat least have the opportunity to). It is not that people exist only for their children—they shouldn't—it is that they see a point to life past their own self-importance and gratification.

Having children is a monumental responsibility, and it is that recognition that often pulls people up short when they consider dumping their marriage. John wrote that he and his wife had been happily married for six years when they ran into some severe problems. It was a combination of his wife lying to him about finances, and his own need to look for something beyond his marriage to make his life more "exciting."

> *"I had worked my way up to saying that the only recourse was for us was divorce and to get away from each other. What happened to stop it? Three simple words: Maggie, Emily, and Joey . . . my kids. I could not do this (divorce) to them. I was responsible for their lives and even though I 'thought' I might be happier without my wife, I knew I wouldn't be happier without them.*

"This doesn't sound romantic or anything special, but it made me stop to look at my life and my wife. The kids made me stop before doing something stupid, but afterward I saw that I truly love my wife; we have good days and bad days, but mostly we just have days together."

I always try to remind callers with children threatening divorce that it won't be just about them and their spouse—it'll be about destroying their children's lives; unless the situation is dangerous or destructive, it should be endured for their sakes. And you know what? When you're there because you've endured, wonderful things can happen—which will never if you leave.

Karl wrote about his experience with his parents when he was ten on a summer's evening in 1978. The family had just come home from a wonderful day, or so he thought. As he played with his new record player and headphones, he was unaware that his parents were in the living room having a bitter argument. Suddenly his father burst into his room and said, "Come in here, son, we need to talk to you." He was annoyed, having to turn off *The Muppet Movie,* and went into the living room. He noticed his mother was in tears and his dad was very serious.

"That's when he hit me with it—'Your mom and I are getting separated.' What? After what was a perfect day in a kid's life, my folks drop this bombshell on me? No. NO! I wasn't going to let them ruin my day (more important to me at the time than the implications of their actions on the rest of my life).

" 'No,' I said with tears starting to well up in my eyes, 'you can't do this to me. Do you know what this is going to do to me? I'll never get to see you together again. We'll never

be a family again. YOU CAN'T STAY TOGETHER FOR ME?' "

His parents started to backpedal by assuring him that this would only be a trial run, and after a few weeks, they'd probably get back together again.

"Well, then why leave at all, if you're going to get back together in a few weeks? Make it work. Aren't I worth it? Keep trying!"

His parents reassured him that they would. Satisfied, he went back to Miss Piggy and the Muppet gang.

His parents will be celebrating their forty-ninth wedding anniversary, and he modestly assumes credit for making it happen!

Oh that more children could/would fight back in such a way.

Most of the time, getting a divorce is just quitting.

As Ann, another listener, wrote, there were three things she knew she had to do to save her marriage from her deep resentment and insecurity:

> *"1. I had to remember why I married my husband—which may not have been because he was such a great provider, but because of his gentle manner, complete emotional support of me, his incredible integrity and dependability—all of which were still there.*
>
> *"2. I had to realize my fears and insecurities were exaggerated because of my childhood and that these were my issues and not him doing something wrong.*
>
> *"3. The greatest lesson I learned and try to tell others is that marriage is like learning 100 Russian words. You can say, 'I can't learn Russian, it's too hard.' But the FACT is that you could if you truly were committed. Each morning you could learn one*

word—after a while, it gets easier and the words can become sentences.

"Marriage takes work; committing to it each morning keeps it from getting away from us and it keeps getting easier.

"The greatest reward is when we ask our three-year-old who he wants to read to him and tuck him in and he says, 'I want Mommy on this side and I want Papa on this side.' "

Commitment has great rewards, especially in the eyes and hearts of your children.

I'M LEAVING OR YOU'RE OUT!

It is sad but true that sometimes the camel has to completely drop down dead before some folks are motivated to be and do better in their marriages.

Jim reported that his crisis came twenty years into the marriage. His sisters and friends kept saying that he had the patience of Job in letting his wife run over him. His wife was very insecure because of a terrible childhood. She was controlling and unloving. He was simply determined never to let the marriage break up while the kids needed them both. He endured.

One day while they were shopping, his wife saw a friend of hers approaching and immediately put her arm around Jim's waist. He was really irritated that she did that as a "show" for her friend; she hadn't hugged him in ten years!

When they got to the car, he realized he had reached his limit, and said,

"Honey, you had no business putting your arm around me that way. If you cannot show me affection in our home, then you

> *need not try faking it in public. You seem to never find anything I do as acceptable or good and I seem to be a great aggravation to you. Life is simply too short for us to be miserable any longer. I am therefore going to release you from your vows to me. I simply love you too much to see you in this agony any longer.*
>
> *"Since I seem to be the source of that misery, we will part. I'll be packing as soon as we get home. Perhaps you will then be able to find another man who will be able to let you be happy."*

She sat quietly all the way home. He held to his promise and began packing. She walked around the house for a time and watched him. When he began putting his tools in his truck and spoke to her about finances, she broke down and began really crying . . . and promising she would change.

She did change and they continued their marriage.

> *"Sure, there were stumblings and slips and occasional spats but we worked through them. She slowly began showing me more respect and honor, and over the next few years things became much better. We now have three grandkids, married 34 years, and our home is continual peace. In fact, today we are as happy as we have ever been in our entire lives."*

I always remind people to never use leaving as a manipulation; it is an ultimatum of the sort that must never be made except in earnest. Leaving should be the very last option. While it is true that many people who won't see they need to change or say/think they cannot change, make huge leaps when confronted with the ultimate rejection, it is also true that some people give lip service to changing once the nest gets secure again.

Nonetheless "leaving" is often a powerful "rebooting" of the marriage, reminding each person that they have obligations to the other, not just a right to expectations for themselves.

Nicole described her marriage as a perpetual fight.

> *"We didn't even want to be in the same room as each other. It took my husband leaving and going to a hotel room to really hit us that this was it!*
>
> *"That night he called me on his cell and we talked for a long time—and for the first time I think we actually heard each other. Funny how it took us being on a phone and not in the same room to be able to get our points across.*
>
> *"He then came home and we just simply started to show each other affection. We knew that we had to work on our issues but that they would not be resolved overnight. We also knew that we once had a very passionate relationship and that we were once very much in love—and the number one reason is we had two boys who needed their mom AND their dad.*
>
> *"The more affection we gave each other and the increase in sex actually helped us. He started to change and so did I. We just reminded each other why we fell in love and what it felt like and that helped us talk nicer and open up a lot more to each other I can now again say that I am so in love with my husband and he is with me too!!"*

Many people get it backward: they think they have to talk everything out, resolve everything completely, and see a ton of concrete changes before they will *maybe* feel in love again. Actually the compassionate, sensitive, and loving *gestures* have to come *before* the feelings. Generally actions drag feelings along and not the opposite. Husbands and wives must treat each other with the tender, loving regard they once had in order to reinitialize positive feelings about their spouse. The more you *think* and *do* loving things, the more you will feel loving.

Does that mean you're being phony? No. It means you're thinking positively and making an investment based on earlier wonderful returns.

As Michelle offered, "*I think the biggest mistake people make in a marriage is forgetting that you can still be girlfriend and boyfriend. We tend to treat each other more like roommates because we get comfortable. We don't give enough compliments and praise. We let our bodies go and think that the other person will love us no matter what. We stop experimenting with new things together and settle into the same old routines. Continuing these activities once married helps keep things together, especially when the times get tough.*"

And this is twice as important when you're on the brink of divorce. Actually Michelle and her husband, both of whom came from divorced families, had been divorced for nine months, ostensibly due to his infidelity. Once apart they realized the magnitude of what they had given up. They were so motivated to not continue their family divorce traditions that they used that energy to break through their fears and really open up to each other. After agreeing to care for one another more tenderly, and never to bring up the past (which can't be changed) as punishment or leverage in an argument, they remarried.

WHAT? IT ISN'T SUPPOSED TO BE ALL ABOUT ME?

The number one most difficult task in the entire world is to think outside the box—when it is yourself that is the box! Don't take it personally; to some degree, this is true for everyone. Your thoughts and feelings are immediately accessible to you—you can know the thoughts and feelings of your spouse only if they tell you. But if they tell you and you refuse to listen, denounce their truths and perspectives, deny any culpability for their feelings, or excuse yourself from having to respond lovingly to their needs because you have hurts too—then, simply, you lose them—even if they are still under the same roof.

I had one such call recently from a woman with two small children who wanted to know what she should do with her husband. It seems he's told her that he needs more attention from her. She refused to admit that his request was reasonable, because in her view she gave him sufficient attention. It is difficult with two small children and a trying day to always be sensitive and accommodating to one's spouse; however, the spouse becomes hopeless when their plea is dismissed.

Try as I might, I couldn't get through to her. She and I ended with this sad exchange:

Caller: Well, I need time for myself.

DrL: If you refuse to acknowledge his loving need for you, then—if he's a decent man—when your youngest is eighteen, he'll be gone—and you'll have lots of time for yourself.

That relationship was going to hell.

Self-centeredness finds many faces. One couple almost had their marriage annulled only after a couple of weeks. Though they were both twenty-eight, she was stuck in her adolescence always wanting mommy and daddy's approval for everything. *"I didn't care too much about my husband's opinion on things. After realizing that my husband was very serious about the annulment, I finally placed my husband as the priority and finally opened up my eyes that he is not the enemy, but now my real, true family."*

Marilyn came to realize that too as her life was all about pleasing her difficult parents, she accommodated them and took her frustrations with that situation out on her husband. She still has familial issues, but she deals with them now as his wife, not their daughter.

Another typical self-centered motivation for tracking a marriage into hell is deciding that your spouse is boring. "*After 3 years of marriage,*" wrote Kris, "*I decided my husband was horribly boring and unromantic. We never did anything exciting, and I somehow felt as if MY happiness was HIS responsibility. I moved out and stayed with a friend and went out on a few dates. This was the life! This was exciting! And after all, as a child of the 70s flower children, I knew it was most important to do what makes you happy, right? Why shouldn't it be all about me-me-me?*"

It took Kris only a couple of weeks to realize how completely selfish she was being. *"All I had to do to save my marriage from the brink of disaster was to stop being an idiot. It's really that simple."*

The thing about bored people, as I mentioned in an earlier chapter, is that they are boring. Once Kris focused in on how wonderful her husband was, and how lucky she was that he was still open to her after her shenanigans, she spent her time making sure that he was well taken care of—never a dull moment after that!

Brian admitted that "*stopping my drug addiction really saved my marriage.*" Taking responsibility for out-of-control, self-focused behavior without blaming your spouse for your actions is a tremendous boost to a marriage teetering over hell. Drinking, drugs, gambling, pornography, video games, and so forth, when compulsively done, are self-centered activities geared toward instant gratification and distraction from problems and feelings that need more constructive forms of attention.

A recent caller, twenty-eight years old, told me that she just finds it too impossible to be nice, loving, and sexual with her husband despite his wonderful nature. They've been married five years and have two little children. She told me she'd been in therapy since childhood concerning sexual abuse by a stepdad, and an unfortunate first marriage to an abusive guy.

DrL: How did all that therapy help you be able to love your husband?

Caller: Well, actually it didn't. I learned that I was a victim, that nothing was my fault, and that probably my husband earned my negative feelings toward him.

DrL: Brace yourself, my dear, for an alternative view. I think you are feeling so safe with this nice guy, that you feel free to be the perpetrator.

Caller: What????

DrL: Exactly. The tables are turned and now you have control and dominance and feel safe. However you're no longer in a situation against which you have to defend yourself. This is payback against the guys—your stepdad and first husband—who hurt you, but aimed at an innocent party AND your own potential happiness.

Don't you see that the first part of your life was taken up by predators and this, the second part of your life is also . . . except that the perp this time is YOU!

Caller: Whoa—I never thought about it this way, but I think you're right. What can I do?

DrL: Drop your guard, trust your husband, and love him up and have fun with him. No more fear—just more fun.

Caller: That sounds absolutely great. No therapist ever told me anything positive I could use to be happy—it is as if they all catered to my ugly history and not any potential for a beautiful tomorrow.

There are some good therapists out there, if you're lucky enough to find one. Mary wrote to me about what happened a decade ago when her marriage was indeed on the brink of divorce because of her husband's adultery.

"What saved it for me was that we entered into therapy with a counselor who thinks an awful lot like you do, Dr. Laura. Without excusing my husband's behavior, she repeatedly redirected my assessments from his behavior to mine. Meaning, every time I wanted to rehash what my husband had done to me, she forced me to examine how I had contributed to the problem.

"Instead of entering into a fast food mentality of 'sit 'n bitch' every week, with fingers pointing at what the other party had done that was so egregious, we were constantly forced to examine our own behavior.

"People go into couples' therapy with an agenda to change the other person. 'If only my husband would just do/not do this or that, then I'd be happy.' Imagine two people sitting in chairs across a room, each one waiting for the other one to change their behavior; each one waiting for the other one to lead!

"Rather than allow us to marinate in our own disillusionment and bitterness with the other, we were directly to examine what needed to be changed about OURSELVES!"

And that is why Mary and her husband are happily back together again.

Abraham wrote about his marital problems, acknowledging

that his angry, critical behaviors were more about people in his past who hurt them, and not his wife, who got the brunt of it. *"Dr. Laura once said on the radio to a caller, 'Expect from your wife only what she can give you today. Don't expect her to make up for other people's abuse or shortcomings. She's your wife, not your mother.' "*

These days Abraham works hard on seeing her positive attributes and always considers her opinion. When he wants to criticize or point out some fault, he thinks long and hard about whether or not it is truly necessary to do so. If he decides that it is important, he thinks a few moments about exactly what he wants to say, lowers his tone, gets straight to the point, and points out that he is in no way trying to put her down. *"I always try to remember that I am not so high and mighty myself either."*

I usually remind listeners who feel some anger at their mate rising up within them to pair each critical thought or judgment with a positive or loving memory of them. It is too easy to do damage to a beloved when that tally sheet is momentarily out of balance. Always balance it in your mind before you speak.

It is also typical for people to just get too embroiled in their own importance with work, charity, children, family, or the problems of friends. These are ultimately all self-centered activities when they clearly preclude time, attention, affection, and respect for your spouse and family.

Personal ego gratification at the expense of family is a no-no.

COMMUNICATION

Mostly learn to "shut up." Just because it crosses your mind, don't assume it should come through your lips. Where did you ever get the notion that free speech meant you didn't have to consider appropriate restraint when dealing with the feelings of a beloved or the well-being of the entire family?

I realize that most discussions about communication have to do with actual "talking," but I'm of the opinion that more people need to learn to shut up than need to learn how to say something stupid or hurtful in a better way.

Certain things once said cannot be taken back. Too many spouses seem to imagine that they have some sort of protective immunity so that they can be cruel—with the excuse of hormones, bad day, need to vent—and there will be no real ongoing consequence. You're going to get only a few "get out of jail free" cards, and then the awe, respect, admiration, and love for you will start to wane.

Before you speak, think first about whether or not this will add to happiness and peace. Better still, cut your communication 15 percent, and fill the other 85 percent of the time with touching a hand, offering a cup of coffee, a neck rub, a hug, a sweet compliment, and so forth. Remember—TALK IS CHEAP and ACTIONS SPEAK LOUDER THAN WORDS . . . unless, of course, the words are mean or lies.

People just want to be treated with warmth, love, respect, and support. They don't want to hassle every detail of life. One quick way to bring your marriage back from the brink is NOT to talk it to death, but to instantaneously just start BEING NICE. You can't convince somebody you've changed . . . you've got to actually change. It might take them a while to believe and trust it, so don't do the "I tried it and it didn't work" schtick. If you want this marriage bad enough—EARN IT!

YOUR SPOUSE IS A SAINT

Some of you have seriously earned being dumped. The only thing that saves the day is that your spouse is a saint. Some of that sainthood might be part afraid to let go and be alone or even seemingly futile hope; maybe they just see more to you than you realize you have and are. Whatever it is, they give you another chance. DON'T BLOW IT!

Russ, a listener, wrote:

> *"When my wife and I got married I was an angry young man with a chip on his shoulder and a bad temper. I grew up in a violent home. This June 19, 2006, will be our 35th anniversary and I thank God every day that she stayed with me and helped raise me.*
>
> *"My wife learned somehow, probably because of my explosive reaction, that challenging me in public back then was not a good thing and she was more effective in a private conversation with me. She was able to make her point, even though most of the time I was more concerned with winning the argument in my eyes than the actual point of the argument.*
>
> *"I was very immature and selfish probably the first 10 years of our marriage. I credit my wife and the Lord for what I am today (not that I think I am special now) and the great relationships we have with our kids, their spouses, and our grandchildren."*

So what makes his wife a saint and not a patsy? It is interesting that Russ suggested himself that one of the typical mistakes women make is accepting poor behavior from their husbands, thinking it will get better. Ironically that is exactly what did happen for Russ. Why? Probably because his wife was not weak—she *didn't accept* his behavior, she dealt with it in a way which didn't cause the situation and his behavior to escalate. They had known each other since they were fourteen and sixteen; she had compassion for his family situation and how it impacted him—she was there to witness it. Her compassion, however, would probably not have stayed intact had he not demonstrated self-control at significant moments.

She made an investment, she took a risk, and her gamble paid off. It doesn't always. Although Russ pointed to that ten-year mark as the turning point for his behavioral changes, I bet it was more consistent and gradual—so she had reason to believe that her way of dealing with him worked.

Stefanie was prepared to leave her husband two years ago. They had been married seven years, and fought the whole time.

> *"The name-calling on both our parts was out of control. Having three small children and both working full-time (opposite shifts so one of us was always home with the kids) was stressing us both out. I also was always 'too tired' to have sex with him. I didn't take care of him. We hated each other.*
>
> *"I had an affair and my husband found out. Rather than kick me out like I deserved, he cried and said, 'You broke my heart.' This coming from the man I thought hated me!*
>
> *"We went to counseling and learned to stop the name-calling. My counselor must have been a Dr. Laura listener because I was told to be happy that my man always wanted to have sex with me and to give it to him whenever he wanted. After all, even if I was 'too tired,' wouldn't I enjoy it too? The counselor said that the fact that my husband still found me incredibly sexy and beautiful after seven years and three kids was wonderful, and that some women didn't have a husband like that.*
>
> *"I did nice things for my man. Two years after the affair, we get along better than ever. Whenever I make the mistake of turning him down for sex because I am 'too tired,' I stop for a minute, think about the past, put on a movie for the kids, and call him upstairs.*

"I am so lucky he stuck with me. I used to hate him, now I would literally give him my heart if he needed it. He is my man, the father of my children, and I thank God every day for him."

If your spouse shows any glimmer of cutting you some slack or supporting your better self—take it humbly, graciously, seriously, and lovingly. Give daily thanks to him/her in every way imaginable. Don't take advantage of a second chance; don't get all defensive and try to even up the score. Don't be stupid; do be grateful and take the opportunity to become a better human being, spouse, and parent. Become the person you'd be more proud to be with, feel safe with, and loved by.

IT'S THE SMALL THINGS, STUPID!

Most people get it into their heads that personal change and marital repair have to be huge, overwhelming issues. KISS: keep it simple, stupid! Or KISS: keep it small, stupid! Both concepts work. Heath wrote to me that he and his wife were pretty much finished. They did little as a team and when things got frustrating, Heath would lash out at her by saying mean things. He felt pretty much reduced to "*a walking paycheck with a penis attached. My job ground me down too. My wife didn't care about that, so long as the MONEY kept coming in and her health insurance was covered. We were finished.*"

What turned things around was something very small. It started with the simple good deed of my wife bringing me a hot lunch during my break time at work. *"Such a small act paid such great dividends as the job didn't seem so life-draining nor did the workday seem as long. Sometimes she'd bring my dog to visit me as well, which really helped me keep things in perspective, that what I was doing was worth SOMETHING."*

What goes around comes around works for good things too. Heath starting finding ways to help her at her workplace, like bringing her a rose or lunch. *"Ultimately, everything turned around. Marriage becomes less difficult when your partner helps you with your struggles. And the sex gets better as well. *wink wink*."*

KISS versus imagining you have to go through the hell of rehashing old hurts and angers. KISS versus thinking you have to wait eons for there to be good feelings back in the relationship. KISS versus believing that there is no hope. KISS . . . yeah, I do mean literally!

Chapter 6

Mother Laura's Marriage Tools

You all have heard the admonition, "If it ain't broke, don't fix it." Well, sometimes folks forget that when it is broke, they should do whatever it takes to fix it rather than give up and throw the marriage away, pull inside themselves, run to someone else for validation, or start attacking in order to look like the one in the right or the victim.

Admittedly there are times though that you might feel so emotionally distraught that it is hard to think of what you should and could do. Combine that with the fear of failure or rejection, and you may just emotionally run and hide.

Here are ten alternatives. Memorize them! Live them!

1. ***There is no "I" in TEAM!*** When your marriage is on the brink of divorce, when there is no communication and you're both miserable and figure you need to do something about it or cut it off then and there, it is time to . . . what? Well this is exactly why there is such a high divorce rate; most folks don't really know what to do at the moment that the feelings are so

high, or low, that you can't imagine anything good coming out of whatever you say or do.

As I mentioned earlier, Aaron, Moses's brother, healed a shattered relationship between two former best friends by meeting separately with each and telling them a special kind of lie. He told each that he had run into the other and heard nice things about them! Now what makes this a "special kind of lie" is that in truth, each *had* nice things to say about each other—for years! It's just that they hadn't said any of those things recently because they were damn angry about something or other. When each heard that the other said something nice about them, it brought back their own nice thoughts about each other. The next time they met in the street, they embraced instead of ignoring each other. There is a lesson here: when the going gets to feeling hopeless and way too ugly, it is time to remember the covenant and your earliest dreams and hope for the relationship. You are a team. Stop thinking only that you are sleeping with the enemy.

Instead of giving him/her a list of their failures, give your beloved a list of your points of appreciation and a list of the things you intend to do for them! That's right—for them! And this is true *even if* (the favorite phrase of many of my callers) you believe you are the victim here. Do it! It will remind your beloved that you are a team and that will be more motivating than forcing them to feel humiliated and beyond redemption.

2. **Down Memory Lane.** Tommy and Coral, listeners, had been just sharing the same house, leading sepa-

rate lives. Coral says she was praying for ages that she could love him again. Basically, however, they were like brother and sister. She is seventy-one, and he a young eighty-two. This was their second marriage (of fifteen years) as both had lost their first spouses.

One day while Coral, who didn't cook anymore, was making dinner for a sick neighbor. Her husband walked by and saw the stir-fry pan and said that he remembered that pan. " *'I fell in love with you when you cooked me dinner in it.' I said, 'Well, I fell in love with you while we were dancing and I don't cook anymore and we don't dance anymore, so I guess we both got gypped.'* "

One week later Tommy wrote "dancing" on Coral's "to do" list. They went dancing.

> *"Tommy is the most fantastic dancer and he has the cutest expressions on his face—it made me fall in love with him all over again. People tell us that we look like a couple of lovebirds. When we are being passionate, I say, 'Are old folks like us supposed to be having this much fun?!' Oh, and I also cook more.*
>
> *"This has been the greatest miracle in my life. My prayer was answered beyond my wildest dreams. I always thought that Tommy should have someone who adored him. I never though that someone would be me."*

Remember back to what made you "fall in love" and make that memory live today.

3. **Mutual Forgiveness.** Kimberly and her husband had the most wonderful, romantic courtship, engagement, wedding, honeymoon . . . but then nothing else

seemed to fall into place after their first year together. Loss of jobs, changed professions, unplanned and difficult pregnancies, having to drop out of college, a severe car accident, family deaths, financial problems, relocations . . . led to a lot of bad, hard feelings between them.

"When we came to our five-year anniversary nothing seemed right. That actual night [of their anniversary] we took our son to a sitter and ended up at home in the worst fight ever. We vented. There was screaming, things were broken, many tears and the word divorce was thrown out on the floor as the solution to our nightmare. However, almost as soon as we realized that it could happen, we verbalized to each other that this was not what we wanted.

"We then did something special that brought healing and the ability to press on. ***We forgave each other. We agreed to let the past die and start over.*** *We went from being on opposite sides of the room, to holding hands and praying together. My husband then led me to where we kept the copy of our vows. We had our own little ceremony. We recommitted and said our 'I dos' again. We hugged and kissed and then went and picked up our son. We went to bed that night in peace.*

"We were poor, there were no gifts or romantic getaways for our 5th anniversary; but I will remember it forever. It was an incredible night about true love and our decision to keep it happily ever after."

4. **Dump Your Prideful Ways.** Most of the time you both probably behave very badly when your beloved tells you how you've hurt them or gives you any criti-

cism at all. You probably don't take the time to really listen, instead you just get all defensive and attack back to try to make yourself look better—and it works the opposite way!

Just listen! By that I mean, listen without speaking—don't explain, excuse, or defend yourself. Just listen! Show respect for the state of mind, perspective, and feelings of your beloved. Keep your lip buttoned and just listen.

After you've heard it all, find some part from 1 percent to 99 percent of what she/he says that holds water and **own it!** Accept that you have failed or let someone down. Admit that you were insensitive, wrong . . . whatever. It is not constructive to try to prove that you are right and they are wrong. Even if you think you have a great explanation or excuse—they are feeling hurt; acknowledge your part in that.

If you **own it,** take responsibility, show true remorse, try to repair it, and clarify how it will not be repeated, then you have given your beloved a gift that will tsunami back with loving rewards.

5. **Ignore the Sometimes Not So Small Stuff.** Everybody has lousy parts of their personality—everybody. Jim wrote that he and his wife were able to avoid divorce by taking responsibility for their own actions and focusing in how to personally change rather than make the other change. Jim would get physically violent when angry; and what made him the most angry, was when his wife would curse at him and use her words to hurt him.

"I made myself accountable by writing a letter to my wife stating that if I ever physically hurt her again, I

would call the police on myself. I also learned how to direct my frustrations more constructively and if I was feeling like I was getting 'heated up,' that it was okay to go for a walk and cool off.

"My wife's main problem was that when she felt like she was getting mad, she would find any word or phrase that she knew would hurt me. I had a problem with taking things from the woman I love very personally. She would provoke with her words, hurt me, I'd get heated up and then things would escalate.

"Now, however, if she swears (and it is rare now) I ignore it and later, as she does now, I know she will come back and apologize for the swearing."

Yeah, I know your beloved can cut you deeper than anyone else has the power to do; that's because you love them and have your emotional well-being attached to their feelings about you. And you are hurt by the seeming rejection that their anger feels like. Nonetheless it is never useful to escalate a situation by reciprocating with your own bad behavior.

6. **You're the Genius! . . . No, Honey, YOU'RE the Genius!** Remember that you two will each have a different point of view about any situation. Try to remember that two heads can be much better than one if you show some respect for the other's head! You might learn something useful, and you just might come up with a better solution together than each of you separately.

   Instead of fighting your beloved's perspective, make the huge effort to find something good about it. That way, your spouse feels heard and appreciated, instead of someone you consider stupid and useless.

Try this: next time you're in a so-called debate about something (money, kids, relatives), instead of trying to convince your spouse that you're right, make a big deal about some part of their point of view that you think is terrific! Watch how quickly s/he will suddenly find something of value in your perspective. This is loving negotiation.

Don't let it get personal. When you discuss problems, make sure you keep it to the issue, some perspective, an idea, a solution, a dilemma, whatever, but DO NOT let it get personal in an ugly way. Avoid the name-calling and bringing up of past mistakes, and so forth. Is it more important for you to have your way than to have a marriage of happiness and peace? If you blow any of this, just say you're sorry IMMEDIATELY and ask for forgiveness . . . then screw up less and less, okay?

7. **Nicer to Strangers.** It is amazing to me how many people treat absolute strangers with more courtesy, kindness, and sensitivity than their own spouses and families! Why is that? Because they know they can get away with it with family—they feel safe from rejection and abandonment. It is all about taking advantage of love and taking love for granted. Don't—you have too much to lose and the potential of too many people being hurt.

   "*We are married because we love and enjoy each other—so why not treat each other as friends first? We practiced kindness, restraint, complimenting, and most important, get-*

ting those nagging thoughts (if they are important) into the open instead of brewing on them for hours or days on end and then ferociously erupting at some later time," wrote Marsha, who revealed that they were on the brink of divorce five years earlier.

You should actually be treating your spouse with infinitely more regard than a stranger due to your covenant, and the gratitude you should have that someone tolerates your nonsense and would mourn your passing. A stranger won't mourn your passing. Don't treat your spouse so poorly that they won't either!

8. **It Is a Far Greater Blessing to Give than Receive.** Mostly when we've had a bad day or are just out of sorts, we *need, want, demand, expect.* Problem usually is that either we don't communicate any of this, that is, ask for hugs, a neck rub, kind words, and so forth, or when/if we get some caretaking, we are critical or rejecting of it, or don't let it help us at all and we stay in a crummy mood.

   I have always found that coming out of yourself at these times, while difficult, is better medicine. Do an errand for her/him. Get your spouse a little gift surprise, write a cute and loving note—you get the idea. You will, I promise, feel better faster than waiting and wanting stuff to come your way.

   Then if you still need a little TLC, ask specifically for it in a reasonable, humble way. And when you get it, make a fuss about how wonderful they are . . . even if it's a little off the mark or doesn't do the trick.

9. **Forget Rewriting History.** "*I realized that the years of resentment weren't going to disappear overnight,*" wrote

Lynette about her marriage. That is such an important point. So many people yearn for the pristine and won't "let it all go" or "get on with today" because they are still marinating in the crap.

Lynette knew that her husband wasn't spontaneously going to get her off the hook for the long-term errors of her ways. He wasn't going to one day soon just blurt out, "I forgive you! I am madly in love with you and I want to be with you forever! I will never leave you again!" Healing takes time and you can't take the temperature of a marriage every five minutes in order for you to feel safe, while forcing your spouse to feel something they're not up to yet.

Best thing you can do when you've messed up is DO THE RIGHT THING FROM THIS POINT ON . . . and pray for the best.

10. **Kings and Queens.** Tracy wrote that "*Ten years into our marriage I didn't feel unhappy, but I knew I couldn't say that I was happily married either. I went home to my Grandma's to 'think' for a week. Grandma sent me back to my husband after a few days saying, 'It's as simple as this: treat him like a king and he will treat you like a queen.'*

    "We are now into our twenty-third year of marriage and I can say without a doubt, I am one happy queen."

    Give him/her what they want and need (unless it's immoral or illegal) *even if* it is not your cup of tea. Assuming you married a reasonable, decent person this will be reciprocated—I promise.

Chapter 7

The Gift of the Magi

Abe Lincoln quipped that "Most people are as happy as they make up their minds to be." In life and in love there are definite attitudes and actions that make people happier: gratitude, optimism, forgiveness, self-healthcare, and speaking positively. Many people hang on to gloomy, negative, and angry states of mind out of pure habit, and habits are difficult to break; difficult, but not impossible.

One recent caller, married only a handful of years and with a small child, called to tell me that she's probably going to end the marriage because they fight about everything and say hurtful things to each other. I asked her to try an experiment: every time she wishes to lash out with her words she was supposed to *first* say *two* things utterly complimentary. If, after that, she still felt like saying something mean—then go for it!

It is a fact that what comes out of your mouth is what sits on your brain. The more you talk to or about your spouse in angry, ugly ways, the more angry and ugly you are to them and feel about them.

Some of you reading this are probably aghast! You probably

can't imagine generating so much self-control from within or getting over the feeling that you'd be letting them get away with something. Well, if your goal is to be happily married, can you afford not to learn self control? Do you really want to make the love of your life feel quite that bad when they've upset you? Do you want this ferociously angry exchange to be the last thing s/he remembers about this marriage as s/he goes to sleep at night?

Rachel, a listener, wrote that she has not gotten along well with her husband's family due to some bad behaviors on both their parts. I was impressed that she did admit that she had responsibility for the family's upset. She didn't have to deal with them more than once every four or five years because they lived in a different state.

The current situation arose since her husband had an important event, and some of his family flew into town to be at this event. Rachel didn't want to go to the dinner.

> *". . . and I just kept thinking what you, Dr. Laura, would say if I had you sitting across from me and I was whining to you about how I did not like these people and how* 'UNCOMFORTABLE' *(I know you always make fun of uncomfortable being used as an excuse since it is a small issue) they made me and why I couldn't just stay at home while my husband went out to dinner with his family.*
>
> *"You would have said that they paid quite a bit of good money to come and see my husband and to be there for him on his big day, and they are his family and he wanted them there on his special day. You would say that a good wife would not do anything to make her husband's life harder and you would ask me if I wanted to be a good wife or a bad wife.*
>
> *"Then you would tell me, 'Smile and be polite.'*

"I made up my mind that I was going to be kind, pleasant, friendly, and polite, no matter what anyone else did at dinner last night.

"Well, I was—and imagine my surprise at how pleasant the evening was. I am not going to delude myself about certain unchangeable facts about these people that make my whole 'Walton's Mountain' fantasy impossible, but they've grown up some and so have I since the last time I saw them. It really was a nice dinner and I look forward to seeing them today . . . to my utter shock!"

As I mentioned in the Preface, this is the point of the Gift of the Magi: to have a lovely marriage, give what is most precious to you. In Rachel's case, she gave of her loving, kind self in spite of her fears and hurts. She did it for the sake of the man she loves. This behavior is called altruism. Married people who display frequent altruism toward their beloveds have happier marriages. Spouses who have this self-sacrificing "put the interest of the other before my own interests" mentality are happier, and more happily married.

Tiffany's husband was studying to be a minister, so money was tight. He had just found a used PlayStation on sale for $40. She knew he loved to relax with a video game in between reading nonstop for his two college degrees. They had a couple of small, unexpected expenses show up later that week, and her birthday was coming up. They didn't have money for him to buy her a birthday present, and she told him it was truly okay, and that he could get her something down the line when the finances eased up a bit.

He asked her what she would have wanted had they the money to get it; she said a body lotion and body spray set that cost about $20. He promised to get it for her when he could.

"The next day, I came home from work and the entire apartment was cleaned and vacuumed, candles were burning, and dinner was cooking on the stove. I asked him what the occasion was. He replied, 'Your birthday, honey! Now let me go get your present.'

"He came out with a gift bag with the lotion and body spray set in the fragrance I had wanted. I couldn't believe it, and asked, 'How did you get this? We have no money!'

"He replied, 'I pawned my PlayStation. I would rather you have a birthday present than for me to have a video game machine.' "

I guarantee you, folks, that as happy as it made her to receive, it made him happier to sacrifice for her. Altruism, self-sacrifice, makes people happy. It also makes them loved. In order to be loved, you must first love. Love is not about you or what you want, it's about giving love without conditions to somebody healthy and kind enough to do the same.

Annette and her husband recently celebrated their twentieth anniversary.

"And as we look around and see people struggle in their marriage, and then we look at each other and we ask, 'Why are things so good for us? We're either in complete denial or things are pretty dang good.'

"Yes, we've had many struggles: infertility, miscarriages, business bankruptcy, moving from our home of 18 years to a new state, moving a business, building a new one . . . but I can narrow down a great marriage to the banishment of two words from our vocabulary and marriage: they are EXPECT and DESERVE.

"Too often partners in a marriage have way too many unrea-

sonable expectations. There is no room for 'high horses' in a marriage, and if we focus on what our ***partner*** *deserves, magically we get everything we need."*

That is the Gift of the Magi.

THE GIFT OF BECOMING "ONE"

The covenant of marriage generally includes the proclamation that two lives have joined into one. I wish more married couples would spend time considering what that really means outside of joint income tax forms and community property laws. Your spouse is not supposed to be your sibling with whom you compete for attention, importance, or power. There is no beauty generated by those motivations.

Danielle wrote that for her birthday, she

> *"sat at the picnic table with all my kids and hubby of 33 years. She thought, 'This is the life!' Yes, we have had our struggles because we are human, yet here we are eating a dutch oven supper my husband cooked for us. We laughed at the past and giggle at the stupids we have all committed, but the most important thing we all realized was that WE ARE A UNIT—AND WE ARE THERE FOR EACH OTHER COME HELL OR HIGH WATER!*
>
> *"I am sure we will do stupid human tricks from time to time, but I can look forward with confidence that MY TEAM that was formed by blood, sweat and tears will be there to get each other through the tough and good times.*
>
> *"It has been worth the trip—believe me—and when all is said and done and we die, the only thing we can take with us is the relationships we've formed and the integrity of our souls.*

I did the right thing and spent the day celebrating with the ones I love . . . unconditionally."

Life can be quite complicated and difficult. It is a blessing and a relief to not have to go it alone. Cherish that.

Linda wrote that she had overspent quite a bit on her credit card, due to less household money coming in. Her husband's business is in a low cash flow position, due to new product development, and he had been worried, cranky, and distant for months. She admitted to spending sneakily because she didn't want to deal with him, and because she has been somewhat ticked off about the distance.

But after hearing me on my radio program giving advice to a woman who had also sneakily overspent about not working *with* her husband as a *team,* but instead treating him virtually like an annoying and potentially punitive parent, she felt guilty enough to face the music.

"I paid bills, took a deep breath, and went to him with the numbers, statements, and credit card. I updated him on the bills, apologized for spending and not telling him, told him I had been wrong and a BRAT, and turned my credit card over to him.

"Dr. Laura, I was stunned by his response! With tears in his eyes, he took my hand, kissed me, and then he TALKED—for an hour. He told me he felt useless for anything but writing checks now that the kids are grown—and since he couldn't even write checks with the money so low, he felt even worse. With college, a wedding, and all the other expenses with three great kids left to educate, he's worrying about retirement. And he misses the kids so much he can hardly stand it.

"So we made a plan to hike more, visit the grandchildren,

and make whoopee!—all free activities. I assured him that I'm very good at not spending money, and would run all purchases by him.

"We are closer than we have been in months."

Linda and her husband went from him & her to we & us, dealing with life as a team—facing challenges and enjoying triumphs as "one."

THE GIFT OF UNDERSTANDING AND COMPASSION

One of the more typical behaviors that hurts the "we" and "team" concept, is the turning on each other when life throws us a curveball.

Amy: I am my two kids' mom. I have five-month-old fraternal twins. I just don't know what to do with my husband. I am working part-time right now and he just lost his job. For a month he's been looking for a job and I don't know if I should just go back full-time to my work and let him stay home and take care of the children.

DrL: Well, whatever you need to do to survive for the time being you need to do. That's what marriage and families do. That's what a team is, and if that's the best decision for right now, then that it what it is. Stuff happens. What did he lose his job for?

Amy: He was on probation and he didn't pass.

DrL: And that was because . . . ?

Amy: He has a back injury.

DrL: Then he was not irresponsible.

Amy: Yeah, but sometimes I get mad at him.

DrL: It's not fair to get mad at him, Amy. You're going to have to control that. You can't take your discomfort with real life out on your man. It's no fault of his own that he lost this job, and in addition, his back hurts and he's got a ticked-off wife. Do you want to just put his head on the floor and dig your heel into it?

Amy: Not really.

DrL: You're supposed to be the one person he can be safe with. And if you're not that person—you lose the marriage even if you stay together.

Amy: Right, and I love him.

DrL: He feels bad enough. There he is, he can't take care of his woman and his two kids because he has a back injury.

Amy: Yeah, I know.

DrL: Okay? A little compassion here. Build up his ego and make him feel better somehow. Tell him what a wonderful job he's doing with the kids.

Amy: So do you think me working full-time and him staying home is okay? That's better than them going to day care, right?

DrL: You have to ask that question? Hired help, virtual strangers already watching over too many screaming kids or one's daddy? I don't know—which do you think is better?!

Dawn called my program very bent out of shape because her husband wants peace and quiet in the home after eight P.M. on weeknights. Dawn pulled the "isn't he controlling" card out of the deck. They have two married children, and an eight-year-old daughter. All he asked for is that weeknights, when he needs to unwind, get rest so he can function the next day, that family and friends not stay past eight P.M.

Dawn: I don't know if I'm being selfish or he's being kind of controlling.

DrL: I don't think there's anything controlling about that. I just love the way women in particular jump to "controlling" when a man just simply wants something like peace and quiet in his home during the week. I don't think you'd call yourself controlling for wanting company to stay till late!

Dawn: Okay, but the other thing I was going to ask you was, like in the mornings—I can't turn on the bedroom light or anything, so I always have to get my clothes out the night before and try not to make noise in the morning.

DrL: Because he needs to sleep?

Dawn: Yeah.

DrL: So what is bad about that? I'm that respectful to my husband too if I have to get up before him. It's a matter of respect, Dawn. When you love somebody you try to accommodate them out of love and compassion—and respect.

That issue of not giving to a spouse because it is "giving in to their control" is a very sad commentary on what ought to be a no-brainer: accommodate your spouse, especially in the areas of peace and happiness.

Carrie called about her husband's desire to change what they agreed would be the name of their baby son, so that the son can be the IV in the family; it's tradition. I asked her why she was so against it.

Carrie: I guess it's an identity thing—like he's just as much a part of me as he is a part of my husband—and I felt I was kind of being controlled into doing it.

DrL: A man wants something and it's controlling. A woman wants something and it is entitlement. I don't have a lot of sympathy for your point of view. This baby spent nine months in your body and gains sustenance from the milk of your breasts? How do we even that up with your husband so that he feels the baby is also a part of him?

It's a simple gift, Carrie, which doesn't make the baby less yours, and it doesn't make him controlling.

Carrie: No, I would agree. But in my defense, he did say during my pregnancy, "Whatever makes you happy."

DrL: Guys say that so their wives won't bitch at them and not give them sex. They're also saying that to avoid a fight and in the hope of ultimate altruism from their wives.

Carrie: Right. So what do I do now?

DrL: Why don't you give him the gift? Make the family happy that it is four generations now. That's kind of cute. You give him this gift, he's going to give you many gifts back.

Carrie: Yeah, you're probably right.

Understanding and compassion—great gifts.

THE GIFT OF PERSPECTIVE

One of the most loving and helpful gifts is that of having or giving of a new perspective on things. For example, Janet wrote that she and her husband were driving home from his family's Christmas celebrations. She and her husband were discussing the obvious inconsistencies in how he and his sister were raised; his sister being the darling "cannot do wrong" sibling who delighted in getting him in trouble, while his boyish misbehaviors were met with severe punishments, bordering on abusive beatings.

Her husband was continuing to bitterly recount the imbalance in his boyhood home and his resentment at his sister even after all of these years.

> *"I looked at my husband and simply reminded him, that he is one of the most compassionate, empathetic people I have ever met. He is kind, gentle, loving, and genuinely a good person. He is by far the best person I have ever known in my life. All those experiences, as horrible as they were,*

seem to have added up to make him the man I fell in love with eleven years ago.

"I also reminded him that his sister is lonely, bitter, selfish, and for the most part, a not nice person.

"My husband then realized, as did we both, thank God for the imbalance. How awful it might have been if he had been the spoiled favorite—and what kind of person would he have turned into under that kind of upbringing; maybe he might have been the narcissistic, unlovable, and unhappy sibling!"

They had a good laugh over that, he felt a feeling with Janet that he never got as a child: ultimate love, respect, admiration, and appreciation—all the while realizing that his pampered sister had none of that. The bitter rivalry melted away, all due to Janet's loving "perspective" check.

Janet could have just said, "You know—get over it already and stop acting like a baby. I'm sick of hearing about your lousy childhood. Grow up!" Instead, Janet, gave him the perspective he needed to let go of that pain. Perspective is a gift.

Giving yourself perspective is yet another way to give your spouse a gift. Amy wrote about her adjustments during the first few weeks of motherhood. It was a time when getting a newborn to sleep at night was quite a challenge. This particular night their daughter wasn't fussy, but when Amy laid her in the bassinet, she was wide awake and squirming. Ryan, Amy's husband, came in to check on them, kissed and petted Eva's forehead, and went back downstairs.

A bit later, Amy was still sitting by Eva, who was quiet, but still wide awake. Ryan came in again, this time to fill up the humidifier for Eva and Amy with fresh water.

"I wanted to say 'Stop coming in here!' because I was afraid the commotion of the door opening, him walking around, etc., would stir Eva again. But I bit my tongue, just glad that he was so helpful.

"After a while, Eva was still awake, but quiet, so I ran downstairs to quickly grab some water. I was dying to be able to sit next to Ryan on the couch for a few minutes, but I had to get back upstairs. So I gave him a quick hug around his neck, kissed him, and told him good night. THEN—and here's where Dr. Laura helped me—I almost said, 'And don't come into her room anymore!!!!—It'll just wake her up!' But I didn't. I didn't let my bitterness that I couldn't relax with him make me snap at him. I am so lucky that he is such an involved dad and that he loves her enough to check on her and give her one more kiss. So I didn't make any rude or snippy comments.

"Eva fell asleep so I crawled into bed and closed my eyes. Ryan came in. My first thought was 'Grrr! What do you want?' but I kept quiet. 'Sleeping?' he whispered. 'Yeah,' I answered. Then he hopped into bed with me and began making love to me! How nice that with all the above, he wanted his wife! It was so great! I'm SO glad I wasn't a bitch earlier. Thank you, Dr. Laura, for helping me to be a pleasant wife. It was you vs. the post-pregnancy hormones—and you (and I) won!"

It is all in how you **choose** to look at it, isn't it?

THE GIFT OF HEALTHY FOCUS

Many married men and women use a million excuses for not making sure that their relationships with their own moms and dads don't infect their marriages. They'll cater to their parents' unreasonable requests and whims, they'll spend an inordinate amount of emotional time and energy fretting over pouty, manipulative, threatening, difficult, and even mean parents—hoping uselessly that they can finally get parental love.

What I remind folks who call me from these situations is "It is a terrible thing that you do not accept and reconcile your destructive past and present issues with parents because you are so narrowly focused on your childlike needs to be perfectly parented, that you don't seem to be even aware of the damage you do your spouse and your children with your constant distressed state of mind!" That is most usually a revelation to them.

But not to Helene:

> *"Reading* Bad Childhood Good Life *gave me the biggest boost of my life. I can't believe I've wasted so many years feeling sorry for myself because I have a cold, selfish mother. I put myself and my family through hell, trying harder and harder to please her, thinking that I could change her into the sweet, kind mother I'd always wished for. But of course she never changed and it only frustrated me to tears.*
>
> *"I used to obsess about this every day with my husband—poor guy. I'm so ashamed that I put him through that. But I'd been pitying myself and in the process I know I was driving my husband crazy. I'm so embarrassed. Honestly, if you hadn't written this book, I would no doubt still be crying about my mother day after boring day to my dear husband.*
>
> *"You're absolutely right that I have a second chance at a happy family life with my own husband and children. And I'm so blessed that I picked a wonderful, caring husband and we have two great kids! So now I remember to count my blessings. I'd been feeding those 'poor me' thoughts for years—but now I finally get it."*

Another source of extended family problems being allowed to negatively impact marriages is when some parent doesn't approve of or like your spouse, or refuses to acknowledge them or treat them with respect. Yes, you have to choose! You need to tell your difficult parent that the price of admission into your life is their respectful and polite treatment of your spouse. Without that—you're gone from their lives!

Give your spouse the gift of your loyalty, and your most healthy psychological self.

THE GIFT OF INTEREST

There is no way in the world that you can really "give a damn" about all your spouse's interests. I know that when and if the discussion gets to cars or sports, my brain clouds over. It probably is the same when I try to explain some technical sail racing technique I've learned, or how I found a new way to work stones in the necklaces I make for charity. Does this mean we're entitled to say "I don't care—shut up and leave me alone?" Well not if you love him/her—and not if you want to be happily married.

> *"Your book* The Proper Care and Feeding of Husbands *helped me to see how completely ONE-WAY I had become in my marriage. I went so far as to tell my husband that 'I didn't care about his job and to stop boring me with the details of his day.' Can you even imagine how he managed to come home every night and be decent to me? He did, but I always felt he wasn't giving ME enough.*
>
> *"Halfway through reading your book, I put it down and looked him right in the eye and told him that I was sorry. He works very hard every day to allow me to stay home and raise our children—and all I could do was tell him to shut up?*

> *"I told him I would always be there and there was nothing too trivial to discuss with me ever. Two days later, on Monday, I met him at the door with a giant kiss and sincerely asked him what his day was like and if there was anything I could do to help him unwind. After he got over the shock, he told me about his day—and listening wasn't hard after all. He then asked me if he could help me with anything. This was new for both of us, but terrific as well.*
>
> *"Since then, I have made him a priority in my life, and the rewards have been immeasurable. My kids are even happier. I look forward every day to seeing my man walk through the door and he tells me he can't wait to get home!"*

That's the power of the gift of showing/having interest—genuine interest is a form of caring; and you ain't a'gonna get some if you don't give some.

THE GIFT OF GRATITUDE

It is way too easy to get yourself all worked up about how you're not getting what you want, exactly the way you want it. Even if you're right, you're missing the bigger picture, and a sense of peace and happiness in your life and marriage.

Andie wrote that she used to think her husband was terribly UNromantic and it made her sad, disappointed, frustrated, and angry. Nothing has changed in terms of her husband's behaviors. But now, miraculously, she thinks he is the most incredibly romantic man and she is deliriously happy! How is that possible?

When they were dating, he brought her flowers only twice: once for her birthday, and another time to apologize for a silly argument. Since they married, she can count on flowers for all special holidays, as long as she goes with him to the supermarket to pick them up. She usually has to plan their activities on these special days as well, as he gets stressed and grumpy about the pressure.

So why is she so in love with him that she still gets butterflies when she hears his ring tone on her phone?

> *"Instead of bringing me flowers, he brought me two children. He gets up before the sun every morning and comes home after dark so that we can afford for our children to have their mommy home with them all day. He went to school for eight years to get a job that he doesn't particular like, so that we can afford to live somewhere that we really love. He takes our family to church every Sunday so that the children will grow up knowing that God loves them and that their daddy loves God. He compliments my cooking—even though I know that I am not a good cook. He tells me I'm beautiful, and means it, even though my body looks like I went through a taffy puller each time I gave birth. He takes Saturdays off so that we can spend the day together, even when he'd like to go out with the guys or get a few more hours in at the office. He tells people (and I've overheard him) that he loves me for staying home and doing the most important job: raising our kids. And the most romantic thing of all is that he has never, not one time, gone to bed without saying, 'I love you.' "*

Young folks today need to learn from Angie what ROMANCE is really about—and it isn't the behavior in a Harlequin novel.

Jonathan's definition of romance is this description of his wife: *"She always makes me feel loved from the moment I walk in the door with a kiss and a hug. She helps me feel like the sexy man in her life."*

Big deal flowers and candy. Bigger deal that your beloved takes care of your soul and psyche.

THE GIFT OF AHA!

Scottie wrote an apology note about her regrets to her husband. She apologized for her misbehaviors toward him for so many years: rejecting his love, being extremely selfish and self-centered, and not putting their relationship first. Her letter was all the more touching because she wrote that it made her feel so terribly sad to remember how she'd hurt him and how sorry she was.

> *"I had a huge aha! moment. That 'aha!' was: all you ever wanted from me is LOVE. I was always attaching a mood of emotion to keep me away from that one thought . . . LOVE. Why didn't you know what I (!) needed; why didn't you say exactly what I(!) needed to hear; why, why why!? I realized that it isn't all about what I'm not getting, it's about what I'm giving that makes the difference. I want to express my love to you fully. I am not looking for anything in return (anymore) . . . seriously, I long for your touch and will make sure you never feel rejected again. It is my pleasure to be your spouse and your lover."*

An aha! moment is one in which you own up in your own mind and heart to your failures, errors, and hurtful behaviors toward the one who should be your most cherished—and then you admit it to your beloved and make changes. It is not good enough to "try" to make changes because that attitude gives you a built-in excuse for any small failure to release you from your obligation to change. The gift of changing requires you to persevere in your changes in spite of any personal discomfort or disappointment in your beloved's instantaneous reaction; it may take some time for him/her to feel trusting and open again to you. You have to have the compassion and fortitude to proceed forward based on what is right, not what gets immediate applause.

Jake, another listener, wrote that he decided to try something he heard me talking about on my radio program to another caller who was having issues with feeling "good" enough to be nice. I suggested that no matter the mood, say something nice. Period. Just do it. So Jake wrote that "*Well, I am learning from listening to you . . . if I can communicate, say something positive like wishing them well with something, that it truly helps 'my spirit' and there is nourishment and freedom in this. A seemingly simple mindset and these little gestures of kindness toward someone else creates freedom and a better life for me too!*"

Jake's aha! was that he can generate a good feeling inside himself—freeing himself up from a darker moodiness and freeing up a relationship from tension—simply by saying something nice.

Whether it's that you have a drinking problem, you allow your parents and family to be too intrusive into your lives, you exhaust yourself so that you have nothing to give to your spouse, you allow your moods to dictate whether or not you are loving, you're too focused in on money, power, and acquisition as the main point of your existence, you keep trying to prove to your spouse that you are smarter, better, stronger, or that you've let your fears and hurts from your past take up residence in your marriage—it's time for you to have an aha! moment.

Admit your weaknesses and wrongs to yourself and to your spouse. Get professional and spiritual guidance to help you morph into your better self with options for a deeper happiness. You know, most of you rue this thought because you believe that if you show your weaknesses and admit your wrongs that you will be disdained and punished forever. Well, that's true only if you're married to a horrible jerk. Most of you are married to decent folks who will be touched beyond imagination by your gift of the aha! You will gain the love and respect you've yearned for and have gone after the wrong way!

Forget pathological or false pride. Remember only the gift of love.

Another source of an aha! moment is anytime you learn. Carly's fiancé picked her up at home and told her they had a special outing. Their first stop was a florist's shop where he picked up six yellow roses. He came back to the car and instead of handing the flowers to her he put them in the backseat. She was perplexed and curious.

They drove across town and he stopped at a retirement/assisted living home. They got out of the car and went to the front desk where he introduced himself and the attendant, obviously aware of their visit in advance, took them down a long hallway where they were shown a door, and told, "They are expecting you."

"My fiancé knocked on the door, which was answered by a lovely older woman who invited us into her home and introduced her husband. I had never met these people but smiled and sat down in her living room. Then my fiancé said, 'Tell us your secrets. . . .'

"I came to learn that he had called and asked if there were couples that were married longer than 50 years and could we come speak with them. The assisted living home found us 6 couples married between 50–65 years for us to speak to—or

rather, to speak to us. They each shared with us their 'secrets' to a long marriage and their advice and best wishes for us. The yellow roses were for each of the women. It was an amazing evening where I learned a lot from 6 couples who had 'been there.' "

On the way back from meeting these couples, her fiancé apologized for not getting her a rose too. She took his hand, and with tears running down my cheeks, thanked him for the beauty that those six yellow roses brought into my life that no single rose given to her could have had.

"I remember the advice from those wonderful couples and, on days when he is driving me crazy (as I'm sure there are many when I do the same for him), I remember those 6 roses and the wonderful gift he gave me before we were married so that we can share our 'secrets' in another 45 years."

There are aha! moments all around you. Open your eyes, ears, mind, and heart to them. Perpetual learning of how to be more caring and loving is a great gift; better than any flower or trinket.

THE GIFT OF DEEP ACKNOWLEDGMENT

"Thank you so very much, Dr. Laura, for encouraging us female types to be feminine, not feminists. I am so lucky to have a husband who adores me, even after 17 years! He tells me often how much he loves me, but the best way to tell me happened the other day.

"He recently got a new computer for himself and went through all the process of installing software, setup up e-mail

accounts, etc. A few days afterward he sent me an e-mail and I noticed something so sweet it made me cry. You see, he listed me in his contacts folder as 'Shannon, the greatest wife ever.'

"How wonderful to be cherished so much—he did that only for himself, but it meant so much to me. Makes me want to be an even better woman for him."

Obviously he had Shannon on his mind. Her husband probably didn't even realize that she'd see her address listing. Finding these things out accidentally is very touching because any sense of "s/he's just being nice out of habit or obligation" . . . or "s/he wants something," is totally eliminated!

Nonetheless deep acknowledgments of admiration are a blessing of incredible proportion! By deep I mean way more profound than the usual platitudes already written in a Hallmark card.

The following fifty-seventh birthday note from a loving husband to a loving wife ought to be a guide for you to come up with your own for your beloved. It is not enough to say "I love you"; it is a far, far better thing to describe "why."

"Happy 57th birthday. I have been thinking about this past year, and decided I should share with you some of the things that you do to make our marriage and life together such a wonderful and thriving relationship. This is not a complete list, but these things are certainly among the most impressionable and important ones.

1. *Scrapbooking—you are at your best when creating, designing, and putting together the material that shows and describes the great family experiences we have.*

2. *Home and yard care—this is an unending and demanding job that you have done for years. You really have made our yard a Garden of Eden.*
3. *Health and nutrition—you are one of the most disciplined people I know for planning and controlling your eating and exercise. You fight one of life's greatest battles with rare conviction and personal self-control.*
4. *Curiosity and interest in learning—I love your unending interest in people, places, and things. It's fun to see how much enjoyment you get from reading newspapers, magazines, and books. I relish in your thinking about things and what they mean.*
5. *Grandmother—what a delight it is to see how much your grandchildren crave you and your attention. Their affection and love is well earned.*
6. *Friend—you are so kind to those who really need friends. You spend hours listening and sharing thoughts and feelings with those most in need.*
7. *Great meals—I can't tell you how much I appreciate having regular meals that are healthy, timely, tasty, and well prepared. It has helped me to maintain good health and I enjoy and look forward to them.*
8. *Religious class—you have a great spiritual depth that you cultivate and grow weekly.*
9. *Home—you have put your talented and creative touch on our home and furnishings and made it so comfortable that I would rather be here than anywhere else!*
10. *Intimate friend and companion—I appreciate your love and affection, your companionship and attention. Thanks for making me the center of your life and focus of all you do.*

"Thanks for a great year. I know there are many more to come and life will only get better. I give you a world of thanks for your love and dedication to me and our family. All of my love and all of my kisses!"

When was the last time you truly and deeply assessed the beauty and the blessing of your spouse? When was the last time you truly and deeply assessed yourself to see if you were earning your spouse's love, admiration, awe, and respect?

THE GIFT OF ALCHEMY

Alchemy refers to the pseudoscience of turning base metal into precious metal. While that is an impossibility, it is quite within your capacity to turn an ugly situation into a beautiful one.

Chris (twenty-eight) and Rachel (twenty-five) called my program after being married for only a year. Chris said, "Well, basically we wondered . . . we have our occasional disagreements. I tend to take them in stride and get over them pretty quick. Rachel tends to get . . . she's pretty sensitive and tends to think maybe there's something wrong with us. I wonder what advice you had for couples on engaging in what amount of disagreements and arguments are okay versus what's too much?"

This is a typical scenario for young people in new relationships. The shock of everything not being delightfully perfect all the time, and the worry that one won't be liked when warts show, and inexperience in thinking as "one" usually cause these rifts.

I suggested that "When tensions first rise, you have to ask yourself a question really fast, 'Did I make a mistake and marry a bad person?' Because if that is what you believe, get out fast. If that is what you know to be not true then ask yourself what is the point of being so ferociously hostile and angry at each other? If you didn't make a mistake in the choice of a spouse, and you really believe that the other person truly lives concerned about your welfare and has the best intentions toward you and has your feelings and your very life in their heart—then there is no point in being so ferociously defensive, hostile, manipulative about hurt feelings, or apocalyptic about a little spat. At the time you are the most angry, the most resentful, the most irritated—do something nice for the other person and something magical happens."

Turning an ugly moment into a beautiful one can happen subtly, simply, and lovingly. Just say, "You know, I'm feeling so angry, hurt, upset that I'm confused. I do know that I love you, you're wonderful and I want us to be calm and comfortable with each other ten minutes from now. I want you to be happy and to be happy with me. How can I give that to you?"

There it will be: dirt into bliss.

Laura, another listener wrote to me that her husband is a great man who takes good care of her, but that his parents are not very pleasant to be around. Since they live but an hour away, they are invited over all the time, and her husband didn't see a problem with going to 90 percent of these events, she was starting to feel drained. Whenever she said she didn't want to go to see his family, her husband would take it personally. She was alternating between feeling bad for him and angry with his family.

After listening to my program a while she decided to put some of my principles into play.

> *"I chose as my 'love attack plan' to try to have Sunday afternoons and evenings by ourselves instead of with his family. In my head, we would still do birthday parties, occasional*

Friday night games and pizza—but I wanted Sundays with my husband.

"So one day after church, we came home, I put a pork roast into the Crock-Pot (his favorite dinner) and I put on something a little 'more comfortable ☺.' I asked him sweetly if we could please ignore phone calls and any visits for a few hours. He agreed. I then asked him if I could have a back rub in the bedroom, and to see what else would happen ☺. He sprinted into our room, lit some candles, and gave me a 15 minute back rub and we continued to share an intimate afternoon. We then had a yummy dinner and watched a movie together. We have continued that Sunday tradition for several months now. A few weeks ago, I asked my husband if he wanted to go up on Sunday night for a dinner at his parents' because we hadn't been there in such a long time. He gave me a big hug and said, 'Thanks, honey, but I LIKE OUR SUNDAYS *more than their Sundays.'*

"Pulling my act together by caring for him allowed me to have the power more than any nagging, anger, or resentment had in our past!"

A great form of alchemy is to, in the immortal words of Vito Corleone, "I'll make them an offer they can't refuse." The best offer is love and attention.

THE GIFT OF . . . YOURSELF

One particular call to my radio program generated a tremendous number of follow-up letters from listeners.

Jennifer: I'm calling because I'm married to an accountant so I'm more or less alone for the next month and a half (tax season). I had been planning for several months to come up with my kids to visit my parents during the month of March for a few weeks. And my husband knew about this, my parents knew about this—it was preplanned. My husband called last night to let me know that his work expects him to go to a social obligation on Tuesday and to bring his wife and I don't feel that it's fair for me to cancel my trip and drive down there.

DrL: You are already at your folks' home?

Jennifer: Yes.

DrL: And you've got three little kids?

Jennifer: Yes.

DrL: Let me give you another perspective on this. He's going to be busting his back for a month and a half. It's certainly nice to come home to have a warm wife and a warm bed and be able to smooch the faces of your sleeping children during this horribly difficult time of a month and a half. I think you looked at it as, "Well, I'm not getting attention anyway, I might as well not be here."

You didn't look at it as a wife.

Jennifer (sighing)***:*** Yeah . . . But he did agree!

DrL: Oh husbands will agree to anything we want just to keep us happy and having sex with them. You know that. You know that he agrees to all sorts of things just to make sure that you're okay with him and he doesn't get punished. Men with wives are like boys with mothers. So don't tell me he agreed with it as the rationale for not acting like a wife. As a wife, you might think to yourself, "Well, you know what—he has just no time for anything and it would be nice if when he walked in the house there were food and warm bodies.

Jennifer: Even though he's working eighteen hours a day?

DrL: Especially when he's working eighteen hours a day. He's not out eighteen hours at a bar, he's working to support you and three kids.

Jennifer: Yes he is. He works very hard and does a great job of it.

DrL: Right, and frankly we could look at it the other way—that you abandoned him.

Jennifer: Oh, ouch!

DrL: If I were you—I'd go home and take care of my man. He misses you, he misses the kids.

Jennifer: Okay, I'll do it. I'll go home then.

Several days later I received a follow up e-mail from Jennifer:

"I called you on Monday about my obligation to my husband while I was on vacation. I wanted to know if I was 'obligated' to drive eight hours home to attend a social function with him for his work. You told me that I was not obligated, but that perhaps I wasn't thinking of this as a wife should.

"When I arrived home last night, he had music and a gourmet dinner waiting for me. And after the kids were in bed, there

was other entertainment . . . Dr. Laura, you have no idea how AMAZING my husband is. Thank you for helping me to remember."

Take a note, Jennifer, "YOU ARE AMAZING TOO!"

As you might imagine, I get a lot of questions from spouses of military, police, and firemen about how to handle their stress. Saralee, on of my listeners, is married to a marine deployed to Iraq. She started getting really frustrated looking at all the work she has to do around the home by herself. She started crying and thinking about how she would love to tell her husband how she hates doing all this yard work.

> *"I wouldn't because there you are on my shoulder telling me how I married a warrior. I have even passed on your advice to other military wives. Then, in the midst of my tears, there you were again today telling a wife that a warrior needs a woman with grit.*
>
> *"I made up my mind that I will not even think about telling my marine about what a bad day I'm having pulling weeds and doing other dirty things. After all, I am positive he would rather be here doing this than dodging IEDs.*
>
> *"I am a proud wife of a U.S. Marine who has a woman at home who wears the crown that says GRIT. I will make him proud for marrying me too. HOORAH!"*

The Proper Care and Feeding of a Marriage is to GIVE, GIVE, and GIVE some more—of your best self.

Epilogue

"My husband stormed into the house the other day, as angry as could be from a frustrating day of melting under the Arizona sun and dealing with incompetent subcontractors. He paced and fumed and poured his frustration out on me. He also made several comments about me, the house, clean laundry or the lack of, and so forth. After a few hours of this, I began to feel very defensive and fought the temptation to lash back at him. I tried to remind myself that it was the anger speaking—not the man—and I did my best to support and love him.

"Yesterday evening, it was I who was depressed, angry, and volatile. My husband came home, took one look at my face, and probably decided that running for it was a good idea. But instead, he gave me a kiss and marched straight for the kitchen. He plowed into the dirty dishes, made an amazing steak dinner for us, and watched our 9-month-old daughter while I hid in the bedroom and ate chocolate chip cookies.

"When the baby was in bed, my husband put his arms around me, told me that I was his Ishah (Hebrew for woman), and that he would carry me when I couldn't walk on my own. I collapsed in tears, and he just hugged me until I could speak

intelligently again. He apologized for his behavior the other day, and said that my gentleness with his anger helped him to calm down.

"We're a team and we cherish each other."

Sincerely, Christine.

For me, that says it all. Now it's your turn.